BEYOND FIVE IN A ROW
VOLUME 1

BY

BECKY JANE LAMBERT

FIVE IN A ROW PUBLISHING · GRANDVIEW, MISSOURI

Beyond Five in a Row, Volume 1
Revised Second Edition

ISBN 1-888659-13-0

Published by:
Five in a Row Publishing
P.O. Box 707
Grandview, MO 64030
(816) 246-9252

Send all requests for information to the above address.

Printed in the United States of America

For my father, mother and sister-
You believed in me when I didn't believe in myself.
Always remember and never forget, I love you!

And for Matt and Megan-
Two of my favorites

Table of Contents

Finding Your Way Around in *Beyond Five in a Row,* Volume 1

We've provided a few simple icons to help you navigate through the teacher's guide quickly and efficiently. There are many lessons about science, history, geography and language arts that comprise the majority of the curriculum that do not have any special or unique identification beyond the section headers. But, there are also a variety of special learning opportunities that invite activities, projects, computer activity, etc. Take a moment to familiarize yourself with the icons below so that you'll be prepared to recognize at a glance the various enrichment activities associated with each unit.

Internet Connection

Drama Activities

Career Path

Art

Cooking

Writing and Discussion Questions

Getting the Most Out of *Beyond Five in a Row*

Welcome to *Beyond Five in a Row,* Volume 1. You're about to begin a wonderful adventure in education built around the concept that the single most important lesson any child can learn is to "love learning." We strongly believe that if a child successfully learns this lesson, all the rest will follow. *Beyond Five in a Row* is a literature-based unit study built around strong, traditional and delightful children's books. In this volume, you will be exploring two books of fiction and two non-fiction selections. These four books will take one semester to complete.

Unlike *Five in a Row*, you will not be studying specific academic subjects on specific days of the week. Instead, you will be guiding your student into a variety of areas each week. Some weeks will have a heavier emphasis on science while others may have greater emphasis on the fine arts, for instance. What you study each week is a function of what chapters you happen to be studying. Overall, your student will receive a comprehensive education in five principal areas: History and Geography, Language Arts, Science, the Fine Arts and Human Relationships. There are several areas you *will* need to supplement including Arithmetic, and the narrow language arts specialties of grammar, spelling and penmanship. These subjects do not lend themselves to a unit study approach and you'll want to be sure to include them each week.

With this type of curriculum, it is not possible to simply read one chapter every day and do the associated lesson activities. Some chapters are brief and you may very well finish the chapter and all related activities in one day. Other chapters, however, may be either lengthy, or filled with an unusually rich field of learning possibilities. These chapters may take nearly a week to explore thoroughly. Your overall goal is to complete the volume in one semester—approximately 90-100 school days. On average, you'll find yourself covering a chapter every two days or so, but part of the joy of unit study is allowing students to follow their interests. You may find some lesson activities such as a personal journal or a leaf collection, for instance, that continue for weeks as you pursue your studies. Other activities may take only 30 minutes to complete. Remember that our goal as educators is *not* to cram facts into children's brains long enough to successfully complete a test on Friday. Our goal is to help children fall in love with learning, to discover the joy of reading, to learn how to find answers and use research tools, to learn to think critically and to assimilate knowledge in a way that is both relevant and memorable.

Inherent in any unit study is the need for good supplementary resources. You'll be making regular trips to the library as your student moves from topic to topic. While *Beyond Five in a Row* provides a tremendous amount of specific, factual content, it will not be enough to satisfy your student who wants to pursue a subject in greater depth. Find a librarian with a heart to serve rather than one who is simply good at checking out books. Explain your needs and what you are doing and then let her know how much you appreciate her support in helping you locate good resources. Bake her a pan of brownies occasionally or bring her an inexpensive "cash and carry" rose from time to time, along with a nice note or card of appreciation. A good librarian is a tremendous resource to any educator!

You will also want to invest in a good set of encyclopedias. That does not mean spending a great deal of money! We recently bought the entire *World Book Encyclopedia* on CD-Rom for our computer for only $20 after the mail-in $20 rebate offer from a local computer store. And of course, you can locate used encyclopedias at bargain basement prices through classified ads, flea markets and used book stores. For 99% of your student's needs, a 1977 encyclopedia works just as well as a 1997 edition. Expect to pay between $25 and $150 for a set. A good encyclopedia, dictionary and atlas are the links between your curriculum guide and the library. These resources do not by any means *replace* the need for regular trips to the library, but they will substantially reduce the frequency and urgency of those trips. Your student can immediately begin to branch out and enrich their studies using the resources at hand. Later in the day, or later in the week when your schedule permits, you can go to the library to look for specific books on the topic.

You will also want to look for opportunities to continue building a personal resource library as time, finances and space permit. Don't rush out and try to fill your library in one week. Get to know the used bookstores in your area and watch the sale tables at major bookseller chain stores. You can often find wonderful resource books for 25 cents to a few dollars. If it's a quality resource, buy it whether you need it now or not. You will eventually appreciate having a book on trees, another on our solar system, etc.

You will discover as you begin Volume 1, that each chapter of the book you are studying includes a "Parent Summary" for your benefit. If you wish, you can "assign" the chapter reading to your student and use the parent summary so that you'll know what has been covered in the chapter. But we also encourage you to read the chapter aloud *with* your student. You can take turns reading, listen while he reads, or read it aloud for him using your best dramatic voices, vocal energy, etc. There is no right or wrong way to do it. Most likely you'll employ a combination of all these approaches.

One important tool for helping pull a unit study together is a timeline. You can purchase good timelines or you can make your own. A timeline can be as simple as a notebook, binder or scrapbook with each page representing 50 or 100 years. You may want to create an adjustable scale timeline covering 100 years per page up until perhaps 1700. Then you can cover 25 years per page up to 1850 and further expand the detail of your timeline by only covering 10 years per page through the year 2000. Whether you purchase a timeline or create your own, the important concept is to help your student begin to locate the place that each person or event has in history. Everything is either *before* or *after* something else. The Spanish Armada was sunk *after* Columbus discovered the New World, but *before* the Pilgrims landed at Plymouth Rock. Each time your student writes down an entry or looks up a date in his timeline, he will begin making those associations of time relationship. He will also begin to discover what things were happening parallel in history–what music was being written at the same time as which war was being fought all while certain scientific discoveries were being made. The world is all inter-connected and timelines are one of the very best ways of grasping the big picture so important in a good education!

You will find a Writing and Discussion Question for every chapter. We strongly believe that learning to communicate clearly is foundational to any good education. Your student may or may not need to understand the complexities of physics in his chosen career field, but he *will* need to be able to communicate with others through both the spoken and written word. Use these questions as a starting point. Encourage your student to write frequently. If you have another idea for a discussion question, by all means use it instead. Assign the length of each answer based on your student's abilities and age. Younger students or students with learning disabilities may only be able to write 1-3 paragraphs. Older students, or those who excel in writing may want to write 1-3 pages or more. Feel free to adjust the assignment length as you find out what works for you. And don't feel obligated to use the same length every day. You may assign a 100-word essay one day and a 500-word essay the next.

You will find Career Paths to explore from time to time. You may choose to study each of them to a limited degree, to at least learn more about what various professions do. Others that particularly spark your student's interest may merit much deeper investigation including a field trip to meet and interview someone in the profession. Again, use the curriculum in a way that works for you and your student.

To further enrich your student's studies, you will find a reminder at the end of each chapter to check our *Five in a Row* website to see links relating to the lessons. It goes without saying that if you have Internet access you'll want to use wisdom and supervise your student's access to the wide variety of sometimes unwholesome material available in cyberspace. On the other hand, there are wonderful resources available from businesses, agencies and universities that can provide a rich resource for learning. Use wisdom and learn about the Internet yourself rather than just turning your student loose with a modem and web browser!

At the back of this volume, you will find a Scope and Sequence detailing the various academic subjects covered. We suggest you mark off each subject as you complete your unit and keep this list as a part of your student's permanent academic record. You may also want to keep a variety of other documentation including your student's essays, reports and projects. You will also find a certificate of completion for you to sign and date when your student has finished this volume. Again, keep this certificate with your student's permanent academic file.

Thank you for selecting *Beyond Five in a Row,* Volume 1. We hope you have a wonderful time using it. If you have Internet access be sure to visit our website at www.fiveinarow.com to exchange ideas with other *Beyond Five in a Row* users.

Now, welcome to the wonderful world of *Beyond Five in a Row*. You are the leader for this adventure, so gather the children around you and have a great time!

Becky Jane Lambert
April, 1997

THE BOXCAR CHILDREN

BY GERTRUDE CHANDLER WARNER

Chapter 1–The Four Hungry Children

Parent Summary

They have a grandfather, but will not contact him for help because they are afraid he is mean. We find the children in a bakery buying bread for their dinner. The children notice benches with cushions in the front window and ask the woman who owns the store if they might stay there for the night. She is suspicious but agrees, planning to keep the three older, orphaned children for help with housework and to send Benny to a Children's Home. These intentions are overheard by Henry and Jessie that night after they lay down, and so without a sound they leave the bakery and go out into the night.

What we will cover in this chapter:

Science: Meal Planning and Proper Nutrition

Science: Health and Cleanliness

Language Arts: Creative Writing—The Element of Mystery

Issues of Human Relationships: Learning to Listen

Lesson Activities

Science: Meal Planning and Proper Nutrition

When the children first enter the bakery, all Benny is interested in are the cakes and cookies. Yummm! But Jessie reminds him that "bread is better for you" (page 8). Use this scene to begin a discussion about healthy eating habits. We know cookies are delicious and sometimes they are just the right treat, but as we grow up, we learn about balance in our diet.

This might be an excellent opportunity to introduce the six food groups (dietitians have recently begun dividing fats into a separate "pyramid slice" and fruits and vegetables separately, expanding the traditional basic four food groups to six). Jessie suggests that "bread is better" and she is right! Nutrition experts suggest 6-11 servings daily of this most important group. We need 3-5 servings of vegetables, 2-4 servings of fruit, 2-3 servings of dairy products, 2-3 servings of meat, eggs or nuts, and tiny bits of fats, oils and sweets. Take time out to go on a *food pyramid* search right now. Look on bread wrappers, cereal boxes, etc., to find the pyramid! Wow, what a lot to remember!

To make this more practical, have your student choose a name for his own imaginary restaurant. He can design the menu, draw pictures, choose prices, etc. But remind him that he must offer a wide range of food choices. After the menu is complete, have your student "order" one day's meals that make up the proper number of servings from each group.

Beyond the basic food groups, you can begin to discuss vitamins and minerals. Perhaps you give your student a chewable multi-vitamin each day. Have him look at what his tablet includes and write down the name of each vitamin and mineral. The 13 vitamins are vitamins A, B complex (which is really 8 different vitamins), vitamins C, D, E and K.

Our bodies use vitamins as catalysts for productive growth (catalysts speed chemical reactions without being consumed by the reaction). We can think of our vitamins as speedy delivery messengers. Without them, vital changes our bodies need would either occur very slowly or not at all. Understanding the concepts of nutrition is a challenge, but a healthy life is our reward! You can use this opportunity to find a simple library book on vitamins and minerals or general nutrition to read with your student.

Science: Health and Cleanliness

On page 13 we find out the children keep their clothes, money, knife, food and a cake of soap and towel. Ask your student why Henry and Jessie think it is important to keep soap. Washing up before dinner and taking a bath before bed aren't just expected duties. Keeping clean is an important part of stopping the spread of disease. Germs are easily passed and washing up is a great way to cut down the risks of getting sick.

We often take soap for granted, but in many countries soap is a precious commodity. Does your student know how Mother Teresa used soap in the early days of her mission? Before she founded her order, she would teach the poor, uneducated children of Calcutta, India how to read. If the children put up a fight or got tired of their lessons, she would promise them a sliver of soap as their reward for doing a good day's study. In their communities, dirt and disease were everywhere. Imagine, using soap as a prize!

But does your student know how soap *works*? Soap attacks dirt and grime in three ways. First, it breaks down the *surface tension* of the water. Surface tension is caused by the molecules of water binding together and making droplets. Soap forces the water to "thin out" and so whatever you're washing (your socks, hands, hair, face) can get good and wet. Next, soap has molecules which attach themselves and bind to the dirt particles, making the dirt "shake" loose from your hands or clothes and stay suspended in the water. Finally, after all the dirt is floating around in the water, soap keeps the dirt floating away from the washed garment or your scalp until you rinse it all off.

If your student is interested in this process, try taking a very greasy pan (perhaps you could fry bacon for bacon, lettuce and tomato sandwiches for lunch). Take the greasy pan and pour a little stream of water down the length of it. Did the grease wash away? Now, dribble a few drops of dish soap. Notice how the dirt is immediately forced away from the soap! Now, pour water down the same area a second time. The grease is lifted! Additional topics for some good, "clean" research might include: how diseases are spread, plagues in history and which countries lack sanitary conditions. Also, take this opportunity to read a simple library book on germs, or Leeuwenhoek, Edward Jenner, Pasteur, Robert Koch or Joseph Lister and discover the relation to this lesson!

[**Teacher's Note**: The scientific names for the explanation of how soap works are *hydrophilic* and *hydrophobic*. Hydrophilic means "attracted to water." This is how detergents break the surface tension. Hydrophobic means "lack of attraction to water" explaining how detergents suspend dirt particles away from the material being washed. If your student seems interested in the properties of soap and is ready for advanced, scientific vocabulary, introducing these two terms might be appropriate.]

Language Arts: Creative Writing—The Element of Mystery

The Boxcar Children begins "One warm night four children stood in front of a bakery. *No one knew them. No one knew where they had come from*" (page 1). How mysterious!

Have your student read or listen to those lines and ask him what it makes him want to know. Of course! Who *were* those children? Where *had* they come from? The element of mystery in stories pulls the reader to the next page. And it's fun! Solving a mystery is like doing a jigsaw puzzle in your mind!

Have your student write the beginning of a story utilizing the element of mystery. Certainly he can finish the story if he wishes, but the exercise in this activity is to think up "mysterious" openings. He might write, "It had been snowing all week. Charlie decided to go sledding. Pulling his sled behind him, he started off down the street. Just as he reached the corner market, he suddenly heard slushy footsteps behind him. He turned around but no one was there." Using mystery in stories is a great way to make them exciting—and they're fun to write!

Issues of Human Relationships: Learning to Listen

Listening when someone is speaking to you isn't simply the polite thing to do. Sometimes it keeps you safe. On page 14, Jessie says, "Sh, Violet! Come! We are going to run away again. If we don't run away, the baker will take Benny to a Children's Home in the morning."

Violet wakes up and does not make a sound. If she had not listened to Jessie, something bad might have happened. A fun activity to demonstrate this skill is called a *Trust Walk*. Blindfold your student. Standing in the yard, living room, park (anywhere besides the street) spin him around a few times to disorient him. Then, simply by speaking to him ("walk, stop, turn left, slow down, stairs are coming up," etc.), lead him around. If you are in a familiar area, you might have your student try to guess where he is now and then.

After doing the activity once, your student might think he has the difficult job. After all, it is sometimes frightening and wearisome to pay attention so carefully. Now switch places and let *him* blindfold *you*. This exercise demonstrates that both listening and leading are difficult jobs, requiring trust.

You can make this same exercise more difficult by eliminating speech and simply using clapping or snapping to indicate directions. By positioning yourself in the direction you want him to walk, hearing the clap will tell him which way to turn. Two claps might indicate stairs, three claps might indicate curb, etc. Take this exercise and have fun with it! There are so many interesting variations!

Writing and Discussion Question

Even though Henry, Jessie, Violet and Benny have never met him, they do not believe their grandfather likes them. They assume certain things about him, but have no real proof. Why is assuming things about people without talking to them first, sometimes dangerous?

Vocabulary Words

catalyst: a substance that causes a chemical reaction while remaining practically unchanged itself

hydrophilic: a substance that can readily absorb or dissolve in water

hydrophobic: a substance that has little or no ability to absorb or dissolve in water

Internet Connections

To view current suggested links relating to this chapter's lessons, see www.fiveinarow.com/connections.

Chapter 2–Night Is Turned Into Day

Parent Summary

After the children leave the bakery, they walk until early morning, looking for a place to sleep. Finally, they find a huge haystack and create four little "nests" around the sides. They drift off as the sun is coming up. Around nightfall they awake and find a farmer's pump for water and eat their next loaf of bread. As they are eating, they hear the baker and his wife coming along the road in their horse and buggy. They hear the baker's wife admit she does not like children. The couple decides to "look for them in Greenfield and that is all." The children walk on to Silver City, knowing the couple will not find them there. As daylight approaches, Henry and Jessie decide to sleep in the woods. They make beds out of pine needles and shut their eyes.

What we will cover in this chapter:

History and Geography: The Dust Bowl Years (see Science lesson—Drought)

Science: Human Body and Sleep

Science: Water Cycle and Drought

Science: Water—A Rare and Valuable Resource

Science: Inventions and Discoveries

Fine Arts: Functional Design

Lesson Activities

Science: Human Body and Sleep

This chapter is called "Night Is Turned Into Day." Henry, Jessie, Violet and Benny sleep during the day. What would it be like to sleep during the day and work all night? A lot of people do just that, including factory workers, police officers, firemen, delivery clerks, telephone operators, etc.

Take this opportunity to discuss sleep and how our body works. We have our own "inner clock" which tells us when we should be up and active and when we need to rest. Rest allows our body to store up energy for the next day. Our inner clock's alarm is set off mainly by daylight and darkness. However, habit also affects our clock. If your bedtime is 9:30 p.m. every night, after awhile you'll begin to get sleepy around 9:30 p.m. every evening, even if you have decided to stay up later.

A person between the ages of 6 and 14 sleeps about one third of the time. As people get older they generally sleep only about one fourth of the time. To prove this, have your student make a chart and keep track of the hours he sleeps for a given week. Record the time he goes to bed and the time he awakens each day. Now add up the hours and divide them by the 168 hours in seven days. What percentage of the time does your child sleep? When our body tells us to get to bed—it means we need it!

Science: Water Cycle and Drought

In this chapter, the children are very concerned with water. Water is vitally important to our bodies. The human body is almost 96% water! Take this opportunity to teach your student about water and the water cycle.

Ask your student to guess how much of the earth's surface he thinks is covered by water? More than 70%! And water never goes away. There is the same amount of water on the earth as there ever was—or ever will be. How can this be? Well, something called the water cycle keeps it all in balance.

To begin, the water cycle includes three distinct stages: *Evaporation, Condensation and Precipitation*. Water in its liquid stage covers the earth in the form of rivers, oceans, ponds, etc. When the sun comes out, it warms the water and the water becomes water vapor. The vapor rises into the sky and begins to cool down again. Clouds form from condensation (water beginning to return to liquid form) and when they cool completely it rains (precipitation) back down into the rivers, oceans, ponds, etc. In this way, the same, fixed amount of water all over the earth recycles itself again and again, but never goes away!

For an activity to illustrate this complex principle, boil water in a tea kettle. When steam (water vapor) begins to form, hold a cool, clear glass near the steam, making sure the steam is going into the glass (being careful not to burn yourself!). Your student will be able to see inside the glass as the water vapor begins to condense into droplets and then runs down the glass like raindrops.

If your student is interested in this subject, you could discuss the lack of water on land (drought). A tragic and scary time in American history occurred during the mid-1930s across the plains of Kansas, Oklahoma, Texas and the adjacent parts of Colorado and New Mexico. This area of the United States became known as the Dust Bowl. The name came from the low annual rainfall and high winds that blew dust and dirt for miles. This time period is also referred to as 'The Dirty '30s.'

During the years 1934-1937, farmers in this area of the country had stripped the land of the natural grasses and planted fields of wheat. Without the aid of the root systems of the natural plants, too much dirt and dust was picked up by the high winds. Soon, dust storms formed and buried entire houses. More than half the population was forced to leave the area. Our government replanted the grasses and trees and helped the land return to its natural state. Self-directed research on the Dust Bowl years can make an interesting science and history project for students.

Science: Water—A Rare and Valuable Resource

Just as the "Dirty '30s" areas suffered drought conditions, many areas of the world today continue to suffer from a shortage of fresh water. In certain regions, water must be carried in jugs and barrels from considerable distances and each gallon is carefully guarded like a treasure. Yet, in America, we often waste water in alarming quantities.

As an interesting exercise just to see how little changes in our behavior can make substantial differences in saving water, try this experiment. Have your student brush his teeth while leaving the water running. While he brushes, you carefully collect the running water into two convenient glasses or cups, alternately filling one while pouring the other into a bucket nearby. When he has finished brushing his teeth, use a milk carton to measure the amount of water wasted. Now let your student do some arithmetic.

Suppose you discover that he wastes one gallon of water while brushing. If he brushes in the morning and at bedtime, that's two gallons of water each day. If he brushes at morning, bedtime and after every meal, that's five gallons of water each day. Now multiply the daily gallons times 365. Your student may waste more than 1,000 gallons of water each year just while brushing his teeth. Now suppose there are six people in your student's family. Have your student multiply his total by six to see how much water his family wastes on this one activity alone. Now calculate the total waste in your city by multiplying the population times the number of gallons you calculated are wasted each year.

Surprising, isn't it? Millions of gallons of water wasted annually over something as insignificant as leaving the water running while brushing our teeth. Many experts believe that water will become our most precious commodity in the years ahead. Practicing conservation is a good idea your student can begin today!

Science: Inventions and Discoveries

On page 18, Violet spies a large haystack. The children decide to use it for a bed. (Ask your student if he thinks a haystack would be comfortable. It seems like an itchy choice, doesn't it?) Take this opportunity to discuss the changes in farm work over the years. A lot of inventions and discoveries have helped farmers get better crops with less work. The change in haystacks is just one example.

The Boxcar Children was written in 1950. On farms today, you won't see haystacks anymore. Instead of mounds of hay loosely piled up, you'll see hay bales. If you live on or near a farm, take some time out to go and look at hay bales. Ask your student if he thinks it would be easy to pull out a "sleeping nest." Probably not.

Balers (farm machines that roll cut hay into large round or rectangular bales and tie them with twine or wire) help the farmer store his hay efficiently. Round bales shed water and can be stored outside uncovered. These bales can weigh as much as 3,000 pounds. Rectangular bales of hay must be draped with canvas to keep out the rain and generally weigh between 50 and 100 pounds.

Another benefit of having hay bales instead of haystacks is transportation. Ask your student how he would move a haystack from the field to a barn. One solution might be to use a pitchfork to load the hay onto a truck or wagon and then haul the hay to the barn. But think how much faster it would be for the farmer to simply pick up a whole round bale with his tractor and drive it over!

Inventions can help people save time, money and energy! If your student seems interested in this discussion, a remarkable book to look through is *Haystack* (appropriate title, isn't it?) by Bonnie and Arthur Beisert (Copyright 1995, Houghton Mifflin Company, ISBN 0395697220). The illustrations are wonderful and it chronicles the interesting heritage of the farmer's haystack.

Of course, there are many other agricultural inventions and discoveries you can talk about with your student. In fact, see how many he can think of and write down. Dairy milking machines, combines, tractors, threshing machines, silos, grain augers, plows, discs, planters, airplane crop dusters—the list is long! A student might like to select one particular invention and research its history, development and impact on agriculture. He could write a paper detailing his research findings, draw diagrams of how the equipment operates or even build a static or working model!

If you live near a farm community, this would be the perfect opportunity to take a field trip! Maybe your student could even interview an area farmer and write a short paper on what invention that farmer thinks has been most helpful to him personally in operating his farm. Perhaps he is old enough to remember farming without the aid of new technology. Remind your student of the benefits *we* reap from today's efficient farms. Food! Yum!

Fine Arts: Functional Design

On page 24, the children find a drinking fountain. In the story, Henry says, "Oh, what a fine fountain this is! See the place for people to drink up high, and a place in the middle for horses, and one for dogs down below." What an interesting idea!

Have your student design a fountain that could accommodate people, horses and dogs. It can be as futuristic or practical as he wishes. He could draw, paint, build, or sculpt a model of his creation. If the model is three-dimensional and waterproof, your student could even pour water down it and demonstrate how it works!

Some fountains are *drinking* fountains while others are just to look at. Does your city have any decorative fountains? Kansas City, Missouri is a city known for its fountains. Showcasing more fountains than any other city in the world except for Rome, Kansas City is lucky to have beautiful sculptures and stone creations surrounded by bubbling water. Some of the fountains are so expansive that in the winter when the water freezes, people from all around the city can ice skate on their surface! If your community has fountains, take some time to enjoy them. Your student might get some great ideas for designing his own fountain.

Writing and Discussion Question

In this chapter, on page 22, the baker's wife admits she does not like children.

Some people do not like dogs. But if you ask them why, they always have a particular reason (i.e., they were bit once by a dog, their dog died when they were a child, etc.). Why do you think the baker and his wife disliked children?

Vocabulary Words

evaporation: the change of a liquid (or solid) to gas form or vapor

condensation: the reduction of a vapor or gas to liquid form

precipitation: moisture in the form of rain or snow falling to the ground as the result of water vapor being condensed into liquid form

Dust Bowl: a section of the south-central United States including Oklahoma and Texas where bare topsoil was blown away by winds during a drought in the 1930s. Also known as the Dirty Thirties.

Internet Connections

To view current suggested links relating to this chapter's lessons, see www.fiveinarow.com/connections.

Chapter 3–A New Home in the Woods

Parent Summary

The children are awakened in the woods to thunder and blowing wind. Jessie, after a little walk, comes upon an old abandoned boxcar. The tracks are rusted and the weeds surrounding the boxcar suggest it is not in service. All four children climb in the boxcar and shut the door. After the storm is over, they discover the boxcar is situated by a lovely brook and the children decide to set up "house" in the old train car. Henry announces he is going into town to buy some milk for Benny. Just as Henry leaves, Jessie tells Violet and Benny she has noticed some blueberries growing nearby. The three get ready to go blueberry picking, but suddenly they hear a mysterious cracking sound in the woods.

What we will cover in this chapter:

History and Geography: The Golden Spike and Railroads

History and Geography: Sources of Shelter for People

Science: Blueberry Bushes and Soil

Language Arts: The Use of Serialization

Language Arts: Using Description—Make your story come to life!

Lesson Activities

History and Geography: The Golden Spike and Railroads

Jessie finds a most unusual "home" in this chapter—an old train's boxcar! Trains are very interesting forms of transportation. Perhaps the single most significant event in the history of railroads occurred on May 10, 1869. That date sealed the joining of the first *transcontinental* railroad.

In 1862 the United States Congress agreed to let Union Pacific and Central Pacific railroads unite and connect the country from coast to coast. It took seven years of hard work. Central Pacific had to lay track eastward from Sacramento, California. This was a difficult task because they had to cross the Sierra Nevada Mountains with rail. The Union Pacific was commissioned to lay track westward from near Omaha, Nebraska. They had the towering Rockies to contend with. Finally, in 1869, the rails were connected at Promontory Summit in Utah. On a momentous day, the last spike (a gold spike!) was driven in and now Americans could travel from one end of the country to the other by rail.

Railroads are fascinating and fun! If your student is interested in trains, why not have him plan his own trip by rail? Amtrak, the nation's largest passenger railroad, offers service between many major U.S. cities. Call or have your student call, 1-800-USA-RAIL for a free *timetable*. After your student has access to a timetable, he can plan all sorts of imaginary train trips all over America. He can decide if he wants to spend four days sitting in a chair car, or if he prefers a sleeper car. The timetable also delineates the luggage costs, amenities offered, etc. Sit down with your student and select several destinations. Then let him research the travel time, costs, etc. What a fun way to learn about railway travel! Bon Voyage!

History and Geography: Sources of Shelter for People

What kind of a home do you have? Maybe a house or apartment? Is your house made of logs, lumber, bricks or stone? Is it shaped like a box or is it a dome? People all over the world have different types of homes. For example, did you know people live in homes made of snow? In some Arctic and sub-Arctic regions people live in homes made of blocks of snow cut with a knife and arranged in a dome shape. People outside the Inuit culture call these structures "igloos." This term in Inuit culture actually refers to any kind of dwelling. Sometimes Inuit people use igloos for temporary shelter when they are away from home hunting, but often they are the primary family domicile and can be built with many rooms.

Another type of home is the traditional shelter of Eastern North American Indians—the wigwam. These homes are made with a framework of poles and then covered with grasses and sheets of bark. In the American Southwest, Native Americans lived in homes called "pueblos," flat-roofed houses made of adobe clay. Ask your student if he would like to live in a house like that? Why or why not? Learning to appreciate the wonderful differences cultures have, as well as the common threads they share, is an important part of growing up.

Perhaps your student would like to build a model of one or more alternative home types. Use sugar cubes or Styrofoam cubes to build an igloo. Use twigs, coffee stirrers or wooden shish kabob skewers as a framework and build a wigwam covering it with bark, moss and lichen. Or use clay to make "adobe bricks" and build a pueblo. Your student can even build a model of your home using balsa wood, cardboard, cardstock or any other suitable material. Cut out the four walls, windows and doors. Then assemble and add a roof. Or perhaps he would like to build a model or draw a famous home—the White House, Monticello, etc. Enjoy!

Science: Blueberry Bushes and Soil

Jessie, Violet and Benny give Henry a wonderful surprise: fresh picked blueberries. Yum! Blueberries grow on a shrub (a round bush with thick foliage) which varies in height from six inches to 15 feet. Before the berries form, the shrubs are covered in beautiful white or pink flowers.

The children found their blueberries growing wild and indeed, they do grow wild in the United States. This variety is found mainly in Maine. Canada is also fortunate to have wild blueberries. They can be seen in the Maritime Provinces (Newfoundland, Prince Edward Island, New Brunswick and Nova Scotia). Interesting names, aren't they? Take a moment and locate these Canadian provinces on a map.

The type of blueberries we buy at the store are known as the "high bush" variety. These are grown by farmers (cultivated), not found wild. The shrubs from the high bush variety generally reach three to six feet. Michigan, New Jersey, North Carolina, Oregon, Washington and British Columbia are where you will find most cultivated blueberries. Have you ever picked blueberries? It is great fun because the berries are beautiful as well as delicious. The blueberry bushes have no thorns like some other berry varieties (i.e., raspberry. blackberry, etc.), and the berries are large and generally very plentiful on a single plant. One healthy plant can produce as many as 20 pints annually.

If you decided to plant a blueberry patch, you should be prepared to tend it for a long time. Can you guess how long a blueberry shrub lives? Many live longer than 50 years! If you live near a blueberry patch, go and see the blueberries. In the southern United States, blueberries are in season from May until June. In the northern states, they are available for picking from June through August. Have your student draw a map of the United States and Canada and ask him to color in the areas where blueberries are most commonly grown with blue crayon or colored pencil.

Ask your student why he thinks blueberries only grow in specific areas. One major consideration is climate (the normal weather conditions of a region). Another is the composition of the soil. Is it hard-packed clay, or water-retaining humus or fast-draining sandy soil? And, yet another reason certain crops grow in specific places is the acidity (acid quality or quantity) of the soil. Blueberry bushes need soil which is high in acid.

What type of soil do you have? For further information and a great kit to test the soil in your area, call the ASCS (Agricultural Stabilization and Conservation Service) in your county. They will send you information and a test packet to do your own experiments.

After you've learned about shrubs and soil, take some time out with your student and make some blueberry muffins or a blueberry pie and think about how surprised and happy Henry must have been when he saw his blueberries!

Language Arts: The Use of Serialization

Notice how this chapter ends: "*But she suddenly stopped, for she heard a noise. Crack, crack, crack. Something was in the woods.*"

Ask your student if he wanted to read the next chapter right away? Chances are he did. This type of "hook" in stories is the common key in the many books, radio programs, television shows and magazine stories known as "Serials." Has your student ever listened to old-time radio programs? (Today, several of these original radio programs are available on audio cassette.) If not, do you remember some? If so, tell him about them. Perhaps your student has seen television movies called "mini-series." This is a form of serialization.

Serials work by leaving the listener/reader with a *cliffhanger* at the end of each installment. A cliffhanger is an exciting, unresolved situation. Have your student write a short story. But instead of ending the story, have him end it with a cliffhanger. If your student is younger, his story might only be one page long. If he is older and is interested in this type of literary device, have him write a three- to four-page short story, perhaps in three different "installments" using cliffhangers at the end of each segment to draw his reader into the next "chapter."

Language Arts: Using Description—Make your story come to life!

Draw your student's attention to page 30. Reread the following paragraph: "All the children looked out into the woods. The sun was shining, but some water still fell from the trees. In front of the boxcar a pretty little brook ran over the rocks, with a waterfall in it."

What a wonderfully descriptive paragraph! Ask your student if he can "picture" this scene in his mind? This is what makes stories interesting—the descriptive details! Have your student write a descriptive paragraph describing a specific place. It could be his special thinking spot, tree house, backyard, bedroom, etc. Encourage him to use as many descriptive phrases as possible.

For example: "*My favorite thinking spot is on a rock at the edge of our back field. Weeds surround the base of the rock. I can see for miles when I stand on my rock. At night, the stars seem very close.*"

Help your student expand on his ideas. You might ask, "What does your rock's surface feel like? Is it rough or smooth? Is it cool or warm? How tall are the weeds that surround it? What do the stars remind you of?"

Then have your student rewrite his paragraph, including the details he told you.

The second draft might read something like, "*My favorite thinking spot is on a long, flat rock at the edge of our back field. My rock feels cool against my legs and has little ripples in it. I trace the ripples with my finger while I think. If I lay flat on the rock and stretch my arms out, I can feel the tops of the weeds blowing against my hands. The weeds are almost as tall as I am. At night, I lay on my back and look up at the stars. They seem very close. They remind me of little light bulbs strung across the sky, shining brightly.*"

What an improvement a few descriptive phrases can make. Have fun painting pictures in your mind with words!

Writing and Discussion Question

On page 31, Benny is frightened at the prospect of living in the boxcar. Ask your student if he can remember why. (Benny is frightened the train will come back and take the car away.) Instead of mocking Benny (saying he is dumb or teasing him for not knowing such an obvious thing), Henry gently calms Benny's fears. Henry understands he is older and therefore knows more than Benny.

When people laugh at you when you ask a question, how does it make you feel? How do you wish they would respond? How did Henry treat Benny?

Vocabulary Words

transcontinental: crossing a continent

timetable: a schedule of when certain things happen (train departures and arrivals, for example)

serialization: a story or production appearing in a series of continuous yet separate segments

amenities: things which add to a person's comfort or convenience (i.e., bathrooms, club cars, luggage racks, reclining chairs, etc.)

cultivate: to grow plants or crops from seed (versus wild)

climate: the average weather conditions of a certain place or region

acidity: acid quality, amount or condition

cliffhanger: a highly suspenseful situation left unresolved in a book or dramatic production

Internet Connections

To view current suggested links relating to this chapter's lessons, see www.fiveinarow.com/connections.

Chapter 4–Henry Has Two Surprises

Parent Summary

Jessie, Violet and Benny investigate the mysterious sound in the woods and discover a dog! The dog has a thorn in his paw so Jessie carefully cleans the wound, removes the thorn and bandages his foot. After that, Violet and Benny pick blueberries for supper while Jessie holds their new friend. When Henry returns from town with milk, bread, and cheese, the other children surprise him twice: fresh blueberries and a new watchdog! Benny names the dog, Watch. After supper, the children decide to make beds out of pine needles inside the boxcar. After they wash by the brook and have a drink of water, they all crawl inside to get a good night's sleep.

What we will cover in this chapter:

History and Geography: Evergreen Tree Regions

Science: First Aid

Science: Dogs—Breeds and Care

Fine Arts: Cooking

Fine Arts: Handmade Watercolors with Berries

Fine Arts: Maps and Models

Career Paths: Veterinarian—A Doctor for Animals

Lesson Activities

History and Geography: Evergreen Tree Regions

Where do the Boxcar children live? The book never tells us exactly, but we get many clues. In the previous chapter we learned about blueberries and where wild blueberries can be found (primarily in Maine and the Maritime Provinces of Canada). In chapter 4, we discover the children use pine needles for beds. Ask your student how he could use these two pieces of information to deduce where the children might live?

We first need to learn where evergreen trees (*non-deciduous trees*) grow. *Deciduous* [dee SI ju us] trees lose their leaves in the fall and winter. Oaks, maples, elms, and butternut are examples of common deciduous trees. Evergreen trees do not lose their needles, but instead stay *"ever green."* This type of tree grows many places around the United States but the main region where both wild blueberries *and* evergreen trees are located is the northeastern states. Have your student continue to watch for other clues in the story as you go along! Find some good books and study this area of botany! Have your student draw a simple map of the United States and Canada and color the regions where evergreens are prevalent using green colored pencils or markers.

Science: First Aid

Jessie carefully cared for Watch's wounded paw. Ask your student if he would know what to do if he had a thorn in his hand or foot? Being prepared for emergencies is important. Does your student know what is included in a proper first aid kit?

Take this opportunity to discuss types of wounds (puncture, laceration, burn, etc.) and the necessary care required for each. This would be a wonderful time to put together your own first aid kit! Have your student research items a kit should include. After he has compiled his own list, here are some additional suggestions: sterile adhesive bandages, safety pins, soap, latex gloves, sunscreen, sterile gauze pads, triangular bandages, scissors, tweezers, needle, moistened towelettes, antiseptic, thermometer, tongue depressors, petroleum jelly, pain relievers, anti-diarrhea medications, antacid, etc.

For more information, contact your local American Red Cross chapter. Another great source for activities and information is the Boy Scouts of America. Call 1-800-323-0732 to order their *First Aid Merit Badge Book*. As this is being written, these books cost less than $5. Besides first aid, the series includes titles covering more than 100 other topics. A great find! The books are small and easy for your student to carry around. Many public libraries keep these books on their shelves, as well.

Science: Dogs—Breeds and Care

In this chapter, Jessie and the children find a great watchdog. Does your student have a dog? What kind of dog is it? What does it look like? Have your student make a list of all the attributes and characteristics he can think of to describe his dog.

Now, have him do some research to discover characteristics of his dog's breed. Temperament, size, color and skills are all a part of a breed's general description. Did his list and the research match up? Why or why not? Learning about dog breeds is interesting and important if you are choosing a new canine friend.

Beyond selecting the type of dog you might want to own, learning to care for an animal is important as well. Have your student list all the things he thinks a dog (or other pet) requires. (Answers might include: food, water, warm bed, bathing, vaccinations, nail clipping, exercise, play time, affection and attention, a good name, etc.) Animals can become longtime companions, but only if we care for them and treat them kindly.

For additional reading, *The Incredible Journey* by Sheila Burnford is highly recommended. This beautiful story tells the tale of a dangerous 250-mile journey made by a bull terrier, a Siamese cat, and a Labrador retriever. It takes place in the Canadian wilderness and is based on actual pets owned by Sheila Burnford. A stunning book!

Fine Arts: Cooking

The Boxcar children thought blueberries were delicious and they are! Try this special recipe for a fantastically incredible bowl of blueberries.

1 bowl fresh blueberries (one pint)
1 Tbs. sour cream
1 Tbs. brown sugar

Stir and serve. You will hear compliments!

Fine Arts: Handmade Watercolors with Berries

Henry is surprised by a wonderful treat—fresh blueberries. But you don't just have to eat them, you can paint with them! Wearing old clothes or an apron, have your student help you at the stove and begin by bringing 1 1/2 cups of water to a boil. Drop in 1 cup of fresh (or frozen) blueberries. Continue to simmer the mixture until the water is very dark and the berries begin to break down (approximately 20 minutes). Strain through a piece of cheesecloth (or very fine strainer) and reserve the "paint" in a glass jar with a lid. This "paint" can be stored in your refrigerator for up to a week. You can repeat this process with a variety of berries for different colors. Raspberries, blackberries, strawberries, and cherries all make amazing watercolors.

If your student is interested in this organic art technique, experiment with vegetables as well. Spinach makes a beautiful green hue and red cabbage a bluish-purple tint. Once the paints are cool, give your student some paper and a brush and let him paint! Even if you are shy of berry stains, put on old clothes and cover your workspace. But do try this fun activity. These types of little creative lessons are what bring children's learning days to life!

Fine Arts: Maps and Models

By this time in our story, we have learned much about the Boxcar children's "home." Begin to record these facts, by making either a map or a three-dimensional model. Let your student's imagination decide where he thinks things are located: the boxcar itself, the brook, the clothesline, the shelf with Benny's pink cup, etc. If your student likes drawing, he might enjoy making "blueprints" of the boxcar and surrounding area. If he is more comfortable building things, let him take an old shoebox and build a replica of the boxcar. As you continue through the story, allow him to add things as they are discovered. If you have more than one student, you will find no two diagrams or models are alike. Imagination is a wonderful thing!

Career Paths: Veterinarian—A Doctor for Animals

Does your student enjoy animals? Jessie took care of Watch. Being able to make an animal feel better and get well makes us feel good. Ask your student if he thinks this

would be a fun job? People who care for animals and make them well are called veterinarians. It takes a long time to become a veterinarian. You must enjoy science and math to complete a degree in veterinary science. Also, you must be a very patient and kind person. Animals cannot speak or tell us what hurts so we must be willing to take the time to investigate their illnesses and injuries. Perhaps you have a family vet and could go and visit his or her office. If you do not, call some area animal hospitals and see if you could "interview" the doctor or get a tour.

Learning about different occupations helps us decide what we want to be when we grow up. If you love animals, a veterinarian can be a wonderful career choice! If this is something your student is really interested in, draw his attention to the James Herriot books. The larger volumes—*All Creatures Great and Small, All Things Bright and Beautiful, All Things Wise and Wonderful, The Lord God Made Them All*—are great read-aloud stories. Herriot has also written a variety of delightful children's stories including *Moses the Kitten, Only One Woof,* and *Oscar—Cat About Town.*

Writing and Discussion Question

Jessie was lucky Watch was a nice dog, but it is always wise to be careful around strange animals. Why might a strange animal sometimes be mean or dangerous, even if you are kind to him?

Vocabulary Words

deciduous: shedding leaves annually

evergreen: having leaves that are green all year

veterinarian: a person who deals with the diagnosis, prevention and care of diseases in animals

Internet Connections

To view current suggested links relating to this chapter's lessons, see www.fiveinarow.com/connections.

Chapter 5–The Explorers Find Treasure

Parent Summary

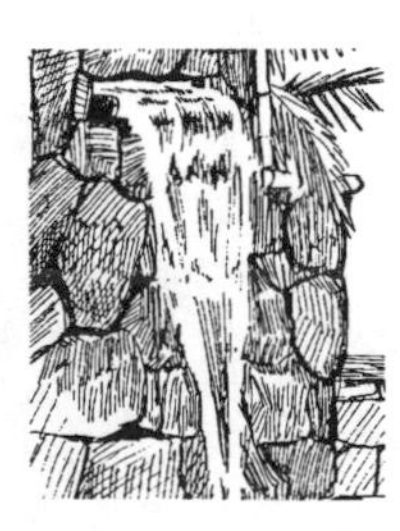

Jessie wakes up and finds the new "refrigerator" by the waterfall works well. The children drink milk for their breakfast and Henry sets off for town to find odd jobs. When Henry leaves, the children set out to find "treasure" at a nearby dump. Dishes, cups, spoons and wheels (Benny especially wants wheels) are what they find, and together they bring their loot back to camp. After carefully scrubbing the rust off things with sand, they eagerly await Henry's return. What a wonderful surprise for Henry! Henry finally returns with many interesting-looking bundles. He builds a fire to sterilize the new dishes and the children prepare to eat.

What we will cover in this chapter:

Science: Louis Pasteur and Milk Preservation

Science: Sterilization and Boiling Water

Science: Building a Campfire

Science: Rust

Fine Arts: Recycled Art

Issues of Human Relationships: Being an Encourager

Lesson Activities

Science: Louis Pasteur and Milk Preservation

Jessie kept the milk behind the waterfall to keep it cold. When she opens the milk, she announces, "It's delicious!" Has your student ever come across soured milk? When milk "goes bad" it becomes very thick and foul-smelling. Jessie kept their milk delicious by keeping it chilled. Many things, however, go into preserving milk.

Take this opportunity to introduce the famous scientist Louis Pasteur [pas TUR] and his discoveries. Have your student take a bottle of milk out of the refrigerator and look at the label. Draw his attention to the word *pasteurized*. This process is one way we preserve and make milk safe and Louis Pasteur invented it!

Pasteur was born in France in 1822. In 1864 (at the age of 42) he discovered milk turned bitter partly because of germs (microbes) inside the milk. After many experiments he learned that if the milk were heated, the heat could kill many of the germs and leave the milk unharmed. This method of heating a substance to kill germs is now known as *pasteurization*.

Pasteur also made great contributions to chemistry, medicine and industry. If your student is interested in this discovery, you might look for a good biography of Louis Pasteur.

Pasteurization is actually the second step of five milk preserving techniques we use before the milk goes to the store. The first is *separation*. In this step, dairy workers separate the cream or fat from the milk. Next, comes *pasteurization*. Then comes a process called *homogenization*. A huge machine puts the milk under great pressure and the cream still left in the milk is then evenly distributed throughout. Next, many dairy plants *fortify* the milk by adding different vitamins or extra calcium. And finally, the milk is *packaged* in sealed containers. The only step we, the consumer, must do to insure freshness is to keep the milk refrigerated. Your student might enjoy doing additional research on the dairy industry, writing a report or drawing a flowchart showing the five steps of milk processing using poster board and colorful markers.

Now, drink a glass of milk with your student and think about all the ways your milk was preserved—and remember Louis Pasteur! You might want to pause during your milk break and phone a local dairy to see if tours are available.

Science: Sterilization and Boiling Water

Why did Jessie need boiling water to get the dishes "really clean?" We learned from our lesson on Louis Pasteur that heat kills many germs. Jessie washed her dishes in the brook, but germs were still present. You might remind your student the boiling point of water is 212° F. This is much hotter than the brook! When we buy bottled water it has been sterilized in this manner.

A new vocabulary word for your student might be '*autoclave*.' This is what doctors use to sterilize their instruments. An autoclave is a container used for sterilizing by means of highly heated steam under pressure. Violet and Benny helped Jessie rub off the rust from the spoons and pans, but they were still dirty. Even if you can't see them, bacteria are still present. Sterilization with boiling water is an easy way to kill many germs.

Science: Building a Campfire

Henry carefully built Jessie a campfire. Fire is not something to play with and building a fire is not something to play at. Learning to build a good campfire and be safe is an important survival skill. If you feel comfortable with your student helping build a fire, the following lesson teaches the safe way to make a fire.

First, you must dig a small pit in the ground and clear away any excess brush or leaves. Never let *flammable* (able to burn) items near the edges of the fire pit. Next, get a bucket of water and a shovel and leave them near the campfire site. In case of emergencies, the water can put out large flames and the shovel can stamp out small flames.

Now, your student must gather three things in order to build a fire. First, he will need *tinder*. Tinder is little twigs, evergreen branches, dry leaves and dry brush. Make a pile of tinder in the middle of your fire pit. Next, he will need to gather *kindling*. Kindling is medium-sized pieces of wood that burn fairly easily. Pine is a good choice. Arrange your kindling in a teepee shape around the tinder. Finally, *firewood* is needed to surround the kindling. Firewood is often a hard wood like hickory or oak.

Now, carefully light the tinder with matches. It will burn first, then the kindling and at last, the firewood. Once your fire is burning, have someone watch it at all times. Never leave a fire unattended. When you are finished with your campfire, extinguish it by first using your shovel to spread the coals out flat. Watch them lose their red glow and begin to sprinkle water from your bucket over the coals. When it is almost out, cover the top with dirt. But never leave a campfire site, until all sign of fire is gone. Many forest fires are caused by careless campers.

Once you learn how to build a successful and safe campfire, have a hot dog roast or marshmallow roast! To remember the important steps of building a fire, have your student make his own "handbook" for building a fire. He can illustrate each step, and staple the papers together. He can even design his own cover. Some students might enjoy building a small "model" campfire using leaves, twigs and small sticks. Use white glue to build your "campfire" and consider using red cellophane or plastic wrap to simulate flames. (The chemistry of fire is covered in *Beyond Five in a Row*, Volume 2, *Skylark*, chapter 6.)

Science: Rust

Why were the spoons the children found rusty? Does your student know what rust is? Rust is formed through a process called *oxidation*. Oxidation is the combination of water and oxygen on either steel or iron. When these elements come together, that reddish-brown coating begins to cover the item. Keeping our steel or iron items dry is one way to prevent rusting.

Perhaps your car has some rust or you have an old bicycle. Take some time to go and examine the spots with your student. Your student might make a list of words describing rust and what he sees (burned, chalky, scratchy, brick-colored, tough, etc.).

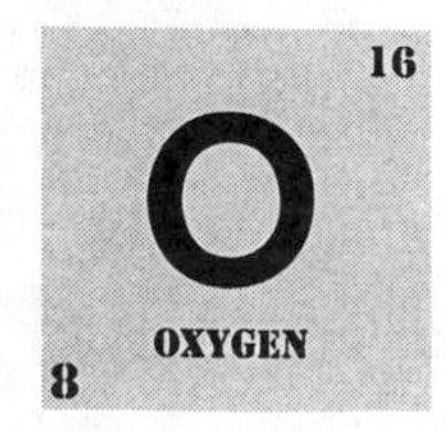

Once rust has begun to form, you can remove it by using *abrasives*. An abrasive is a substance with gritty pieces that help you scrub the rust off. What did Jessie use? (Sand.) Sand works well, but you can also buy products that help you remove rust. If you own something rusty and don't mind some untrained removal attempts, you might allow your student to try some sand and elbow grease on it. It is harder than it sounds! Think how long it took Jessie and Violet to clean all five spoons! Now let your student try sandpaper! It's easier when the sand is held in place by the paper, isn't it?

Fine Arts: Recycled Art

What did Violet use as a vase for her flowers? An old cup! Many things can be used for vases. Bottles, coffee cans, saucers, milk cartons, jelly jars, etc. Have your student look through the trash in your house (supervise the situation making sure no broken glass or jagged metal is present) and let him find something that was going to be thrown out. Then see if he can paint, cover, wash or modify the item to make something useful.

For example, an old cereal box might make a fun frame for a picture on the refrigerator. By cutting "frame-like" pieces out of the box and painting them you can make something very unique. An old plastic milk jug can be cut and revamped into a scoop for birdseed. An old peanut butter jar can be used for a storage container for paper clips. Your student can be so creative with this project. Take this opportunity to remind your student of the old adage, "One man's trash is another man's treasure." All too often we throw things away that might be recycled into beautiful art or functional items. Have a ball with this project!

Issues of Human Relationships: Being an Encourager

On page 49, Benny spots the dump first. Jessie says, "Oh, Benny. You saw the treasures first. What should we do without you!" Jessie encouraged Benny by telling him he was needed. Sometimes we forget to encourage each other.

Remind your student that as he gets older, he has more opportunities to encourage younger children. It is so much fun to make others feel good about themselves. Thinking of mean things to say to one another is destructive. Learning to build others up is more enjoyable for everyone.

Nothing makes us feel better than to know we are needed. Draw your student's attention to moments where encouragement can be given. Have your student draw a self-portrait of himself when he is sad. Then have him draw a picture of himself after someone has encouraged him. When we remember how good it feels to be uplifted, we eagerly look for opportunities to share that special feeling with others!

Writing and Discussion Question

Benny was very excited about finding those wheels at the dump. What do you think he was planning to do with them? What would you make with those four wheels?

Vocabulary Words

pasteurization: the process of heating milk to kill germs

separation: the process of separating milk from cream

homogenization: forcing milk through a pressurized system to evenly distribute cream droplets

fortification: adding vitamins and minerals

packaging: placing in sealed, sterile containers

autoclave: a machine used to sterilize instruments by using steam

flammable: able to burn

tinder: dry, easily flammable materials used for starting fires

kindling: small pieces of dry wood used for building fires

oxidation: the union of a substance with oxygen

abrasives: substance used for grinding or polishing

encourage: to build up, to give hope, to instill confidence, to support someone else

Internet Connections

To view current suggested links relating to this chapter's lessons, see www.fiveinarow.com/connections.

Chapter 6–A Queer Noise in the Night

Parent Summary

Henry shows the children what he has in his bundles: brown bread, milk, dried meat and a bone for Watch. While the four Alden children happily eat their meal, Henry tells them about his day. Having decided to go into Silver City instead of Greenfield, Henry says he walked through the town. Noticing a man pushing a lawn mower, Henry offered to finish the job. The man, Dr. Moore, is very tired of working and gratefully hands Henry the mower. After finishing the lawn and doing more odd jobs later that afternoon, Dr. Moore pays Henry one dollar and asks Henry to please come again the next day. The children finish their wonderful dinner, thankful Henry has found work. That night, as they get ready for bed, however, Henry and Jessie hear a strange cracking sound in the woods. Concerned, they listen closely. Finally, they decide it is just an animal sound and the children finally fall to sleep.

What we will cover in this chapter:

History and Geography: Pioneer Life in America

Science: Inventions—Motorized Lawn Mowers

Science: Nutrition—White versus Whole Wheat Bread

Language Arts: Learning to Write in Chapters

Fine Arts: Make a Collage

Issues of Human Relationships: Generosity

Lesson Activities

History and Geography: Pioneer Life in America

Pioneers in the early days of America lived very different lives from you and me today. They did not have refrigerators, microwaves, department stores, and many other modern conveniences we take for granted. In this chapter, Henry buys dried meat (page 58). Henry knows it will be easier for the children to eat it with their hands and it will last longer.

Because the Boxcar children live in the woods, they do many things like pioneers did. Pioneers often dried meat to preserve it. They would slice it into small chunks or shave it thin and lay it in the afternoon sun to dry. Then, once it became dry and leathery, they could easily pack it in saddlebags or keep it in their pockets. Sometimes, instead of drying the meat they would thread it onto sticks and hold it over a flame to smoke it. Sometimes with chicken or pork, the meat was put in barrels of brine (heavily salted water) to cure (preserving by soaking in brine). Ask your student if he has ever had dried meat. Today, it is often called jerky. If not, a trip to a grocery store or neighborhood convenience store will yield a wide variety of dried meats. Buy a package and try eating it together as you discuss the challenges of pioneer life!

On page 62, Jessie enlists Benny to help make a broom. Pioneer women had to make their own cleaning tools. Dusters were made of real chicken feathers. Brooms were made of long sticks and pine branches or twigs fastened to the end. This type of broom is called a besom.

Today, most of our brooms are made with plastic bristles. Take some time to examine a broom. How are the bristles fastened to the handle? How long do you think a modern broom lasts? How long do you think besoms last?

On page 63 Henry gives Violet the new tablecloth he bought. Violet takes out her workbag and begins to hem the cloth. In pioneer days, families could not run to a store and buy a new tablecloth. Just like Violet, they had to buy the material and then finish it themselves.

Has your student learned to sew simple stitches? You might take a small piece of material and try to sew a little edge. Then fold it over and hem it. Think how long it must have taken pioneers to hem a tablecloth long enough for a large table!

Henry buys fresh, sweet butter and brings it home (page 63). Ask your student to make a list of all the things he loves to eat with butter (toast, baked potatoes, pancakes, popcorn, corn on the cob, noodles, biscuits, etc.). The book tells us it had been many days since the children had eaten butter.

In pioneer days, people made their own butter. A tool called a churn helped them make the butter. A churn is shaped like a slender barrel with a lid. The lid has a hole in the center, and a long handle and plunger is set down into the barrel. Fresh milk is poured in and the operator pumps the plunger up and down until the butter forms.

Making butter at home today is really very simple. Have your student get a mason jar with a very tight lid. Pour in heavy cream. Now, start to shake. If you have several students, this is a great sharing activity. Perhaps while you're reading aloud your students can be passing the "butter jar." After a long while (45 minutes or so) you will see little dots begin to form in the milk. Keep shaking! When the butter is done, you will see a big lump of butter and a lot of clear liquid. That clear liquid is called buttermilk.

Your student will probably notice the butter is not yellow. You can make your butter that sunshine color by boiling a few carrot peels in a small saucepan. Use some of the strained liquid to tint your fresh butter. Yumm! Just like Jessie says, "Oh, butter!"

For a special treat and delightful fun, you and your student can make a "Boxcar Children Lunch." Gather brown bread, fine yellow cheese, blueberries, dried meat, milk, butter and brown cookies. Perhaps you could make your own butter and bake the bread and cookies. Spread a tablecloth on the floor (or even better, outside) and feast! Think of how thankful the children were for their delicious meal! Reflect on the hard work the pioneers did for their food and tools. Take time to read a simple book from the library on pioneers.

Science: Inventions—Motorized Lawn Mowers

Look at the picture of Henry mowing the grass found on page 59. Has your student ever seen a lawn mower like this? It is called a push-mower and you can still buy them. It is much harder to cut the grass with a push-mower because all the power must come from you! The blades are arranged along a cylinder and are attached to a long handle. As you walk, the cylinder rotates like a wheel and the blades snip off the grass.

Today, most people have lawn mowers with motors. These machines run on gasoline and in many cases, even the wheels turn themselves. All you have to do is guide as you follow along behind. Some people even have lawn mowers on little tractors. You drive them like a car! Imagine how much easier it would have been for Henry if he had been able to use a motorized lawn mower! Imagine how tired the doctor was before Henry arrived! If you have the opportunity, go to a well stocked hardware store or lawn mower store and look at all the different varieties of mowing machines.

Science: Nutrition—White versus Whole Wheat Bread

Henry and the children eat brown bread. Ask your student if he eats whole wheat (brown) or white bread? Probably both. Which type does your student think is better for him? Is there a difference? There is a difference, but to understand it you must learn about the primary component of bread—wheat. Wheat is a grain and is grown on huge farms. When the wheat is harvested it is cleaned and taken to a mill. There it is milled (ground into flour) with huge stones or steel wheels. The wheat is crushed and ground into flour. Whole-wheat flour is brown because it includes parts of the hull that surrounded the grain. The bread you make from brown flour, or what is often called whole-wheat flour, is slightly heartier and sometimes even a little crunchy. Find a picture of a wheat grain and have your student draw the parts and label them. Also, you might research flour milling, wheat farming, or bakeries, etc.

It wasn't until the late 1800s that mills were able to mill white flour at an affordable price. Before, in order to get pure white flour, the wheat had to be ground by hand. White flour makes softer bread and is better for cakes and pastries. But is brown bread better for you? Yes! By using the whole grain (whole-wheat flour) the flour retains most of the fiber and vitamins found in the wheat originally. When the flour is picked over and bleached (white flour) the result is a flour lacking in nutritional ingredients.

Today, our white breads are enriched with vitamins and fiber. In other words, the bakers add the important nutrients back into the bread after the flour is ground. But natural is often better. Show your student some whole-wheat flour and white flour. Talk about the differences. If you have time, perhaps you could bake a loaf of each. Now sit down and sample your results and think about the nice brown bread the children ate!

Language Arts: Learning to Write in Chapters

Now that your student is several chapters into *The Boxcar Children*, take this opportunity to go back and look at the end of each chapter. Notice how the last sentence of the chapter leads into the next. It is not always a mysterious ending as we have discussed in previous lessons, but it naturally flows to the first sentence of the next chapter. For example, draw your student's attention to the last sentence in chapter 5, page 56, "Now I know they're clean enough to eat from," she said happily."

Now look at the first sentence of chapter 6, page 57, "At last it was dinner time, and the children sat down to see what Henry had in his bundles." This simple technique is how authors often join chapters together. Tying the idea of *eating off of clean utensils* into *the beginning of mealtime* makes sense.

Have your student write a story about whatever he'd like. Now have him divide his story into several shorter segments, ending and beginning each chapter with sentences that lead to the next chapter.

Fine Arts: Make a Collage

Art is emotion. When you look at a painting you can sometimes tell what the artist was feeling by the colors, shapes, shadows and subject he chose. If you listen to classical music you can pick out the joyful feelings and the foreboding notes.

A collage is a specific art form. It is created by taking pieces of paper (hand-colored, newspaper, magazine, etc.), flower petals, twigs, small items, buttons, or anything else you want and gluing them to a larger piece of poster board or stiff paper. The idea behind a collage is not to create a specific picture, but instead, to suggest a feeling or idea.

On page 66, Jessie and Henry are frightened by a strange noise in the woods. Ask your student about times he has felt frightened. Fear is a strong emotion. An interesting project might be to create a collage that represents "fear" to your student. Encourage him to choose colors, shapes and designs that remind him of that emotion.

Then have your student create a collage that represents safety. Knowing you are safe is an equally powerful feeling. Remind your student as he works, that a collage cannot be wrong! Anything he chooses to include is important because it means something to him! Creating a collage takes time but the finished work is worth the challenge!

Issues of Human Relationships: Generosity

Being generous means being willing to share. It is an important character issue and makes us stronger, kinder people. On page 65, Benny is generous by offering Henry the use of his precious wheels. Perhaps Benny had planned on using those wheels for something else, but he decided to share.

On page 61, the kind cook gave Henry ten fresh, delicious cookies! She was being generous. Draw your student's attention to these examples, and encourage him to look for opportunities to be generous!

Writing and Discussion Question

Henry used a push-mower to cut the grass. Today, we have motorized lawn mowers. What are some other ways (both realistic and humorous) we could cut a lawn?

Internet Connections

To view current suggested links relating to this chapter's lessons, see www.fiveinarow.com/connections.

Chapter 7–A Big Meal from Little Onions

Parent Summary

The morning after hearing the strange noise, Henry and Jessie discuss the situation. Deciding it must have been a person in the woods, Henry advises Jessie not to leave the younger children unattended. Jessie agrees and after a brief conversation with Benny about a new "building" project, Henry leaves for work. When he arrives at Dr. Moore's home, he is quickly put to work thinning vegetables in the garden. Mrs. Moore, the doctor's mother, gives him a dollar at noon, compliments him on his job, and asks him to return after lunch. Henry is able to take the little vegetables he thinned home with him and on the way purchases some meat.

While he was at work Jessie and Benny worked on a new fireplace! When he gives Jessie the meat and vegetables she immediately starts a stew for supper. After lunch,

Henry goes back to the doctor's house and is told to organize the garage. He does a wonderful job and Dr. Moore gives him one of four hammers Henry found along with a bundle of old nails. Henry collects another dollar and heads home, head high and heart glad. He excitedly shows the children his new hammer and they all sit down to enjoy a wonderful meal. After dinner, Henry takes Benny's wheels and his new hammer and builds a cart. Then they all go to sleep, well fed and happy.

What we will cover in this chapter:

Science: Classification and Organization

Science: Creating a Garden

Language Arts: Compare and Contrast

Language Arts: Literary Enrichment—Stone Soup

Language Arts: Point of View

Fine Arts: Dramatic Interpretation of Inanimate Objects

Issues of Human Relationships: Being a Good Worker

Lesson Activities

Science: Classification and Organization

Henry did a wonderful job organizing Dr. Moore's garage! He came up with an organization system (tools in one box, nails in another) and followed it. Take this opportunity to begin a dialogue with your student about organization.

An interesting project might center on a box of family photographs. Hand your student the box and instruct him to organize the pictures. He might choose to put them in piles according to the date of the photo, location of the photo, last name of most prominent person in the photo, etc. The possibilities are endless!

If your student enjoys organizing things, you might give him one drawer out of the kitchen (we all have that "junk" drawer) or a shelf in your linen closet. By providing him with eggshell cartons, little boxes, coffee cans, baby food jars, etc., he can have a splendid and imaginative time creating his own system.

Remember, some children are more adept at this than others. If your child was born with a card file in his hand, this might be quite enjoyable! If your child is more creative and less organized, this might be more of a challenge. However, having order in our lives is a learned life skill. We can all benefit from activities that encourage us in this area.

Classification Acronym:

***K**eep*	(Kingdom)
***P**ulling*	(Phylum)
***C**orn*	(Class)
***O**ut*	(Order)
***F**rom*	(Family)
***G**ramma's*	(Genus)
***S**ack*	(Species)

Once this project is finished, you may choose to share with your student about the way science classifies (or organizes) nature. Every insect, mammal, bacteria, plant, etc., is placed in a specific category. Ask your student why people have chosen to classify nature? Why did Dr. Moore want his garage organized? It is much easier to find things!

In scientific classification there are seven main categories. They are (1) kingdom, (2) phylum, (3) class, (4) order, (5) family, (6) genus, and (7) species. The largest group is called the kingdom and the smallest is the species. Every plant or animal known to man is classified in this way. Each animal belongs to the kingdom called *Animalia*. Every plant belongs to the kingdom called *Plantae*. (Acronym for remembering the order of the classifications is at left sidebar.)

At this point, it isn't necessary for your student to fully comprehend every aspect of the method of scientific classification. It is important to be familiar with it. Have your student choose a specific animal (for example, a chipmunk) and research which phylum, class, order, etc., it belongs to. It is an amazing thing to learn each living organism has it's own special place!

Science: Creating a Garden

Mrs. Moore's garden is both beautiful and bountiful! Is your student interested in gardens and growing things? If you have the space and inclination (this will require both time commitment and assistance from the teacher), have your student plan his own garden. If realizing this project is not feasible, creating the "perfect imaginary garden" can still be great fun.

Your student can render his plans in drawings, on a computer, with a three-dimensional model, etc. Have your student do research on seeds and vegetables. He will need to learn what types of vegetables he wants and what is practical with the space he has. For free information and catalogues on vegetables/seeds/regional zones, call Burpee Seeds at 1-800-888-1447.

After he has chosen the size of his plot, location, and what plants or seeds he will need, he can begin to plot out his planting schedule. By using a calendar, he can note when he will need to plant the different vegetables or fruits, and when harvest can be anticipated. This project is so delightful because *planning* a garden is almost as much fun as actually *planting* one!

If your family has a garden every year and your student is familiar with what goes into preparing it, perhaps planning a garden for a *different* region of the country would be an interesting project. If you live in Florida, planning a garden for North Dakota is very different! May your plans, the work of your hands, and your harvest be blessed!

Language Arts: Compare and Contrast

On page 72, Mrs. Moore tells Henry he is a good worker. What makes a person a good worker? Have your student make a list of all the characteristics he feels contribute to being a good worker (diligence, cheerfulness, efficiency, carefulness, knowledge, creativity, honesty, etc.). Now have your student make a list of all the qualities which a poor worker might have (laziness, complaining attitude, dishonest, untrustworthy, lack of integrity, etc.).

When the list is finished, you can introduce the concept of compare and contrast. This is a skill that is necessary throughout life. Being able to organize differences and similarities regarding any given subject helps us in our jobs, homes, relating to different cultures, politics, etc. Explain to your student how learning to compare and contrast an issue allows us to focus our thoughts on specific ideas. Instead of saying, "A good worker is someone who does a good job" (a vague statement), your student can say, "A good worker is someone who commits to a specific project, and happily completes his obligation" (a concrete sentence). Think up other topical lists for your student to compare and contrast, e.g., what makes a winning or losing team, what makes a home comfortable or uncomfortable, etc.

Language Arts: Literary Enrichment—Stone Soup

Jessie makes a wonderful stew for the children using Henry's meat, vegetables and salt. Does your student like stew or soup? A classic children's story (one which is considered a part of our cultural literary heritage) is the tale of stone soup. Do you remember? There are many versions of this old folk tale. Go the library and find a copy of this story. Now sit down and read it with your student over a nice hot bowl of soup for lunch.

Language Arts: Point of View

Review this chapter's events with your student. After Henry leaves for work, we see the rest of the day from Henry's *point of view*. What happens back at the boxcar while Henry is at Dr. Moore's house? A writer must choose a point of view from which to write. Sometimes this point of view shifts as each character is explored.

Gertrude Chandler Warner, the author of *The Boxcar Children*, has chosen to write chapter 7 from Henry's point of view. Have your student rewrite the chapter from Jessie, Violet or Benny's point of view. While Henry is thinning vegetables and organizing hammers, Violet and the other children might have walked Watch, swept the boxcar, found a hidden treasure chest, climbed the tallest tree to see if they could spot Henry, made a hopscotch board in the dirt, discussed how much they missed their parents, talked about what they think happened to the baker and his wife, etc. Imagine all the possibilities! What a wonderful exercise in point of view! This activity could be a long-term (one- or two-week) assignment or shortened for your younger student.

Fine Arts: Dramatic Interpretation of Inanimate Objects

Your student is probably familiar with the concept of playing a character in a play or movie. Pretending to be another *person* is challenging but makes sense—it is realistic. Imagine pretending to be an inanimate (or not living) thing! Let your student's creativity run wild with this project!

Ask your student to pretend he is one of the turnips from Mrs. Moore's garden. Have your student think of an action and a sound that he thinks a turnip would make. Make a list of all the different kinds of vegetables in a garden, and come up with one dramatic presentation (action/sound) for as many as you can. What might a carrot sound like? How would a rutabaga walk? Do parsnips jump or crawl?

This is a lesson in abstract thinking and dramatic art. If your student is confined by his realistic and analytical thinking, his imagination may suffer. Encourage him to be silly and daring in this fun exercise! You will have a fantastic time! This is a wonderful beginning drama project because no memorization is required. There are no lines! This is also an excellent activity for the student who is shy or introverted. Every sound or movement is correct because they are entirely up to your imagination!

Issues of Human Relationships: Being a Good Worker

Henry is invited to come back to Dr. Moore's house every time he works. Both Dr. Moore and Mrs. Moore tell him he is a good worker. What does your student think is involved in being a good worker? Ask your student to make a list of all the attributes he believes are included in being a good worker. (If he did this exercise in "Compare and Contrast" earlier, have him get out the list he wrote at that time.) Is being a good worker different from doing good work? Spend some time exploring this topic. Encourage your student to be a good worker! Having favor with your employer and friends is important to happiness and success!

Writing and Discussion Questions

1. On page 73, Mrs. Moore asks Henry if he has chickens. The book tells us Henry was glad he did not have to answer that question. Why?

2. On page 78, Dr. Moore tells Henry he could use many workers to help pick cherries the following Monday. Then he looks at Henry in a "queer way." Why?

Internet Connections

To view current suggested links relating to this chapter's lessons, see www.fiveinarow.com/connections.

Chapter 8–A Swimming Pool at Last

Parent Summary

The next morning Henry, Jessie, Violet and Benny begin on the swimming pool project. They measure the depth of the pool and, discovering it is one foot, they determine they will need three feet for a good swimming hole. Then, using Benny's cart to haul stones, they begin to build the dam across the brook. After a lot of hard work, the children successfully create a three-foot deep swimming pool.

Jessie and Violet cook lunch while the boys take the first swim. After a wonderful lunch of leftover stew, they set off for a walk. Exploring the woods, Benny finds an abandoned chicken's nest (he saw the chicken running away). They collect the five eggs, and Jessie makes a wonderful dinner from Benny's discovery!

What we will cover in this chapter:

History and Geography: Bells as Signals

Science: How We Measure—Distance, Time, Volume, Land, Water

Science: Calories and the Food We Burn

Science: Eggs

Science: Dams

Fine Arts: Drawing A Scene

Fine Arts: Cooking

Issues of Human Relationships: Being Flexible and Having Fun

Lesson Activities

History and Geography: Bells as Signals

On page 88, when Jessie rings her dinner bell, Henry and Benny hear it and come running for their meal. Has your student ever been around a dinner bell? Bells, historically, have served as effective mealtime signals. On large farms and ranches, the cook often rings a bell to signal lunch or supper. The workers, far off in a field or in the stables, can hear the bell and come home. In wealthy mansions, butlers sometimes walk the halls, ringing a little bell and notifying the family dinner is served. And in the old west, the chuck wagon cooks would strike a giant triangle to call the "cowpokes" home. Your student might have seen this on an old western movie or television series.

Perhaps your student would enjoy implementing this into one of your meals. You might even have your student go to different rooms in the house, outside in the yard, in the basement, etc., and see how far the sound of the bell reaches.

Besides calling for mealtimes, bells are used on ships to signal the end of a work shift. Your student may have noticed the reference to the mill bells in chapter 7 (page 72). On ships, bells help the sailors tell time. A 24-hour day on a ship is divided into six, 4-hour watches. Midnight to 4 a.m., 4 a.m. to 8 a.m., 8 a.m. to noon, etc. Every sailor's watch (or work shift) lasts four hours. The men then have eight hours free before the next watch. The ship's bell rings once for every half hour during one watch. For example, a sailor begins his watch at noon. At 12:30 p.m. he hears one bell. At 1:00 p.m. two bells sound. When the sailor hears eight bells signal at once, he knows his watch is over. If your student seems interested in any of these bell uses, go to the library where he can do more research.

Science: How We Measure—Distance, Time, Volume, Land, Water

How did Henry measure the depth of the swimming pool (page 84)? With a stick! This might seem like a primitive method of measurement but it is quite effective and used in many areas of life. For example, have your student watch you check the oil in the car. By using a tool called a "dipstick," we can see the level of oil. Just like Henry saw the level of water! When gasoline trucks deliver gasoline to the filling station they use long rods to check the levels in the underground tanks. If they are low, the trucks fill them up.

This is a good opportunity to discuss various aspects of measurement with your student. Measurement does not have to involve rulers. For example, people measure the height of horses by "hands." A hand equals about 4 inches, the average width of a grown man's hand. A horse is measured from the ground to the highest point of the shoulder.

Another example is a "foot"—the distance between the heel and the big toe. A "fathom" is the distance between the tips of your third fingers when your arms are stretched out. A "palm" is the distance from one side of the hand to the other. Have your student measure the length of your kitchen using these types of measurement.

Your student can also invent his own methods of measurement. He might use a fork from the silverware to measure the length of your dining room table. If it takes 14 repetitions of laying the fork end to end, then your table is "14 forks" long.

Of course, we usually use rulers and exact figures to measure things. (Why? Because these measurements are more widely accepted and uniform so we can communicate more effectively.) Discuss inches, feet, yards, miles, etc., with your student. These are ways we measure the distance. Time is measured in seconds, minutes, hours, days, weeks, months, years, decades, centuries and millennia. Volume is measured in teaspoons, tablespoons, cups, pints, quarts, gallons, etc. Land is measured in acres. Lakes and other large bodies of water are also measured in acres. They are measured by how many acres of land the water covers. If your student already understands these concepts, you might wish to introduce the metric system.

If you discuss many of these measurement concepts, your student might like to create his own chart (poster board works great for this) of all the different types of measurements. He can simply make lists of terms and definitions or he can illustrate each type of measuring device. This is fun to create and helps him remember all he has learned!

Science: Calories and the Food We Burn

On page 89, Jessie tells Benny their food tastes so good because they "worked so hard." Why is this so? Why, when we play outside, go sledding, ride our bike or help work in the garden, do we feel so hungry? Why does our food seem to taste so much better?

Our bodies run on a fuel called "energy." Energy is stored in fat. Fat comes from food and the amount of energy we glean from our food is measured in "calories." The word "calorie" is a Latin word, and is used to define a single unit of energy in our body.

[**Teacher's Note**: If you want to be more specific, a single calorie involves the amount of energy it takes to raise the temperature of one gram of water by one degree Celsius.]

When we work hard (or play hard) our body burns the energy it has stored (or burns the calories). After awhile, our body begins to run out of fuel. It tells us by making us hungry. So, when Henry and the children had worked so hard all morning, by the time they ate lunch their bodies needed additional energy—and everything tastes better when we're hungry!

Your library has many books on the human body and the way we use calories. Go to the library and do more research if your student finds this interesting! A great research project might be for your student to research the number of calories needed for his age, size and lifestyle. Now have him keep track of the calories he consumes for a day or two, looking up the calorie content of each item from packages or from a simple, paperback calorie book readily available at the grocery store.

Interestingly, one pound of body weight is equivalent to 3,500 calories. If we want to lose one pound of body weight, we must reduce our caloric intake by 3,500, or increase our energy output so as to burn up an additional 3,500 calories. You can easily calculate how long it might take you to gain or lose any given number of pounds based on how many calories you burn, or leave out of your diet each day.

Science: Eggs

The egg is an amazing thing! You can eat an egg or allow it to be incubated and watch it hatch into a bird! In our story, Benny finds eggs in the woods—abandoned by the chicken mother. Jessie cooks the eggs and the children have a wonderful meal! (page 90) Does your student know all the parts of an egg?

First, an egg has a hard shell. Does the shell feel smooth? Have your student look at it with a magnifying glass. It is actually covered with little bumps. How interesting! Next, under the shell is an extremely thin *membrane* (or skin-like covering). Under that is the white of the egg or the *albumen*. Finally, in the center lies the yellow part, or the *yolk*. This part of the egg is actually the food and nourishment supply for the growing chick. When you eat an egg yolk, you're eating baby chicken food! Locate a book at the library that shows the parts of an egg and the growth process of a baby chick.

If you look in the grocery store at the egg cartons, you see eggs are graded by quality. (Grade AA, A, B and C determine how watery or thin the egg is.) Eggs are also sized. Jumbo, Large and Medium are all common sizes for eggs. Jumbo eggs are about 2 1/4 ounces and small eggs are about 1 1/2 ounces.

Your student has probably seen eggs both raw and hard-boiled. How can you tell the difference without breaking them? Well, a long time ago a process called "candling" was discovered. Candling is used to detect blood spots, cracks and the size of the yolk. For our purposes, however, candling can be used to check to see if an egg is raw or cooked. If you hold a hard-boiled egg and a raw egg up to a candle flame in a darkened room, you will see more light go through the raw egg. You can also tell the difference by spinning both eggs on a flat surface. The hard-boiled egg will spin a lot faster and longer, because the loose yolk in the raw egg acts like a brake.

Many fun science experiments can be done using an egg. One includes fairly warm water, salt and a raw egg, in the shell. Put the egg in a bowl and cover it with about 2 cups of nearly hot water. Now, have your student dissolve about 1 teaspoon of salt in the water. Continue adding salt. When you have put in almost 12 teaspoons of salt the egg will float in the water! Why? Salt water is much denser than plain water and so heavier things become more buoyant. Even *people* float better in the ocean (salt water) than in lakes.

Another experiment involves a match, a peeled hard-boiled egg, and a glass bottle with an opening slightly smaller than the diameter of the peeled, hard-boiled egg you've chosen. Have your student set the egg pointed end down on the mouth of the bottle. Can it fit? No! Now, with your help, have your student light one or two kitchen matches and drop them down the bottle. Quickly, place the egg back atop the mouth. When the flame uses up the oxygen in the air of the bottle, it will create a vacuum and suck the egg down into the bottle! Amazing! Have fun doing experiments with eggs!

Don't forget, eggs make delicious meals—omelets, fried, hard-boiled, soft-boiled, over-easy, sunny-side-up, scrambled, poached, and more! Make an egg any way you like it and enjoy!

Science: Dams

Henry uses rocks to dam up the water for the swimming pool. This incident provides an opportunity to discuss the subject of dams. Of course, you know that beavers are animals that have the wonderful ability to construct intricate dams. By stopping up the water, they create a pond or lake in which they build their homes. Find some interesting books at your library on these fascinating animals.

Then if you are interested you can begin to explore man-made dams. Find some information on the Hoover Dam, located on the Arizona-Nevada border damming the Colorado River, or the Aswan Dam which dams up the floodwaters of the Nile. Look for a video at your library on one of the famous dams, and perhaps there is a smaller dam nearby that you could actually visit.

Fine Arts: Drawing A Scene

Drawing is so much fun! Sometimes we draw a picture of one particular thing—a vase, horse, house, flower, etc. But a more advanced drawing skill is to draw a picture of a scene. A scene is where action is happening—a child reading a book, mother making lemonade, father mowing the lawn, etc.

On page 88 we see a wonderful picture opportunity in the scene involving Henry and Benny splashing in the pool and Jessie and Violet cooking dinner over the fire. Have your student draw how he envisions this scene. Drawing a scene with action in it is challenging. Be as imaginative as you can! Again, if you have more than one student, expect a wide variety of drawings since each of us pictures the scene differently in our minds.

Fine Arts: Cooking

Here is a recipe for Strawberry Shortcake:

(This luscious shortcake is just a batch of biscuit dough with added sugar.)

2 cups flour
1/3 cup sugar
4 tsp. baking powder
1/2 cup (1 stick) cold butter or margarine
1 cup milk
sugar for sprinkling
3 1/2 cups fresh strawberries, divided
2 Tbs. sugar
whipped topping

Combine flour, 1/3 cup sugar and baking powder. Cut in butter or margarine. Add milk and stir till dough balls up. Grease an 8" or 9" round cake pan and spread the dough evenly in the pan. Sprinkle sugar on top. Bake at 425° F. for 12-15 minutes or until it is rich brown on top and done in the center. While the shortcake is baking, crush 1 1/2 cups of the strawberries with the 2 Tbs. sugar; let set. Slice remaining 2 cups strawberries, sprinkle with sugar; let set. When the cake is baked, cool 10 minutes on wire rack, then cut the shortcake in half horizontally so that there is a top half and a bottom half of the cake. Now take the still warm bottom half of the shortcake and pour the crushed strawberries over it. Add whipped topping and a few of the strawberry slices. Put the top on the shortcake, cover it with sliced strawberries and add more whipped cream. Serve at once. Make sure everyone has a spoon and dig in! What a glorious morning!

Issues of Human Relationships: Being Flexible and Having Fun

At the beginning of this chapter (page 83), Henry and the children sleep in! Sleeping in is wonderful fun! Having a schedule and getting up on time is necessary for an organized life, but every once in awhile getting to sleep in is like a special treat! Give your student a special, flexible holiday by allowing him to sleep in one morning. You might even curl up under the covers and read a story together late in the morning and eat breakfast in bed! One of the author's fondest memories was sleeping in, and having her mother fix strawberry shortcake for breakfast. (Strawberry shortcake can actually be quite healthy, consisting of bread, fruit and dairy products—and it's very delicious!) Break the daily grind with an official sleep-in day and have fun!

Writing and Discussion Question

Henry is excited about making a swimming pool. What is something that *you* would like to build at *your* house? Explain what the project is and how you might accomplish it.

Vocabulary Words

watch: the period of time a person (perhaps sailor) is on duty to guard, lookout, protect, etc.

calorie: the term used for amount of heat or energy produced by food

shell: outside layer of egg

membrane: skin-like covering of egg-white, second layer of egg

albumen: the white part of egg, third layer

yolk: the yellow portion of egg, the food supply for the chick; fourth layer

candling: the process by which a person holds an egg up to a candle flame (or today, electric light) and detects blood spots, cracks, yolk size and whether or not it is hard-boiled

Internet Connections

To view current suggested links relating to this chapter's lessons, see www.fiveinarow.com/connections.

Chapter 9–Fun in the Cherry Orchard

Parent Summary

The day Dr. Moore had invited the children to pick cherries arrives, and they decide to all go and help. Concerned that someone might spot four children walking and

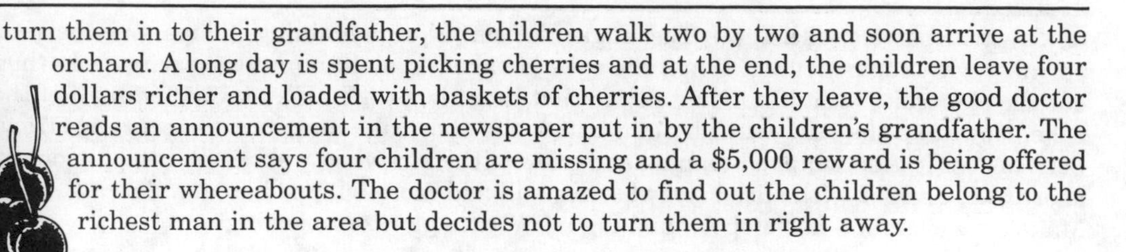

turn them in to their grandfather, the children walk two by two and soon arrive at the orchard. A long day is spent picking cherries and at the end, the children leave four dollars richer and loaded with baskets of cherries. After they leave, the good doctor reads an announcement in the newspaper put in by the children's grandfather. The announcement says four children are missing and a $5,000 reward is being offered for their whereabouts. The doctor is amazed to find out the children belong to the richest man in the area but decides not to turn them in right away.

What we will cover in this chapter:

History and Geography: Different Fruit Regions

Science: Orchards—Types, Care and Tending

Language Arts: Periodicals—Newspapers

Fine Arts: A Poem and a Picture

Issues of Human Relationships: Finding Your Place to Help Others

Lesson Activities

History and Geography: Different Fruit Regions

In the previous lessons, we discussed possible regions where our story might be taking place. We discovered wild blueberries grow most often in Maine and the Maritime Provinces in Canada. However, wild blueberries are also found in the state of Michigan and this state is also the leading state in cherries and their production!

Perhaps Henry, Jessie, Violet and Benny live in Michigan! Ask your student what state he lives in. Does he know what fruits, if any, grow there?

There are three main divisions in the fruit world—temperate, subtropical and tropical. Temperate fruits require a yearly cold season to grow well. Therefore, these fruits grow in the majority of regions in the United States. Temperate fruits include apples, pears, peaches, plums, and some small fruits—strawberries, grapes, cranberries, etc.

Subtropical fruits require a mainly warm growing season and can stand an occasional light frost or cool snap. These fruits are oranges, limes, lemons, kiwi fruits, avocados and figs. The leading producing state of these fruits is California. The seasons are warm and rarely get cold (below 40° F.).

Finally, we have the tropical fruits that cannot handle even the slightest frost. These are grown primarily in the tropics (nowhere in the United States) and include pineapples, bananas, mangos, etc. Find a map showing the tropics and note the countries and what fruit is grown there.

Learning where different fruit regions are is interesting and helps us understand why certain fruits are more expensive than others. Go to your supermarket and buy some fruit from each region. Perhaps your student could make a map of the United States and draw the different fruits and where they grow. For more information on this topic, consult your encyclopedia or local library.

Science: Orchards—Types, Care, and Tending

Dr. Moore had a rich and plentiful cherry orchard. Is your student interested in how we grow fruit? There are three steps to growing fruit in an orchard. (These steps are similar to those of growing produce in any basic garden.) Planting, tending and harvesting are the three required steps.

In a garden, you plant seeds. In an orchard, you must start with trees. A farmer will gather the saplings (young trees) for his crop and plant them a specific distance apart, in a special area (good sunlight, shelter, etc.), making sure everything will still be adequate when the trees are full grown. Then, when his trees start growing, he must train and prune the branches. Training means to stake or tie the branches in a specific direction so they will grow straight and strong. Pruning (cutting off) is necessary at least once a year to eliminate sick or unproductive branches.

Sometimes farmers must use pesticides (a substance which kills bugs and insects) on their trees to keep the fruit from being eaten before it can be harvested. Some farmers feel the pesticides can be harmful to people when they eat the fruit, so they practice what is called "organic" farming. Organic farming uses natural aids, instead of chemicals, to protect the trees.

Finally, after months of hard work, the farmer harvests his crop. Most fruit is hand picked, but with the rising costs of raising crops, some farmers use special machinery to pick the fruit. With hard fruits such as apples and pears, the harvest season is longer. There is more time to get the fruit off the tree. With soft or fleshy fruits, like Dr. Moore's cherries, the fruit will rot on the tree if you don't harvest it quickly and birds can carry off a great deal of the fruit. This is why Dr. Moore wanted all the help he could get and the workers worked all day long.

If you live near an orchard, take a field trip and do some picking of your own! Nothing tastes better than a fresh apple right off the tree, or a peach pie made from peaches you picked! Consider planting a fruit tree yourself! Using the research you conducted on fruits and their regions, decide what kind of tree will grow well where you live. Eat your fruit in good health and think about the hard work Henry and the children did for Dr. Moore!

Language Arts: Periodicals—Newspapers

Dr. Moore saw an announcement in his newspaper about Henry, Jessie, Violet and Benny (page 99). People sometimes place reward notices for lost items in their newspapers. If you've lost your bicycle or dog, advertising in a newspaper is a good way to inform many people to watch for your lost property.

Learning how to use a paper is a valuable and necessary life skill. Have your student begin by learning about the different sections of a paper. Sit down with your student and flip through a newspaper (local, weekly papers aren't as good for this project as a larger, daily paper). Make a list of each section as you come to it. National news, local news, sports, entertainment, op/ed (opinions and editorials), classifieds, obituaries, and whatever else you see. Discuss with your student what is included in each of these sections.

Spend some time just looking at the classifieds. Your student will probably be amazed at the diversity of offerings you find in this section alone. Job opportunities, rewards (just like the Doctor found in his paper), cars for sale, cameras, livestock, house pets, homes, apartments, boats, music lessons, etc.

To teach your student the various sections of a newspaper send him on a "Newspaper Scavenger Hunt." Browse through the paper yourself first and make a list of 5-25 headlines, statistics, quotes, etc. (depending on the age of your student). Then, give the paper to your student, along with the list and have him try to find each item.

[**Teacher's Note**: You can adjust this activity to the age of your student. Major headlines are easier to spot than obscure quotes in the editorial section. This can be a 10-minute game or a challenge that lasts an entire afternoon. If you wish to steer your student away from the hard-core news stories, simply limit your search to the sports page or classifieds. If you have more than one student, perhaps you could hand them identical papers and lists and time them. Whoever finds the complete list first, wins!]

If your student enjoys writing, a great exercise is to have him write his own newspaper! He can create his own name, masthead and format. He can center the news he reports on the family and get direct quotes, opinions and facts from other family members. Discuss with your student the concept of "news worthiness." If his dog just had a litter of puppies, this isn't newsworthy to your town, but is of great interest to his family! News worthiness directly correlates to whom the event affects.

If tackling an entire newspaper is daunting to your student, perhaps writing one news article is more manageable. Study, with your student, the unique, specific style in which newspaper articles are written. Personal opinions shouldn't be voiced—only facts. Direct quotes are used for supporting evidence and specific details like the time and place of an event are important!

If your student is interested in the opinion/editorial section of your paper, he might even wish to compose his own letter to your paper's editor regarding a topic of interest to him. If he chooses to send it in, there is no guarantee it will be printed, but you never know!

Another great learning experience is to study the papers of other countries! Most large, major bookstores carry foreign newspapers. You can learn about the financial outlook, auto sales, fashion, national crises, etc., of each country's paper you read. Often you'll learn a great deal about a country by reading the display and classified advertising sections. You'll learn about jobs, wages, housing prices and rents, grocery selection and prices and much more.

Newspapers are a daily snapshot of our world! Select a country that interests your student and then bring home a paper and explore all you see!

Fine Arts: A Poem and a Picture

Here are four lines from Dorothy Frances Gurney's (1858-1932) poem "God's Garden."

The kiss of the sun for pardon,
The song of the birds for mirth,
One is nearer God's heart in a garden
Than anywhere else on earth.

Have your student study (and perhaps memorize) this short four-line stanza. Then, using whatever medium he chooses, have him draw what he sees in this poem. When the artwork is finished, perhaps you could hang a copy of the poem beside the picture. If your student is a budding poet, he might choose to write his own garden-inspired poem and illustrate it. What is important in this art lesson, is to clearly link the text and the picture together—each expanding on the other.

Issues of Human Relationships: Finding Your Place to Help

On page 95, Henry and Jessie conclude Benny is too young to help pick the cherries. Dr. Moore understands even young children can help with big projects, however, and finds a task for Benny. Discuss with your student all the ways young people can be useful in areas that might seem too difficult for them.

For example, it would be difficult for a ten-year-old to paint the house by himself, but pouring paint into buckets, washing brushes, and carrying ladders are all things that he could do! If your student has younger siblings, encourage him to find ways to include them in projects. If your student is the youngest, have him be looking for ways he can be involved! Everyone can find a place to help others, even when it seems impossible. Everyone is needed, even if they are young!

Writing and Discussion Question

Dr. Moore doesn't choose to reveal who Henry, Jessie, Violet and Benny are right away when he finds the reward notice (page 99). Why? Why wasn't he motivated by the monetary reward?

Internet Connections

To view current suggested links relating to this chapter's lessons, see www.fiveinarow.com/connections.

Chapter 10–Henry and the Free for All

Parent Summary

James Henry Alden (the children's grandfather), along with three other wealthy men in the area, annually sponsors a Field Day for the towns of Silver City and Greenfield. Field Day is a major event and even the mills close down and everyone comes out for the various footraces.

Henry is cutting Dr. Moore's grass when the doctor tells him to go to the races. The doctor can't go, but wants Henry to tell him who wins. When Henry gets to the races, he hears about the final race called the Free-for-All. This race is open to everyone. Henry enters and wins the silver cup and a $25 prize! His grandfather (unbeknownst to both of them) hands him the prize. Henry returns home, exuberant from his victory, and gives Jessie the money. Henry retells the tale of the race and the children eat a wonderful dinner of baked potatoes!

What we will cover in this chapter:

History and Geography: Philanthropy

History and Geography: Mills and the Industrial Revolution

History and Geography: Marathons and Footraces

History and Geography and Science: Potatoes

Fine Arts: Cooking

Fine Arts: Charcoal Drawing

Fine Arts: Potato Prints

Issues of Human Relationships: Problem Solving with Inventions

Lesson Activities

History and Geography: Philanthropy

The children's grandfather, James Henry Alden, is an extremely rich man. Often, people who have considerable wealth choose to give some of their money to charitable events, sponsored activities and institutions. When someone gives a large amount of money in this way, they are known as a *philanthropist*. Philanthropy [fuh LAN thruh pee] is the use of money to benefit large institutions or whole cities. (*Charity*, in contrast, usually benefits one or a few individuals.)

The United States has benefited greatly from the generosity of her philanthropists such as John D. Rockefeller and Andrew Carnegie. Take this opportunity to share with your student examples of such giving.

James Smithson, in 1829, donated the funds to establish the Smithsonian Institution. Benjamin Franklin, in 1790, gave money to build a fund for young American men with promise. Cornelius Vanderbilt gave $1 million to Vanderbilt University in Nashville, Tennessee. In 1907, John Pierpont Morgan loaned New York, a city nearly bankrupt, $30 million to regain it's foothold, and at a time when the U.S. Treasury seemed close to hitting bottom, he loaned the country $62 million to help right the tumbling economy.

Today, according to the *World Book Encyclopedia*, the leading United States Foundation is the Ford Foundation, founded in 1936 and based in New York City. The foundation's total assets exceed $5 1/2 billion.

[**Teacher's Note**: A wonderful resource for more information about philanthropists and their place in U.S. history (along with much, much more!) is the incredible series entitled *A History of Us* by Joy Hakim. This ten-book series is filled with fascinating details, thousands of photos and a student-friendly format. Children love it and adults learn just as much! The title in this series that has much information about U.S. philanthropists is book eight—*An Age of Extremes*. This series is available in both hardback and paperback, as well as at your local library!]

Perhaps your student is interested in a particular philanthropist. Have him select a specific person, do some research on his own and write a report. Learning about the art of giving is a wonderful way to inspire generosity in our young people and pay respect to the great givers of our time!

History and Geography: Mills and the Industrial Revolution

Mills play a big part in the employment opportunities of Silver City and Greenfield. Our book doesn't tell us what type of mills they are. Did you know there are many different kinds of mills? Discuss with your student the many different products that are made in mills: steel, fabric, flour, lumber, etc. Again, as we've studied before, these mills are centered in certain regions of the country. If your student is interested, you might research some mills and, using the reproducible U.S. map located in the back of this book, mark which types of mills are commonly found in the various regions of the United States using markers or colored pencils.

Mills played a major role in our history as a nation during the time known as the Industrial Revolution. The Industrial Revolution began in the 1700s in Europe and spread to North America in the 1800s. Before the Industrial Revolution, most goods (clothing, lumber, tools, etc.) were made by hand or simple machines people owned. People made their own things at home. The Industrial Revolution changed all that. By creating factories and mills, the building processes were taken out of the home and put into huge assembly-type work arenas.

More than just the shift in manufacturing, the Industrial Revolution brought the prices paid for goods down considerably. Life for the citizens of America and Europe was changed for the better and forever. However, there was a downside to the changing industrial world, as well. As different machines and mills became more costly, having wealthy *capitalists* (someone who is willing to risk his own money up front in order to share profits) became vital. If they were not available, costs for goods went up.

Another dramatic negative effect of the massive factories, was the lack of personal commitment from the management toward employees. With as many as 1,500 employees working in a single mill, the owners could not possibly keep in contact with their needs. People were forced to work long days (12-14 hours) and wages went down. Children (as young as ten years old) began working in the factories. No one protected their rights, and they were often injured by unsafe equipment and strenuous labor. This would be a good opportunity to introduce Charles Dickens. A good, simple biography (Diane Stanley wrote a great one, ISBN 0688091105 TR) will allow you and your student to see how Dickens' writings about poor working conditions in England helped end much factory abuse.

Eventually these negative aspects of the Industrial Revolution became less of a problem. The tide of progress caused by the Industrial Revolution moved on. Encourage your student to continue doing research on this revolution, if he is interested, and perhaps make a timeline of the significant events you find regarding this remarkable period in our history!

History and Geography: Marathons and Footraces

Henry ran in an exciting footrace called a free-for-all (page 108). Races involving running take many forms. Discuss with your student hurdles, relays, sprints, long distance tracks, etc. The modern-day equivalent of Henry's free-for-all (similar not in distance, but in the selection process) is called a marathon. Anyone can enter and although training is almost certainly required in order to win a marathon, it is not required for participation.

Marathons are an ancient concept started by the Greeks. Marathon [MAIR uh thahn] is actually a plain in Greece on which one of the decisive battles of history was fought. The plain is approximately 26 miles (40 kilometers) northeast of Athens, and there the Athenians and their allies, the Plataeans, defeated the army of King Darius of Persia in 490 B.C. Legend says that a man ran the 26 miles from the battleground to Athens to tell of the victory. Thus, the modern-day races are called marathons and are always approximately 26 miles in length!

Discuss with your student the various marathons the United States offers. The Boston Marathon, which takes place every April, is a famous footrace anyone can enter. New York City also offers a marathon, and of course, the Olympics have international marathon events that are amazing spectacles of human strength. Is your student interested in running? Why not measure a track in your neighborhood (any distance from 50 yards to 1/2 mile) and have him race. If you have several students, a footrace is exciting and a great physical fitness activity.

[**Teacher's Note**: Buy an inexpensive stopwatch (these can be found for under $10, if you don't have a digital watch with built-in stopwatch already) and time your student's races. These stopwatches can also be great assets for timing math drills, science experiments, etc. Invest and enjoy!]

History and Geography and Science: Potatoes

Henry brought home "some fat brown potatoes" for Jessie and the other children. Does your student like potatoes? For many years, the potato has ranked as America's favorite vegetable, perhaps because of the many ways it can be cooked. Potatoes can be mashed, french-fried, baked, scalloped, made into potato salad, boiled, and much more. What is your student's favorite way to eat potatoes?

Potatoes are called *tuber* [TOO bur] vegetables. The edible part of the plant grows underground on the stems. The potato plant above the ground has many green leaves covering its thick stems and small pink, white or lavender flowers. Potatoes are not grown from seed, but instead from tiny potatoes called "seed potatoes." In the United States, potatoes are grown commercially in almost every state. However, the state of Idaho is the leading producer of potatoes in America.

There are several hundred varieties of potatoes. Take some time at the market and look at all the different types. Yukon gold potatoes have a pale yellow skin and are very smooth when cooked. Russet potatoes are what many people think of as "baking" potatoes. You can also find red potatoes, purple potatoes, small "new" or "boiling" potatoes, sweet potatoes, and many more varieties at your local market. Choose one or more unusual types of potatoes and bring them home for dinner!

Potatoes were brought to the United States by English explorers (the Spaniards from South America had already brought them to the English) in the 1600s. However, it wasn't until the Irish immigrants came in the early 1700s that potatoes became an integral crop in America.

In terms of history, perhaps no other country has been so affected by the potato as Ireland. Share with your student the story of the great potato famine, which occurred in Ireland from 1845-1848. Because of the lack of industry, the Irish relied mainly on agriculture for both their livelihood and their food. Potatoes became the main staple for most of the impoverished Irish people. A plant disease attacked the potato plants in 1845, and for the next three years people died from lack of food. Approximately one million people lost their lives due to what is now know as the "Great Potato Famine." Another result of the famine was mass immigration to the United States by the Irish. Draw your student's attention to a world map and discuss where Ireland is located.

An interesting book which talks about the Great Depression in America (and potatoes!) is entitled *Potato: A Tale From the Great Depression* by Kate Lied (Copyright 1997, Publishers Group West, ISBN 0792235215). The story centers on a family seeking work during the Depression and their employment as "potato diggers." Written by eight-year-old Kate Lied, the book is fresh and heartwarming! An excellent find!

Next time you eat a potato, talk about the way we got them and the Irish who love them!

Fine Arts: Cooking

Potatoes certainly can be fixed in many ways. There are even some cookbooks devoted entirely to unusual potato recipes. If your student is interested in cooking, make it a project to locate several new potato recipes and try one.

Jesse enjoys cooking and makes a stew with the vegetables and meat that Henry provides. Has your student ever made a "Pocket Stew?" Here is one recipe:

Wash potatoes and cut into 1/4-inch slices. Peel carrots and slice into circles. Make thin hamburger patties out of lean hamburger. Take an 11" square of foil and place hamburger patty on it. Salt and pepper the meat. Now, top with a portion of the sliced potatoes and carrots and seal up the edges. Place in a pan in the oven at 350° F. for 40-50 minutes or place into the glowing coals of a campfire! (Check in 30 minutes.) When meat, potatoes and carrots are done, open up the foil packet and have a feast. (The quantities will vary with the amount of people served. Each foil packet is an individual serving.)

Fine Arts: Charcoal Drawing

Jessie and Violet made a wonderful book for Henry using a charred stick as a writing instrument (page 112). A fascinating medium for drawing (similar, but much easier to use than a burned stick) is charcoal. Obtain some simple charcoal sticks (these are available inexpensively at any art supply store) and have your student experiment with this unusual medium. Unlike crayons or markers, shading becomes extremely easy with charcoal. Creating textures and shadows is exciting, as well. If you are adventuresome, you might try a charred stick and compare it to the modern charcoal pieces. Think of Benny's book and have fun!

Fine Arts: Potato Prints

An easy and delightful art form is potato printing. Have your student cut a potato in half. Then, with your help, have him draw a design on the cut end. After the design is set, again with your help, carve the design in relief. This means to cut away all the potato surrounding your design. Now, touch your potato to an inkpad and begin stamping! You can create your own wrapping paper, greeting cards, murals, etc., all by using a simple potato. Another fun application is to carve the initials of your student into the potato. Then, with all of his artwork, he can stamp his signature at the bottom. Be creative and enjoy this inexpensive art form!

Issues of Human Relationships: Problem Solving with Inventions

Jessie feels it's time for Benny to learn to read (page 111). But Benny can't attend school and Jessie has no textbooks. Encourage your student to examine the creativity Jessie exhibits by creating her own textbook. Being inventive helps us solve many problems. Perhaps your student would like to be inventive as well. If he seems interested, have him create a textbook for a younger sibling or friend. He can make it out of cloth with markers or fabric paints. He can also design it on a computer or draw it by hand on paper. Remind your student that being inventive is the way people solve many of their problems. Have him look for ways to invent his own solutions when problems arise!

Writing and Discussion Question

Henry ran a good race and finished a winner! We can't always be winners, but we can always do our best. How do you feel when you succeed at something? What is something you are very proud of accomplishing? Explain.

Internet Connections

To view current suggested links relating to this chapter's lessons, see www.fiveinarow.com/connections.

Chapter 11–The Doctor Takes a Hand

Parent Summary

Days go by and the children are happy and well. Jessie makes Benny a stocking bear out of his old stockings! Benny decides to cut Watch's hair. The result of the haircut is so funny looking Violet begins to laugh. Jessie laughs, too, but Violet doesn't stop. She begins to cry and shake. Jessie, worried, puts her in the boxcar and covers her with pine needles. When Henry returns from work, Violet is no better. Afraid to go to the hospital, Henry goes for Dr. Moore. The good doctor immediately rushes back to the boxcar, and without Henry's directions, seems to drive right to it. Bringing Violet home to his house, he and Mrs. Moore arrange beds for all the children. Dr. Moore stays up all night with Violet. The following morning the doctor notifies the children's grandfather, James Henry Alden, that he has some information regarding the children.

What we will cover in this chapter:

Science: Fever—What It Is and How It Works

Language Arts: Letter Writing—The How-To's

Fine Arts: Sewing and Design

Issues of Human Relationships: Grandparents

Career Paths: Becoming a Doctor

Lesson Activities

Science: Fever—What It Is and How It Works

On page 122 Violet becomes ill. She is hot all over and Jessie tries to cool her head with wet towels. Later that same evening, Violet begins to shake and is chilled. No matter what Henry and Jessie do, they cannot get Violet warm. What is going on? This is a great opportunity to discuss with your student the way our bodies fight infections through fever.

Your body has an internal thermometer, which is supposed to stay at about 98.6° F. Get a thermometer and take your student's temperature. Let him take yours. What do you find? Violet had what is called a fever. Inside her body, her temperature was much higher than 98.6° F.

A fever, in and of itself, is not a sickness. Actually, our bodies use fevers to stop bacteria and sickness from spreading. For this reason, most medical experts do not encourage people to try to lower a fever until it gets above 100° F.

When a fever rises above 100° F. it is considered a sickness in itself. This is what happened to Violet. She was hot, and then she was very cold. Without proper treatment, a fever out of control can be very serious. For more information on fevers and the ways our bodies work, go to your library or encyclopedia. Your student can easily spend several days learning more about the body's amazing reaction to illness and infection. Next time your student has a fever, perhaps it will be a little less frightening.

Language Arts: Letter Writing—The How-To's

Learning how to write a letter is an important part of growing up. More than jotting down a note, composing a proper and interesting letter is something which will serve your student his whole life.

By taking a blank piece of paper, begin by charting the basic sections of a letter. Remind your student to remember a letter includes the date, the writer's name and address, a salutation (greeting—like Hello, Dear, Dearest, My friend, etc.), the main body of the letter, a closing (sincerely, with love, warmest thoughts, etc.) and the writer's signature. Remembering each of these sections is important.

Have your student practice writing a couple of letters. Don't forget to have your student proofread every letter before mailing, checking his work for spelling, grammar, clear language, etc. A fabulous resource for information on writing letters, grammar, creative writing and much more is a book entitled *Writers INC*, by Patrick Sebranek, Verne Meyer and Dave Kemper. This is an invaluable handbook for you as a teacher and can be used by your student to check any writing problem.

Letter writing has increasingly become a lost art in the last century. With telephones (in our homes, offices and even cars!), fax machines, e-mail and pagers, writing a nice, long letter to someone isn't as popular as it once was. Encourage your student to continue this special literary art and write wonderful letters! Remind him he can illustrate his letters too!

Fine Arts: Sewing and Design

Jessie makes Benny a darling little bear out of an old sock (page 118). What a creative and delightful idea! Sewing and designing fabric projects is an ancient art. Has your student ever done any sewing? Take this opportunity to try making a sock-doll just like Jessie did. Don't worry about having perfect measurements or stitches, have fun creating whatever you want. Add a tail like Benny requested, or some button eyes.

Check your library for a book on beginning sewing projects. Perhaps your student would prefer to begin with a sketch. Whatever he chooses, let him design it just the way he wants. Just as beautiful as Jessie's created bear, was her kindness to Benny by making it just like he wanted.

Issues of Human Relationships: Grandparents

James Henry Alden is a good grandfather. He cares about Henry and the children and is trying to find them. Does your student have grandparents living? Discuss with your student what you remember about your grandparents. Reminiscing is the way we pass information, stories and laughter to the next generation.

If your student is interested, this is a great opportunity to start creating a family tree. Begin by helping your student write down as much information and facts as he can. This may include names of siblings, parents, grandparents, aunts and uncles. You will be able to help him record birth dates and birthplaces for these people, as well. Now your student can do some interviews with his grandparents, aunts, uncles, etc., to gather additional information. Working on a family tree provides a wonderful sense of 'belonging.' Beyond learning about his grandparents, your student will surely obtain a fascinating look into history. As anecdotes and memories are shared, your student will be gleaning facts about the times long ago.

Another topic to share with your student is how much grandparents love to hear from their grandchildren! Grandfather Alden missed his grandchildren very much. Imagine how much your student's grandparent would love to get a letter from him telling all he has been doing! Encourage your student to keep in contact with his grandparents. Perhaps after learning how to write a good letter (the Language Arts lesson in this chapter) your student could make a commitment to write his grandparents at least once each month. Even if it seems difficult at first (writing good letters takes practice), thinking of interesting things to include will become much easier the more letters he writes. Grandparents will love this and it will bless them greatly!

Career Paths: Becoming A Doctor

Dr. Moore was able to help Violet get well. When we help someone feel better, it makes us feel good too! If your student is interested in medicine and health, a career path worth exploring is that of physician.

Your student probably thinks of a pediatrician or family practice physician when he discusses doctors. Talk with your student about the many types of medicine doctors can practice—internal, pediatrics, optometry, podiatry, obstetrics, plastic surgery, general surgery, neurology, trauma, immunology, and much, much more.

To become a doctor, you must attend approximately 6-8 years of college and then take part in what is called a 'residency.' A residency is a time when a new doctor can take care of patients with a more experienced doctor watching him. Residencies normally last about two years.

A person must excel in math and science to become a doctor. If you are able, take a tour of an area hospital or doctor's office. If you know a doctor or nurse, have your student interview him and perhaps write a report.

[**Teacher's Note**: If you wish, this might be a good time to introduce Hippocrates (the famous Greek, father of medicine) and the Hippocratic oath (a high moral code physicians must accept).]

Remind your student being a doctor is more than knowing a lot of information and finishing a medical degree. To be a good physician, someone must also have a kind heart and a willingness to listen to people. When someone is sick, they want to be cared for and made comfortable. A doctor who is good at what he does, just like Dr. Moore, helps us feel better in spirit, as well as body!

Writing and Discussion Question

Why didn't Dr. Moore take Violet straight to a hospital?

Internet Connections

To view current suggested links relating to this chapter's lessons, see www.fiveinarow.com/connections.

Chapter 12–James Henry and Henry James

Parent Summary

Without telling the children, Dr. Moore invites Mr. Alden over to the house. The two men decide to let the children get to know their grandfather before introducing him. He slowly gets acquainted with Benny and then Violet. Henry, after hearing Mr. Alden say "my boy," remembers he was the man who was at the free-for-all. Putting pieces together, he introduces himself to his grandfather. The moment of truth arrives for all the children and the happy family is finally reunited. When Violet is well, the four children, their grandfather, Dr. Moore and his mother all go and see the boxcar. After a final meal by the brook, the children and Watch set off to spend some time with their grandfather at his house.

What we will cover in this chapter:

History and Geography: Names and Your Lineage

Science: Grow a Vegetable in a Bottle

Fine Arts: Design and Illustration—Grandfather's House

Issues of Human Relationships: Moving

Issues of Human Relationships: Going the Extra Mile

Issues of Human Relationships: Seeing Past Differences

Lesson Activities

History and Geography—Names and Your Lineage

Draw your student's attention to Henry's name and Mr. Alden's name (page 135). Henry James Alden was named after James Henry Alden. Many times people hand names down through generations. Often the first son of a couple will bear the same name as his father with a "Jr." added at the end. Perhaps your student is a junior. Mothers and daughters can share names, as well.

The author of *Beyond Five in a Row* has a unique type of name heritage. The author's grandmother is named Billie *Jane*. The author's mother is named *Jane* Claire. The author's name is Becky *Jane* and she hopes to have a daughter named *Jane* to carry on the tradition.

What is your student's name? Is there a specific lineage attached? Where did the name come from? Is he named after a famous person? Have your student do some research into his family's name. If the interest is there, this name information could be listed in the data gathered for the family tree (covered in chapter 11).

As a side note, share with your student some interesting facts about the names used in our book. The name "Alden" is a famous name belonging to a man named John Alden. Mr. John Alden sailed from Essex, England on the *Mayflower* to America. He married Priscilla Mullens and their courtship was described in the famous Henry Wadsworth Longfellow poem *The Courtship of Miles Standish*. (If your student is interested, you might find that poem and read it together.) John Alden made it through the first winter at Plymouth (a winter which killed half of the Pilgrims) and served as assistant governor of the community until his death in 1687. You can visit his final homestead in Duxbury, Massachusetts. If you live near Massachusetts, take the time to go and visit this site.

In *The Boxcar Children*, the fictional city of Greenfield shares its name with the famous home site of Henry Ford, inventor of the Model T.

[**Teacher's Note**: Remember this fact when you study the next book in *Beyond Five in a Row* about Thomas Alva Edison. Edison and Henry Ford were dear friends late in life and spent much time at Ford's estate, Greenfield Village.]

Learning about names and their origins can be very enlightening. Encourage your student to begin paying attention to the names he hears and sees in his own family and community.

Science: Grow a Vegetable in a Bottle

Grandfather Alden had the most interesting thing in his garden—cucumber in a bottle! (page 131) Take this opportunity to explain to your student how a cucumber can be grown in a bottle. If there is interest, discuss the type of bottle you would need. A clear glass or plastic bottle would let the sunlight in and be ideal. Many vegetables can be grown this way and then picked when they fill their bottle. If you have a garden, try this with a cucumber, tomato or small squash.

If you are planning a special summer dinner or party, a fresh picked "bottle" encased vegetable makes a unique and interesting centerpiece. If you do not have access to a garden, try growing a cucumber or tomato plant in a pot indoors. Just wait until the vegetable blossom is starting to form fruit. Now stick it in the mouth of a bottle and watch it grow!

If you have not studied plants in awhile, get a simple library book or good colorful reference book. Chose one topic and learn about the parts of a flower, or the parts of a leaf, or the parts of a fruit and how it grows. You might find a good book on vegetables, too!

Fine Arts: Design and Illustration—Grandfather's House

Henry, Jessie, Violet, and Benny are going to see Grandfather's house (page 140). They probably tried to imagine what it would look like. Ask your student what he thinks it looks like?

If your student is interested in architecture, you might introduce him to floor plans. Many home and decorating magazines include simplified floor plans of different houses. Show your student how the architect indicates stairs, doors, windows, porches, etc. If your student enjoys this, encourage him to try designing a floor plan of what he thinks Grandfather Alden's home will look like.

[**Teacher's Note**: The following and final chapter does not include any specific details on the style or look of Grandfather's house. Therefore, any design concept your student decides on could be correct.]

Have a delightful time with your student as you discuss and design Grandfather's home.

Issues of Human Relationships: Moving

On page 142, we see the children leaving their boxcar home and moving to their grandfather's house. Has your student ever had to move? Has your student ever experienced a good friend moving away? Leaving our old home for a new one is often very sad.

Talk with your student about the feelings of loss and fear when we leave someplace familiar. It is sometimes difficult to adjust to a new neighborhood or town. New faces and experiences can be frightening, even for an adult. If your student has had this experience, you might have him write a short personal memoir on his feelings and how they were resolved. Learning to enjoy new experiences and the unknown is a part of growing up. Encourage your student to be open to new things!

Issues of Human Relationships: Going the Extra Mile

Dr. Moore took good care of the children. He offered Henry a job, paid the children well, gave them cherries, vegetables, a hammer and nails, checked up on them in the woods, made sure they had enough food, took care of Violet when she was sick, made sure Grandfather Alden was a kind man, etc. Instead of just stopping at finding them a home, he invited them into his own home and cared for them.

Talk with your student about going the extra mile for someone. Caring for someone above and beyond the normal call of duty is a noble thing to do. Give your student examples of ways he can go the extra mile for his family or friends. For example, if he is hanging up his coat and he sees other family members' coats laying around, he might choose to hang them all up. If a new friend in the neighborhood is shy, he could include that person in an outing and introduce him to the other children. Let your student think of other ways, as well.

Instead of just doing what we are obligated to do, a person of good character does whatever he sees is needed. Dr. Moore exemplifies this character quality. Encourage your student to cultivate it also!

Issues of Human Relationships: Seeing Past Differences

Draw your student's attention to the interesting exchange between Mary, the maid and Dr. Moore on page 130. Mary is nervous to cook for Mr. Alden because he is "a very rich man." Explore with your student reasons people are sometimes intimidated by differences in others. Whether it be social standing, money, level of education, race or religion, people are often nervous about being with someone who is different. Mary didn't know what she could fix for Mr. Alden that would be special or fancy enough. Mary didn't understand that when we do things in a way that makes us true to ourselves (cherry dumplings and chicken were *her* specialty!), others can appreciate it! People are not impressed when we try to be something we're not! Encourage your student to look past differences in people and instead, look for what makes that person unique! This is a sign of real maturity!

Writing and Discussion Question

On page 142, Gertrude Chandler Warner leaves the reader with this sentence, "They did not know ... what good times they were going to have." What types of good times do you think they had?

Internet Connections

To view current suggested links relating to this chapter's lessons, see www.fiveinarow.com/connections.

Chapter 13–A New Home for the Boxcar

Parent Summary

The children see their grandfather's mansion for the first time. He has each of their rooms redone to suit them—Violet's room with violets everywhere, Benny's room with toys and a train set, and even Jessie's room has a bed for Watch. The children learn to love their grandfather and his home, but as time goes on they begin to miss the boxcar and their old things. Mr. Alden comes up with a plan. With the children away, he has the boxcar brought to his home and placed in the back garden. Complete with the old stump, everything is just as it was in the woods. The children are delighted and they all live happily ever after.

What we will cover in this chapter:

History and Geography: A Rail Car in Your Backyard

Fine Arts: A Portrait of the Aldens

Issues of Human Relationships:
Making Friends—Learning About Their Interests

Lesson Activities

History and Geography: A Rail Car in Your Backyard

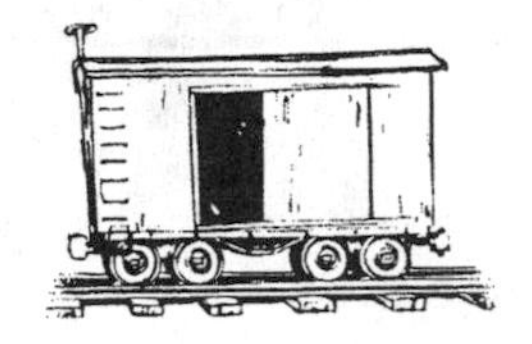

Wasn't it wonderful of Mr. Alden to move the boxcar into his garden! Surprisingly enough, today it is not that unusual for someone to have a rail car in his backyard! Extremely dedicated railroad enthusiasts enjoy collecting old rail cars and renovating them. Many people house the cars in their backyards or as an attached room on their house. Some restore the cars to their original condition, and others renovate them into guest houses, offices or entertainment rooms. Boxcars are collected as well as dining cars, passenger cars, engines and cabooses!

A popular chain of restaurants in the 1980s, named Victoria Station, were all constructed of many railroad cars hooked together to create linked dining rooms. Ask your student if he thinks it would be fun to have a boxcar in the backyard? Check and see if there are any railroad associations or clubs in your city. You might even be able to arrange a visit to a train museum or restoration area. It's fun to know we could have a boxcar in our backyard too!

[**Teacher's Note**: Student rail enthusiasts can find the routes of major railroads past or present and enjoy mapping them out. There are also many great videos of trains, old and new.]

Fine Arts: A Portrait of the Aldens

When your student finishes *The Boxcar Children*, ask him what he thinks the children and their Grandfather Alden look like. We are given some clues on page 8 regarding Violet, but for the most part, that piece of the story is left up to our imagination! If your student is interested, encourage him to draw or paint a family portrait of the Aldens. Your student may want to include Dr. Moore and his mother, as well. The backdrop for the picture could be the boxcar or the orchard or even Grandfather's house.

An additional idea would be to pick something from the story to draw around the portrait to "frame" it. Cherries, pine needles, or pink cracked cups might be fun. Encourage your student to think about the different family photographs or portraits he has seen. Some are formal, sitting pictures and others are outdoors or action poses. Be creative and different—And don't forget Watch!

Issues of Human Relationships: Making Friends—Learning about Their Interests

Draw your student's attention to Grandfather Alden's careful choices for the children's bedrooms (pages 144-145). He knew Violet would like flowers (especially violets!) and soft colors. He was certain Jessie would want Watch by her bed, and so he provided a special place just for him. And Benny loved the animals and train set!

Grandfather Alden wanted his grandchildren to love him and become his friends. When we make friends, it is important to learn about what they like. If we continually talk about our own interests, the person will tire quickly and not feel valued. Encourage your student to seek out new friends, and in so doing develop an interest in what the new person enjoys. Not only will the friend feel comfortable and special, but your student might learn all about something new!

Writing and Discussion Question

Gertrude Chandler Warner doesn't describe how the grandfather decorated Henry's room. What would you have chosen for Henry's room? What do you think his interests are?

Internet Connections

To view current suggested links relating to this chapter's lessons, see www.fiveinarow.com/connections.

THOMAS A. EDISON YOUNG INVENTOR

BY SUE GUTHRIDGE

Chapter 1—An Idea That Didn't Work

Parent Summary

We are introduced to six-year-old Tom Edison. The Edison family resides in Milan, Ohio and the year is 1853. One morning, Tom has a great idea. Since warmth is what causes baby goslings to hatch and Tom is much larger and warmer than his goose Lulu, Tom concludes that if he sits on the eggs they will hatch quickly! Grabbing some ham and biscuits to sustain himself, Tom runs out to the hen house to test his idea. After sitting carefully on the eggs for most of the afternoon, Tom's Mother, Nancy, comes out to find him. Finding him sitting atop the eggs, Nancy Edison laughs and laughs. Realizing his experiment isn't working, Tom heads back to the house to help with the chores.

What we will cover in this chapter:

History and Geography: The Great Lakes

History and Geography: The Erie Canal—How It Came to Be

History and Geography: Making a Map of Edison's Life

Science: Incubating Eggs

Science: The Scientific Method

Language Arts: Descriptive Word Choices

Language Arts: Creative Writing—Living on a Canal

Language Arts: Classic Connection

Fine Arts: Music—Folk Song "The Erie Canal"

Lesson Activities

History and Geography: The Great Lakes

On page 12 we learn about Lake Erie and the barges. Take this opportunity to explore the Great Lakes with your student.

The Great Lakes are the five largest fresh-water lakes in the world. The names of the lakes going from west to east are Lake Superior, Lake Michigan, Lake Huron, Lake Erie, and Lake Ontario. Of the five, only Lake Michigan is entirely in the United States.

The other four share a common border between Canada and the U.S. The depth of the Great Lakes differs greatly. Lake Superior (its name comes from being the biggest) is over 1,300 feet deep. Lake Erie, the smallest lake and the one cited in our story, is only 210 feet deep.

Your student might have heard of many Great Lakes locations including Niagara Falls (the falls are caused by level differences between Lake Erie and Lake Ontario), Straits of Mackinac (pron. Mack i naw, between Lake Michigan and Lake Huron) and Lake St. Clair (mentioned in our story in chapter 2). If you live near the Great Lakes, by all means take a day trip and visit! Such a massive body of water is always an awesome sight. If you do not, perhaps your local library has videos or books on the Great Lakes. Locate the reproducible map of the Great Lakes in the Appendix and begin your studies by labeling each of the Great Lakes.

History and Geography: The Erie Canal—How It Came to Be

On page 12 Lake Erie is mentioned. Take some time to talk with your student about the famous Erie Canal. The man behind this huge project was named De Witt Clinton. Mr. Clinton became governor of New York in 1817 and on the Fourth of July, 1817, men broke ground in Rome, New York for the canal. It took eight years to build and was completed in 1825. The first ship to traverse the canal's full length was the *Seneca Chief* on October 26, 1825. The canal cost over $7 million and was paid for entirely by the state of New York. Interestingly, during the 60 years while tolls were collected (tolls were abolished in 1882) over $121 million was collected by the state!

If your student is interested in the Erie Canal, he might enjoy the book *The Erie Canal* by Samuel Hopkins Adams (Copyright 1953, Random House, Landmark Book Division). This is an older book, available at most libraries, with an easy to read and informative style.

A different type of book on the same subject is *The Towpath* by Arch Merrill (Copyright 1945, Heart of Lakes Publishing, ISBN 1557870012). This book is the autobiography of a tugboat operator. Included are photographs, maps and diagrams. The diary entries trace the tugboat operator's steps down the towpaths of several canals, including the Erie. Filled with valuable and interesting facts, it is a book for more advanced readers, but portions of this book would make a great read-aloud.

If your student seems interested in all of this, you might want to delve into the study of other important canals. The Panama and Suez are two of the more famous. Go to your local library and find some books on each. One such resource you should look for is entitled *Locks, Crocs & Skeeters: The Story of the Panama Canal* by Nancy Winslow Parker (Copyright 1996, Greenwillow Books, ISBN 0688122418). Including excellent maps, description and interesting details, this book makes the Panama Canal come to life! (Also, you may want to consider comparing the dates of the building of the Erie, Panama and Suez Canals as well as their locations.)

History and Geography: Making a Map of Edison's Life

Throughout this story you will read about many towns, regions, lakes and sites which were a part of Thomas Alva Edison's life. Take the reproducible Great Lakes regional map located in the back of the book (you may already have the Great Lakes labeled) and as you read about a specific site, mark it on the map. By looking at a real map of the state or region you can then visually locate it on your map.

For this first chapter your student might want to map out several of the locations mentioned, including Milan, Ohio, Huron River, Lake Erie, Detroit, and New York City. As our study of Edison's life continues, you will be reminded to continue to identify additional landmarks on your map.

Science: Incubating Eggs

Tom Edison thought he could hatch an egg! He knew warmth was necessary (page 18) but he thought he could speed up the process! What is involved in hatching an egg?

The story of Tom's experience with the eggs centers on unhatched goslings—baby geese. The usual incubation period (time the mother has to sit on the eggs) for geese is 28-32 days. Chicken eggs, a more common variety for most of us, have an incubation period of approximately 21 days. A hen will lay one egg a day, until she has a full nest (generally 6-10 eggs, but never more than one a day). If the eggs become cold, even for a few hours, the chicks will die. The hen only leaves the nest for a moment at a time to feed. As the mother hen sits on the nest, she will routinely turn the eggs over.

If you have the opportunity, try incubating chicks for yourself. Many state conservation offices rent or loan incubators and fertilized eggs in return for the chickens. Watching this miracle take place is absolutely amazing and your student will never forget it!

If you don't have this opportunity, look for a science video or detailed book on the subject at your library. The important thing to remind your student is that store-bought eggs are not fertilized. No chick will ever hatch from an unfertilized egg.

[**Teacher's Note**: You can take the discussion of "fertilized" versus "unfertilized" eggs to whatever level of reproductive knowledge you wish with your student.]

Tom Edison was not able to hatch eggs himself—that job was better left to Lulu, the mother goose!

Science: The Scientific Method

Edison had a specific thought process regarding those goose eggs. He knew it took warmth to hatch them (observation and reasoning). He thought that perhaps his body would be warm enough to speed up the hatching process (hypothesis). He tried sitting on the eggs for an entire afternoon (tested the hypothesis). He finally concluded it wouldn't work (evaluated and expressed his findings).

As young as age six, Edison was already thinking in logical terms. These four simple steps make up a critical skill used in science called the *Scientific Method*. Every discovery Edison will make throughout our story will follow these four steps. Encourage your student to make lists of each discovery/invention of Edison's as he reads about it, and then record the steps of the Scientific Method he can see Tom using. Every experiment includes these four phases. Challenge your student to point out the Scientific Method whenever he sees it applied! There is a page in the Appendix that may be reproduced and used whenever your student would like to make a record of times when he is "Thinking Like a Scientist!"

You and your student might discuss how you use the Scientific Method in your own lives. You might share with your student, for example, that you recently *observed and reasoned* that bread rises when warmth activates the yeast. You *formed a hypothesis* that perhaps bread might rise more quickly in a bowl suspended in warm water. You *tested your theory* and discovered it worked, reducing the rising time for bread by more than 50% and you *evaluated and expressed your findings* (told) to your next-door neighbor.

Ask your student if he can think of any recent examples when he has used the Scientific Method. Encourage him to look for opportunities to use Tom Edison's method in the future.

Language Arts: Descriptive Word Choices

Draw your student's attention to page 17. At the bottom of the page, it says Mrs. Edison "opened the door with a quick jerk." Instead of simply saying "opened the door," this author chose a descriptive phrase. Using action words (quick) and unique words (jerk) adds life to our stories.

As an exercise in using descriptive language, have your student make a list of all the phrases he can think of to describe the way a person can open a door. Answers might include: slowly drew the door open, gingerly pried the door open, slammed the door back, etc.

If your student is having trouble thinking of ways, have him walk over to a door and try opening it in different ways. Then, help him find words to describe what he did. This last idea may be a better plan for students who struggle with abstract thinking.

Language Arts: Creative Writing—Living on a Canal

Have your student imagine (based on his research of the topic) what it would be like to live and/or work on a canal. Let him write his imaginings into an essay or a story.

Language Arts: Classic Connection

Do you remember the incident when Mr. Toad was disguised as a washerwoman in *The Wind in the Willows*? Your older student might enjoy this "canal life" portion of the famous story by Kenneth Grahame.

Fine Arts: Music—Folk Song "The Erie Canal"

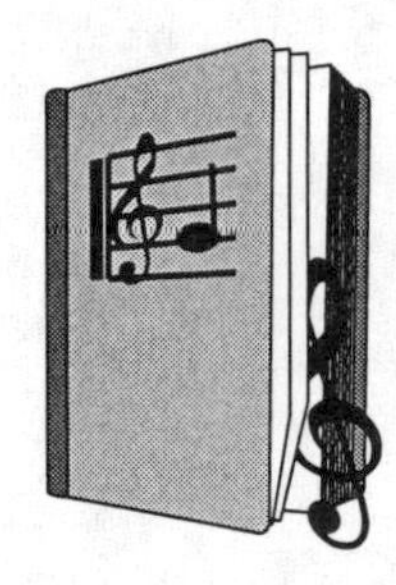

When you study about the Erie Canal, be sure to learn the song with the same name. One enjoyable way to learn this song is to find a copy of "The Erie Canal" by Peter Spier (1970, Doubleday and Co.). This book follows the lyrics to the famous American folksong "The Erie Canal." There are many fascinating pictures of this canal done in Spier's inimitable style. There is also a valuable history page in the back which covers family life on the canal, travel costs, barge speed limits and much more!

[**Teacher's Note**: For a cassette copy of the "Erie Canal" and audio lessons on its history, check out *History Alive Through Music—America 1750-1890* by Diana Waring. With fun sing-alongs and lively lessons, your student will learn about the Erie Canal as well as many other important historical facts through song (Copyright 1990, Hear and Learn Pub., ISBN 1879459019). This whole series is great!]

However you choose to learn the song, enjoy it together. Sing it with gusto, as you remember what life was like on the Erie Canal.

Writing and Discussion Question

Can your student remember a time when he acted like Tom? Has he ever believed he could "improve" something and found out his idea was rather silly? What happened?

Internet Connections

To view current suggested links relating to this chapter's lessons, see www.fiveinarow.com/connections.

Chapter 2–Tom Visits the Shipyards

Parent Summary

We discover in this second chapter of our story that Tom is full of questions! He visits his friend, Mr. Anderson, at the barge landings and peppers him with questions. Tom discovers, after watching Mr. Anderson pound nails with a hammer, that he doesn't hear the hammer strike for several seconds. This leads to a discussion of the speed of light versus the speed of sound. Tom is enthralled! He is just beginning to understand what Mr. Anderson is saying when his brother Pitt arrives at the dock. Pitt is beaming and shares with Tom some very important news. The Edison family is moving away from Milan, Ohio. The new railroad being built is bypassing their town and business will be lost. Tom is so excited to be moving! After the boys arrive back at home, we learn Tom's birthday is coming. He will be seven and it will be his last birthday in Milan.

What we will cover in this chapter:

History and Geography and Science: Pitch—What It Is and What It's For

History and Geography: Parlors—A Room of the Past

History and Geography: Your Map of Tom Edison's Life

Science: Speed of Light and Sound

Language Arts: A List of Travel Options

Language Arts: The Day You Were Born—Autobiographical Writing

Fine Arts: Cooking—A Birthday Cake for Tom

Issues of Human Relationships: Listening to People Who Are Younger

Lesson Activities

History and Geography and Science: Pitch—What It Is and What It's Used For

Sandy spread pitch on the underside of a little barge (page 22). Does your student know what *pitch* is? Tom doesn't know what it is (page 24). Pitch is actually the substance created when coal tar is distilled (heating the coal tar to separate its parts and then cooling it and condensing the vapor leaving a pure substance). The result is a sticky, water repellent, gum-like paste that can be used for roofing a house, patching a boat, paving a road and much more. Pitch is black, gooey and unattractive. However, until this century pitch was the only effective method of waterproofing or patching objects. Today, there are many synthetic, high-tech products of urethane and polymers used on boats, houses, etc.

Remind your student of the *Scientific Method* and discuss his *observations* about the effect of sun and rain on wood. Form a *hypothesis* about what would happen to two pieces of wood if one was protected from weather, and the other piece was exposed to the sun and rain. Now *test your hypothesis* by sealing a small piece of wood (a 6" piece of lumber is sufficient) using any sealant convenient, such as paint, varnish, etc. (If you have several different sealants and several different wood blocks you might try more than one variety. Be sure to label each block as to which type of sealant was used.) Now set one piece of unprotected wood and your freshly-sealed sample outside and continue to observe your experiment's results during the next few weeks. Have your student write a report evaluating and expressing his findings at the end of the semester.

History and Geography: Parlors—A Room of the Past

On page 26, Pitt and Tom find their parents talking in the parlor. The word *parlor* is an old-fashioned term and it means a formal room set aside for guests. Parlors were generally decorated elaborately compared to the rest of the house, and the family generally reserved it for company or special occasions. Today, some people have rooms like this in their homes, but it is unusual.

Here is a wonderful description of a parlor in the book *Farmer Boy*, by Laura Ingalls Wilder (Copyright 1933, Harper Collins, ISBN 0064400034).

"They tiptoed in, without making a sound. The light was dim because the blinds were down, but the parlor was beautiful. The wallpaper was white and gold and the carpet was of Mother's best weaving, almost too fine to step on. The center-table was marble topped, and it held the tall parlor lamp, all white-and-gold china and pink painted roses. Beside it lay the photograph album, with covers of red velvet and mother-of-pearl. All around the walls stood solemn horsehair chairs, and George Washington's picture looked sternly from its frame between the windows... when company came, they had to sit in the parlor... then they looked at the shells and the coral and the little china figures on the what-not."

It is not as practical in today's world to have an entire room set aside just for guests, but it is a luxurious concept. If your student wishes, have him draw a picture or build a simple model (perhaps inside a shoebox) of what he thinks the Edison's parlor looked like. Parlors are a beautiful part of the past.

History and Geography: Your Map of Tom Edison's Life

If you are making use of the reproducible map in the back of this book, continue to mark rivers and cities the Edisons discuss. In this chapter we can add Detroit, Lake St. Clair, St. Clair River, Michigan, and Port Huron.

Science: Speed of Light and Sound

In this chapter, Edison's observations lead him to a discussion about the speed of light versus the speed of sound (page 20). Mr. Anderson talks to Tom about lightning and thunder. Has your student ever noticed he can see the lightning first? That is because light travels faster than sound. To understand this phenomenon, begin by explaining the basics to your student. Both light and sound travel in waves. The speed of the waves depends on the material the waves are passing through. Did you know that sound travels faster through water than through air? Even more interesting, sound will travel faster through sea water (salty water) than through fresh water. No matter what the material is, a light wave will always be faster than a sound wave—almost *one million* times faster, in fact!

In 1926 an American physicist named Albert A. Michelson measured the speed of light as 186,282 miles per second. Scientists today believe Michelson's figure was so accurate it is probably less than 2 miles per second off. How far is 186,282 miles?

(As you discuss this question, you might want to remember that the United States is approximately 3,000 miles across, and the earth is approximately 24,000 miles in diameter. You may also want to discuss with your student the fact that the moon is approximately 238,000 miles away from Earth. How many times could light cross the United States in one second? How many times could it circle the world? How long does it take for the reflected sunlight from the moon to travel to Earth?)

Sound travels at approximately 1,100 feet per second. (Light travels nearly one million times faster than sound!) No wonder we see the lightning before we hear it! The next time you have a good thunderstorm, have your student count the seconds between seeing the flash of lightning and hearing the sound of thunder. Now, divide the number of seconds by 5 and you'll know approximately how many miles away the lightning struck. (Sound travels approximately one mile every five seconds!)

If your student is interested in science, you might take this discussion further by talking about a light year (the distance light travels in a year—5.88 trillion miles), supersonic speeds (jets traveling faster than the speed of sound—approximately 760 miles per hour), sonic booms (shock waves on the ground from supersonic jets), and much more. Go to the library and find additional books on these fascinating topics.

Language Arts: A List of Travel Options

On page 28 Tom is so excited about traveling by both train and boat. Have your student list all the means of transportation he has used thus far in his life. The list might include car, bus, train, airplane, bicycle, tricycle, etc. Encourage him to keep adding to this list every time he travels by a new mode.

Begin an interesting list of every way your student can think of to move from one point to another. For example, walking, running, skipping, jumping, roller skating, skate boarding, go-carting, surf boarding, or riding a dune buggy, motorcycle, jeep, tank, etc. Place this list on the refrigerator and have the whole family keep adding to it. You will amaze yourselves! Can you think of 100 ways to move? Can you think of 500 or 1000? List making is a beneficial skill in many areas of life and exercises like these are good practice as well as fun.

Language Arts: The Day You Were Born—Autobiographical Writing

Tom's father recalled what the weather was like and the time of day when Tom was born (page 27). It is exciting and interesting to learn about the events surrounding our birth. If possible, have your student find out about the events surrounding his birth. The hospital or location, time, weather, name of doctor, etc., are all interesting facts. If you want to get even more information to add to the story, go to a library which has newspapers on microfiche and look back at the edition which came out on your student's birthday. In this way, your student can learn what events took place in the world on the day of his birth.

When all the information is gathered, have your student write an autobiographical paragraph (or even several pages, depending on his age) describing his birthday. Talk to your student about *biographies* versus *autobiographies*. The book we are reading now is a biography of Thomas Edison. It is the story of his life. An autobiography would mean he wrote it himself. Autobiographies generally are written in first person (using the word "I").

[**Teacher's Note**: This assignment for younger students can be a quick discussion about the day they were born and a 15-sentence paragraph. For older students it can become a major assignment lasting a week or more and including interviews of several relatives and additional research. If your student lives near his birthplace, he may even want to take a picture of the hospital and include that along with pictures of himself as a newborn in his report.]

Learning about our first day in the world can be a satisfying project as we learn more about ourselves while we develop our research and writing skills!

Fine Arts: Cooking—A Birthday Cake for Tom

Cooking is a delightful and delicious art. Preparing great meals for loved ones is a wonderful way to nourish both body and soul. Tom's birthday is coming up (page 27) and he wants a "hickory-nut cake with burnt sugar icing." While hickory nuts are not commonly available, the following recipe is a type of nut cake with burnt sugar icing that is delicious and easy to prepare. Supervise your student as you talk together about Tom's adventures so far and bake and enjoy the birthday cake!

Tom's Birthday Nut-Apple Cake with Burnt Sugar Icing

2 cups flour
2 cups sugar
4 eggs
3 cups peeled, grated apple

1/2 cup raisins
1 cup chopped nuts (pecans or walnuts work best)
1 tsp. vanilla
3/4 cup corn oil
2 tsp. cinnamon
1/2 tsp. salt
1 tsp. baking powder
2 tsp. baking soda

Preheat oven to 350° F. Grease a bundt pan with butter and sprinkle liberally with granulated sugar; set aside. Mix the dry ingredients (flour, sugar, salt, soda, baking powder and cinnamon) together well. In a separate bowl combine the apples, raisins, nuts, vanilla, eggs, and corn oil. Now, stir this mixture into the dry ingredients. Don't over-blend. Pour batter into prepared bundt pan and bake for approximately 50 minutes or until toothpick comes out clean. Turn cake out onto a plate. This cake is best when it is cooled and then stored in an airtight container overnight. Ice the following day.

Burnt-Sugar Icing

2 egg whites
1 1/2 cups sugar
2 Tbs. burnt-sugar syrup*
1/3 cup cold water
dash of salt
1 tsp. vanilla

Place all ingredients, except vanilla, in double boiler. Cooking over boiling water, beat constantly with portable mixer or very fast with wire whisk till soft peaks form, about 7 minutes. Remove from heat; add vanilla. Beat until spreadable consistency is reached.

*Burnt-sugar syrup

Melt 1/2 cup white sugar in heavy skillet over low heat till dark brown and smooth. Remove from heat and add 1/2 cup boiling water. Return to heat and stir till it looks like molasses syrup.

Issues of Human Relationships: Listening to People Who Are Younger

Mr. Anderson and Sandy were extremely patient with all of Tom's questions. Sometimes older people can be uncaring and ignore children just because they don't feel their questions and comments are important. Encourage your student, even at his young age, to listen and care for younger children and siblings. He probably knows what it is like to be ignored by someone older. It makes us feel unvalued.

Writing and Discussion Question

Have you ever seen a big thunderstorm? What was it like? Were you unafraid like Tom? (This is a great opportunity for your student to use descriptive language (adjectives and adverbs) as he describes the storm and his feelings.)

Vocabulary Words:

pitch: a black, sticky substance made of coal tar and used for waterproofing

parlor: a room set aside for entertaining guests

light year: the distance light travels in one year; 5.88 trillion miles

biography: the story of a specific person's life

autobiography: the story of your own life, written by you

Internet Connections

To view current suggested links relating to this chapter's lessons, see www.fiveinarow.com/connections.

Chapter 3–A Birthday to Remember

Parent Summary

Tom's birthday finally arrives and he awakens to frost-covered windowpanes. At breakfast he opens his gifts and finds new ice skates, colored pencils and a sketchpad. Excited, Tom finishes eating, does his chores and then grabs his skates and heads for the frozen canal. After greeting his friend Sandy and receiving some words of warning about thin patches of ice, Tom sets off. Enjoying himself immensely, he begins to skate in broader figure eights. Before he knows what's happening, the ice breaks and Tom plunges into the icy water below. Sandy soon sees him and with his help Tom is able to get out of the canal. Frightened but still smiling, Tom heads back home in Sandy's arms to get in bed for the rest of his birthday.

What we will cover in this chapter:

History and Geography: Ice Skating

Science: Ice Skating—How it Works

Science: Dew Points and Frost

Science: Health and Safety—Hypothermia and Frostbite

Science: Non-Homogenized Milk

Language Arts: Literature—Hans Brinker and The Silver Skates

Fine Arts: Colored Pencils—Creating Color by Blending

Issues of Human Relationships: Obedience

Lesson Activities

History and Geography: Ice Skating

Until he fell in, Tom certainly had a wonderful time ice skating on the canal (page 40). Has your student ever been ice skating? Take this opportunity to explore with him the rich variety of ice skating sports. Begin by sharing a brief history of the sport.

Ice skating isn't a new idea! We know that crude ice skates made from wood and using animal bone for blades have been recovered in Roman ruins more than 2,000 years old. Ice skating didn't become a recreational (just for enjoyment) form until the 12th century in Britain. Before that, many Scandinavian countries used ice skating as a common source of transportation down the frozen canals. Skates had wooden blades until the 15th century when the Dutch began forming steel blades. In 1850, E.W. Bushnell of Philadelphia created the first pair of all-steel skates. And another American, ballet dancer Jackson Haines, began to create a new, modern form of skating that came to be called "figure skating" by combining dance movement with ice skating in 1870.

Now, there are many forms of ice skating in addition to traditional figure skating. Done by both single skaters and pairs, this sport is known for its beauty, grace, spectacular jumps, lifts (one partner lifts the other) and spins. Your student may have seen figure skating competitions on television or at an area ice rink. Some of the most famous names in figure skating are Scott Hamilton (U.S. male singles), Peggy Fleming (U.S. female singles), Dorothy Hamill (U.S. female singles), Dick Button (U.S. male singles) and Sonja Henie (a three-time Norwegian Olympic Champion in 1928, 1932 and 1936 female singles).

There are more sports using skates. Speed skating is very popular in the United States, as well as world-wide. In this sport, the blades on the skates are much longer than figure skates and the sport consists of race competition. The object of the race is to be the first to cross the finish line. Unlike figure skating, where part of the score is always subjective (a decision based on personal preference or feeling), speed skating is purely objective. Men and women always compete separately in speed skating and the races vary from 500 meters to 3,000 meters in length. This sport requires excellent balance, rhythm and powerful leg muscles.

Discuss other sports involving ice skates with your student. Hockey is an extremely popular sport in the northern United States and throughout Canada. Ice dancing (similar to figure skating) is also popular.

Broaden your student's awareness to include the delightful world of skating! Watch some televised competition—or go to a rink and skate yourself!

Science: Ice Skating—How It Works

Does your student know how ice skates work? It seems simple. The blade somehow glides across the surface. But how does it actually happen? Ice is a liquid (water) that has been changed into a solid by freezing. However, when a solid is compressed (having high pressure focused on it) heat is created. This is a scientific principle—compression produces heat.

As you glide along on that thin metal blade, your entire body's weight is pressing down on the blade. The pressure created by your body's weight momentarily melts the frozen (solid) ice back into a liquid (water). The water quickly refreezes once more as soon as you have passed by. This principle—ice melting under pressure and then refreezing when the pressure is lifted—is called *regelation* [REE juh LAY shun].

[**Teacher's Note**: If your student is older and very interested in math, you can have him calculate the pounds of pressure per square inch on his ice blades. For example, if his skates were 1/8 inch wide and 11 inches long, that is 1 3/8 square inches. If your student weighs 80 lbs., that is more than 58 pounds of pressure per square inch—assuming you are skating on one foot at a time.]

To demonstrate how ice skates actually work at home, create a block of ice by freezing approximately one inch of water in the bottom of an empty ice cream carton so you can peel away the paper. Now set it on a tall coffee can or pedestal. Then cut a piece of waxed sewing thread long enough to lay across the block of ice with several inches hanging down on either side. Attach weights (ball fishing weights, small magnets off the refrigerator, or even two spoons) on each end of the thread. Lay the thread across the surface of the ice and leave it alone. Ask your student what he thinks will happen?

This is going to be his *hypothesis*. In actuality, the compression of the weighted thread will slowly melt through the ice (much faster than the entire piece of ice will melt—due to the regelation factor). Before you know it, the ice block will be cut in half. This is just the kind of experiment Tom would have loved!

Science: Dew Points and Frost

Tom woke up to frosty windowpanes. What is frost? Many people think frost is frozen dew. This is not correct. Since this is common error, begin by explaining what dew is and then explore frost together.

Dew is the little droplet of water we see on the grass in the morning. Dew is formed by the condensation of water vapor (humid air) near the ground. During the day, the ground absorbs heat from the sun. When the sun goes down at night, the surface of the earth cools down quickly. As it cools, the humid air right next to the ground chills as well. When the temperature of this air decreases to a certain point (known as the dew point) the air can no longer contain all of its humidity (vapor) and moisture condenses, forming dew. Therefore, a scientific definition of dew point is the lowest temperature at which the air can still contain all its vapor.

This temperature, unlike the boiling point (212° F.) or freezing point (32° F.) of water, is variable. It depends on the amount of humidity in the air. There are two main conditions that must be met for dew to form: clear skies and no winds. Cloudy skies prevent dew because they form a barrier. When he sun goes down and the earth's surface begins to give off heat, it is trapped by the clouds and returns to the earth, preventing the surface from ever reaching the dew point. Wind prevents the water molecules from staying in close enough contact to form droplets.

There is an old weather-watcher's poem your student can memorize which, although not fail proof, gives good indications of weather patterns:

When dew is on the grass
Rain will never come to pass.
When grass is dry in the morning light
Look for rain before the night.

Even though the temperature of the dew point is variable, there is a way to average a week's dew point temperature in your area at home.

Take a fairly thin, glass container (drinking glass, vase or beaker) and fill it with ice cubes. Then fill it with water. Using a good science thermometer, record the temperature reading at the point when you first see condensation (dew) form on the outside of the glass. Because the humidity in the air changes every day, do this experiment every day at the same time for a week. At the end of the week, average the results to determine the average temperature for the dew point that week.

If you watch the weather report on television with your student, meteorologists sometimes tell the average dew point each day.

Now that your student understands the general principles of dew, explain that if frost were frozen dew, it would form perfectly round frozen drops on the blades of grass and our windows. But we know this isn't true.

What Tom Edison saw on his window is what we see on a frosty morning. Feathery, flat patterns of frozen water vapor. Frost is formed when the air near the ground's surface drops in temperature so rapidly the humid air bypasses the stage of condensation (liquid) and turns directly to solid.

The next time your student notices frost or dew, talk about what you learned in this lesson and remember Tom's birthday morning windowpane!

Science: Health and Safety—Hypothermia and Frostbite

Tom was extremely lucky that Sandy was able to retrieve him from those icy depths quickly (page 44). Has your student ever heard the terms *frostbite* or *hypothermia*? These are both dangerous physical conditions that can arise when the body is exposed to very cold temperatures. Learning to protect ourselves from harm and how to treat ourselves in case of emergency is another sign of maturity. Share with your student some simple first aid steps to care for frostbite.

Frostbite actually occurs when ice crystals form *in* your skin. In more severe cases, the crystals form deep in the tissue below your skin. The signs of frostbite are tingling and numbness. The skin may appear reddish in color or even bluish-white. An old-fashioned remedy was to rub the tingling area of skin with snow. This is dangerous! The affected skin might be further injured. Instead, begin to bathe the finger, toe, foot, etc., in fairly warm, but not hot, water (approximately 100° F.). This may cause severe pain in the affected limb, but it will subside. Then keeping the frostbitten area elevated, have the person rest, lying down.

Hypothermia is caused by accidental (Tom's falling in the canal) exposure to cold temperatures for an extended period of time. The body's temperature gauge falls below the normal level of 98.6° F. As the body loses heat, the internal organs begin to slow down. In severe cases, the person may die. Elderly people or people who are thin and frail are especially susceptible. To treat hypothermia, allow the victim to soak in a warm bath and then wrap the person in several layers of warm blankets.

[**Teacher's Note**: You may wish to refer back to the lesson on fevers and temperature in *The Boxcar Children*, chapter 11 lesson.]

Both frostbite and hypothermia can be prevented under normal circumstances. Remind your student that wearing warm winter clothing is not just something our mothers bother us with. It is an important part of keeping our bodies safe. Health experts now say instead of just wearing one extremely thick wool sweater, wearing several layers of natural fibers (cotton, silk or a blend) is better for our bodies. It allows the air to circulate and keeps us warm. Mittens are warmer than gloves because our fingers touch one another and the body heat is transferred from one to the other. Hats which cover the ears are important, and two layers of warm socks and a pair of boots finish off our winter wear. These tips can keep you safe and warm, especially if you are sledding, shoveling snow or hiking in the winter!

Science: Non-Homogenized Milk

On page 36 we are told Tom's glass of milk was flecked with golden dots of cream. If you chose to do the science lesson on dairy product preservation in *The Boxcar Children* (chapter 5), remind your student that Tom's milk is *non*-homogenized. The milk is whole and has not been shaken so the cream droplets are combined. If you did not do that lesson, now might be a good time to go back.

Language Arts: Literature—*Hans Brinker, or The Silver Skates*

Part of enriching your student's knowledge of the world is introducing him to well-known literature and literary vernacular. Perhaps one of the most famous tales worldwide is the story of Hans Brinker and his silver skates. *Hans Brinker*, or *The Silver Skates*, written in 1865 by Mary Mapes Dodge, is filled with adventure and vivid details. The story centers around a young boy, Hans, and his sister, Gretel. Their father is sick, and to help raise money for their family the children enter Hans in a skating race. The outcome is exciting and good, strong family values are portrayed throughout. Take some time and read this wonderful story with your student. There are many good abridged versions available, if you don't want to read the somewhat lengthy original.

Fine Arts: Colored Pencils—Creating Colors by Blending

One of Tom's beautiful birthday presents is a set of colored pencils. Colored pencils are wonderful art tools because by shading one color over another you create different hues and textures. It helps to have a quality set of colored pencils.

[**Teacher's Note**: Cheap colored pencils from the discount store aren't the best for this project. Go to an art supply store and ask for an inexpensive, but good quality set for a student. Another delightful medium, similar to colored pencils, is watercolor pencils. Used dry they work just like ordinary colored pencils, but when you add water you can paint with them. A good brand is called Aquarell and is available at most art stores.]

Once your student has experimented with different colors, encourage him to try drawing a picture of the canal where Tom was skating. The areas where Sandy warned Tom the ice was thin should be lighter in shade. Challenge your student to explore creating depth and shadow in the canal by using different layers of colored pencil drawing.

Issues of Human Relationships: Obedience

Ask your student how Tom might have prevented his accident in the canal? He could have listened to Sandy's advice. When adults or peers offer advice, it is often for our own good. Ignoring what our parents say and trying things on our own is foolish at best and can be dangerous as well. Encourage your student to look at obedience in a new light. Instead of thinking of obedience as a slave-like role, have him consider it as wisdom from people who care. When we were little and our mother said not to touch the stove, she was trying to protect us. Even when we don't understand why our parents or teachers are telling us something, we must give them the benefit of the doubt. It is usually easier to swallow our pride and trust their good judgment, than to fall in the canal like Tom did.

Writing and Discussion Question

When Tom returns home, the author tells us very little about the conversation Tom must have had with his parents about his accident. What do you think the conversation was like? Use written dialogue to write what you think Tom's parents might have said and what Tom might have said in reply.

Vocabulary Words

regelation: the term for ice melting under pressure and refreezing when the pressure is lifted

dew point: the lowest temperature at which the air can contain all of its vapors

hypothermia: dangerous condition occurring when the body's temperature falls below the normal range of 98.6° F.

frostbite: numbness and possible loss of affected area which occurs when skin is exposed to severe cold

Internet Connections

To view current suggested links relating to this chapter's lessons, see www.fiveinarow.com/connections.

Chapter 4–Off For A New Home

Parent Summary

Moving day has finally arrived! The Edisons are busy at work, packing everything they own into crates. Bustling around the house, Mrs. Edison shouts out last-minute orders about coats and hats. As they are about to leave, Tannie, Tom's sister, finds a suspicious looking box in the attic. The top of the box is covered in holes. Tom begs his mother to let him take the box, and before discovering what is inside, Tom's mother is distracted by the wagon arriving and goes outside. In the box is Tom's special goose Lulu!

Much to Tom's relief, Tannie agrees to keep Lulu under her lap robe and they all climb in the wagon. With a final look and wave, Tom says good-bye to the little red brick house in Milan.

What we will cover in this chapter:

[**Teacher's Note**: Due to its brevity and content, this chapter is somewhat of a transitional break for you and your student. Enjoy the light lessons listed below and review anything you may have missed up to this point.]

Science: Inventing Packing for Breakables—Modified Egg Toss

Fine Arts: Drawing Illustrations—The Edisons' Home

Lesson Activities

Science: Inventing Packing for Breakables—Modified Egg Toss

Tom's family had to pack everything they owned very carefully into boxes and crates. It took a lot of time, but think of the waste if they arrived in Port Huron and their possessions were broken! Has your student's family ever packed boxes and moved? Sometimes it takes inventiveness to think of how to pack something securely for shipment or transit. That's what this activity is all about. This project can be absolutely hilarious, as well as practical.

Take approximately one dozen raw eggs (hard-boiled eggs defeat the purpose of this exercise!) and go outside with your student. Your student will think you're crazy, but ask him to toss the egg across the yard. Of course, it will break upon impact. Now, give him the assignment to try to invent 'packing' that will allow the uncooked egg to be thrown without breaking. The 'packing' might include a shoe box filled with cotton balls and taped shut, a balloon (the egg tucked inside) filled with water, paper towels wrapped around the egg a "zillion times", etc. Have your student vary the distance he tosses his wrapped egg. If you have more than one student, organize a competition to see whose egg can be thrown the greatest distance without breaking.

This experiment could take the better part of an afternoon and the entire dozen eggs, but it will be unforgettable and a great way to spark your student's creativity. Encourage your student to record his findings and come to a conclusion regarding the best way to wrap a breakable egg! Have fun!

Fine Arts: Drawing Illustrations—The Edisons' Home

Your student should be familiar with what an illustrator does for a book. An illustrator takes passages from the author's text and illuminates it through art. Draw your student's attention to the wonderfully descriptive paragraph at the end of this chapter.

Pay particularly close attention to the following details: "...little red brick house on the hillside. Behind it he could see the silver thread that was the canal which led out to Lake Erie." Encourage your student to be the 'illustrator" for this chapter. By drawing this scene and following the author's description, he can make a beautiful scene—adding his own embellishments, of course!

Writing and Discussion Question

How do you think Tom is planning to care for Lulu on the train and boat? What would you do if you had a goose on a trip?

Internet Connections

To view current suggested links relating to this chapter's lessons, see www.fiveinarow.com/connections.

Chapter 5–Tom's First Train Ride

Parent Summary

The Edisons arrive at the train station. Unable to contain his excitement, Tom races ahead and begins to ask the engineer, Mr. Benjamin, many questions. Mr. Benjamin likes the young boy's energy, and says Tom may ride in the engine with him for a few miles. Mr. and Mrs. Edison agree and Tom is joyous. His ride with the engineer goes quickly, and Tom learns all about how a steam engine works. When he is back with his family, Tom relates his experiences to them and the rest of the trip to Detroit goes by quickly.

What we will cover in this chapter:

History and Geography: People's Signature Trademarks

History and Geography: American Rail History—Harvey and Pullman

Science: Pollution—Air, Water and Ground

Science: Speed—How Fast Is Fast?

Language Arts: Famous Sayings

Issues of Human Relationships: A First Time for Everything

Issues of Human Relationships: Observation—Keeping Your Eyes Open

Lesson Activities

History and Geography: People's Signature Trademarks

On page 55, Tom is pulling his right eyebrow in excitement. Draw your student's attention to page 13 and page 21 in the book. Thomas Edison always pulled at his right eyebrow when he was thinking or excited. This type of unusual movement is known as a signature trademark. Most of us do something when we think: chew our lower lip, twirl a piece of hair with our fingers, drum our fingers, etc. Most of the time these habits are performed subconsciously.

Tom's habit of tugging on his right eyebrow stayed with him through his lifetime and became well-known. Talk with your student about little movements and nuances he sees people doing. Sometimes famous entertainers and personalities choose something as their signature trademark. Your student will not remember, but you might tell him about Carol Burnett (pulling on her right ear lobe meant "I love you" to her mom), Minnie Pearl (who always said "Hoooowdee!" and wore a price tag on her hat), and Johnny Carson (famous for subconsciously tapping his pencil). There are many, many more. Becoming aware of people's signature trademarks is both interesting and great fun!

History and Geography:
American Rail History–Harvey and Pullman

Tom's family was amazed at the power and performance of the railroad! They were able to travel at much faster speeds than before and in considerably more comfort. In comparison to horse-pulled wagons, rail service offered comfortable benches to sit on, candy and beverages for refreshment, and you weren't blown around by the wind or dust. For the Edisons, this method of travel was a vast improvement! But rail service would eventually offer even more comfort and luxury!

Take this opportunity to share with your student the changes which occurred during the next forty years (1860-1900) in both the types of amenities passengers could enjoy and the jobs available on the railroads.

Two important names in the late 19th and early 20th century world of railroads were George Pullman and Fred Harvey. George Mortimer Pullman was chiefly a businessman. He was born in New York in 1831, but moved to Chicago when he was 23 years old. It was then that he saw a need for improving the sleeping quarters on trains. At that time, people were forced to sleep sitting up in their seats, with no privacy or comfort. Ask your student if he would like to sleep on a wooden bench next to a lot of other strangers?

Mr. Pullman and a friend introduced a new kind of sleeping car they called the *Pioneer*. It featured bunkbed-like berths, which pulled out from the wall. In this way they could be folded up during the day, allowing for more room, and pulled out at night. The beds were made up with soft sheets and blankets. It was an amazing invention! Before George Pullman was 34 years old (1865), his new discovery, the comfortable berth, was standard on the Chicago & Alton Railroad. Also, the name for his invention, the *Pioneer*, was soon changed to the *Pullman*.

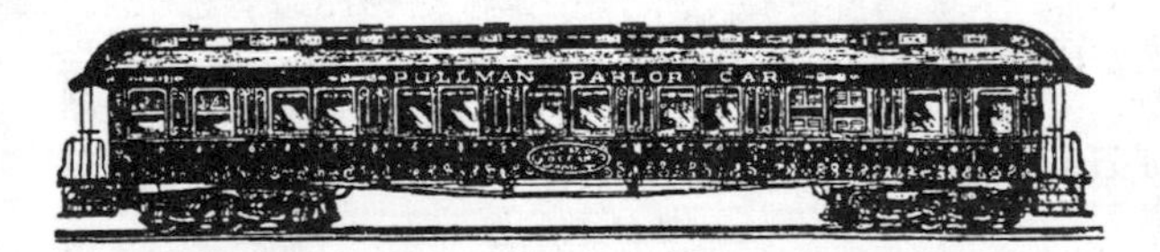

To this day, sleeping cars on railroads are known as Pullman cars. By 1899, Mr. Pullman had a monopoly on the sleeping-car business. His cars were used on every railroad in the country. Imagine what Tom would have thought of sleeping in his own little bed on the train! If your student seems interested in this topic, you might continue the discussion by getting books at the library on George Pullman and railroad service.

Another major name in railroad service was Fred Harvey. During the time Tom's family rode the railroad, people had to pack their own food or eat at the food stops along the way. At that time the food service offered at the stops was really awful! Bad meat was often served and stale, soured breads and beverages were customary. For this reason, most travelers opted for the "pack your own lunch" choice. But, this terrible food service was about to change! In 1876 a man named Fred Harvey went to the Santa Fe railroad with a proposal. Harvey suggested he hire employees, operate food service stops and serve decent food at a fair price along the route of the Santa Fe. He only needed the railroad to buy the restaurant spaces for him and charge him no rent. He said he could pay his employees and then would split his earnings with the railroad 50/50!

Santa Fe took Harvey up on his offer and soon railroad food stops were changed forever! Mr. Harvey insisted on his lunchrooms being impeccably clean, his food of the highest quality and his workers (all women) of the utmost moral character. Becoming known as Harvey Houses, his restaurants became the standard by which all other restaurants were judged within the railroad industry. Offering fresh fruits, vegetables, seafood and even ice cream and serving them on china and fine linens made the Harvey House extremely popular.

The servers, known as Harvey Girls, had to have at least an eighth-grade education, be able to speak clearly, have a pleasant manner and a clean appearance. Some of these young women worked for Harvey House restaurants for years! They were paid well and were highly respected. Besides the staff of Harvey Girls, the Harvey House staff also included bakers, butchers, managers, housemaids, and many others! What would Tom have thought to sit down at a beautifully set table and eat ice cream!

If it is possible, have your student ask their grandparents or even great-grandparents if they have ever eaten at a Harvey House restaurant. There's a good chance they will have! Maybe one of your student's relatives was once a Harvey Girl! If your student is able to interview a grandparent, older friend or neighbor, perhaps he could write a paper summarizing his conversation.

Isn't it interesting how creative men like Pullman and Harvey see a need and find a way to fill it? Both the names Pullman and Harvey have become a part of the American vernacular for the benefits they gave to society. Go and look for more information on both these men and their inventions at a local library.

Science: Pollution—Air, Water and Ground

On page 56, Mrs. Edison makes a comment about the railroad's smoke and its effect on nearby homes. Tom thinks the puffing, black smoke is exciting, but his mother is also right. The soot and smoke of the railroads creates a new type of air pollution. Before the railroads, not much interrupted the clean air of the country other than the smoke from fireplaces.

In today's world, pollution has become a significant problem in most cities and urban areas. Talk with your student about the pollution problems your area faces. Also, you may want to take this opportunity to discuss several current pollution problems facing many areas of the world—acid rain, landfills and smog. All three of these dilemmas are in the news almost daily and your student may have heard of them already. Talk about each briefly.

Acid rain is caused by the water vapor in the air mixing with the exhaust fumes of cars and chemical compounds released by factories. Affecting many regions of the United States, acid rain is polluting our rivers and streams, killing fish and plants. The problem is most severe in the northeastern region. Scientists are working every day to find ways to neutralize these damaging rains and restore the purity to our water supplies.

Landfills are massive "dumping" grounds for garbage and waste. In many cities, landfills are overflowing with plastics and glass, items that could be recycled but instead are thrown away. Most of these items are not biodegradable (capable of decomposing naturally) and will continue to be in landfills for many centuries to come. Cities are struggling with decisions on how to eliminate such massive amounts of waste in their communities. It is a significant problem.

Finally, smog is a type of air pollution created by excessive amounts of exhaust fumes and chemical compounds released into the air and trapped by warm air or mountain ranges. Smog is particularly serious in major cities. Smog poses a serious health threat to people and greatly diminishes the beauty of the skylines in our cities.

Have your student research recent newspaper or magazine articles about pollution control projects that may be underway in your community, state or region. Have him write a report about his findings. Learning about our environment and how to protect it is vital to preventing future problems. Tom's mother thought the smoke from the steam engine was bad. What would she think of acid rain, air pollution and overflowing landfills?

Science: Speed—How Fast Is Fast?

On page 63, Tom thinks the train is going very fast. He asks Mr. Benjamin and finds out it is going 15 miles per hour. Ask your student if he thinks that is fast? If he can't relate the number to actual speed, take him out in a car and drive 15 miles per hour. Does he think it is fast now? What speed does your student consider fast. Remind him of the lesson on the speed of light in chapter 2. Now, that is fast!

Some exotic airplanes can travel in excess of 5,000 miles per hour and commercial airliners routinely go approximately 500 miles per hour. Why did Tom think the train was going so fast? Compared to walking, running, riding a horse or boat, it was fast! If your student is interested in this topic, go to the library and find additional books on trains, airplanes, attempts at world speed records, etc. Speeds continue to increase as technology has progressed. We will certainly continue to travel faster in the new century ahead. Hold onto your hat! (Also consider comparing the speed of light, sound, etc.)

Language Arts: Famous Sayings

Part of mastering a language includes becoming familiar with the "sayings" of that language. For example, someone unfamiliar with English would not understand the saying, "this meal is *on the house*." They might imagine that dinner was going to be served on the roof!

Show your student the opening line of this chapter. Tom assumes there must be a fire because he sees smoke. A famous saying is, "where there's smoke there's fire." Explain to your student what that means. It generally means that when we see certain symptoms, it's usually wise to assume the obvious conclusion about their cause. Hence the statement, "wherever you see smoke, there's undoubtedly fire nearby that is causing it."

Be on the lookout for more common sayings as they present themselves. Share them with your student and encourage him to listen for unique sayings himself. Learning about these special language devices will enrich your student's cultural literacy and increase his understanding of conversations around him.

Issues of Human Relationships: A First Time for Everything

Tom was very excited about his first trip on a train! Imagine what he must have thought about riding with the engineer on his very first trip! Ask your student about things he's done for the first time. Has he ever flown on an airplane, gone sailing, fishing or camped in a teepee? There is a first time for everything. If your student is interested, have him make a list of all the things he wants to try, but hasn't yet done. For an extension of this lesson, refer to the Writing and Discussion Question for this chapter.

Issues of Human Relationships: Observation—Keeping Your Eyes Open

The book tells us Tom wanted to be sure to see everything (page 57). Being observant helped Thomas Edison be the great inventor that he was! Noticing people, places and activities are all a part of being observant. Keeping your eyes open is a major part of learning all about the world around you. Encourage your student to record interesting things he notices around him, using a journal or notebook. He might observe a baby bird, a diesel truck, an old woman with long braided hair, etc. Sometimes the best inventions are born from careful observation.

Making lists of details we notice can also help us in our writing. Have your student take one or more of the items on his list of observations and write a paragraph about them. His paragraph might describe the old woman with the braided hair in greater detail and describe what she's doing, who she's talking with or what she's saying, etc. Challenge your student to become more observant, just like Tom!

Writing and Discussion Question

Tom's first train ride was exciting! Write about something you remember doing for the first time. What were the sounds, sights, feelings, smells or tastes of your experience?

Internet Connections

To view current suggested links relating to this chapter's lessons, see www.fiveinarow.com/connections.

Chapter 6–The House in the Grove

Parent Summary

The Edisons complete the final chapter of their journey to Port Huron. They pass the area schoolhouse on their way to their new home. His parents tell him he must go to the school soon. Finally, they turn onto a narrow road and see a large white house straight ahead. Mrs. Edison is shocked by how big their new house is and Tom runs off to explore the grounds. Soon they begin to move things into their new home, and Tom and Pitt spend the better part of the day helping their mother insulate the floors with straw. After the family eats supper, they decide to name their new home "The House in the Grove." The next afternoon, Mr. Edison takes Tannie back to the train station and sends her back to Milan. That evening, the family sits and listens to Mr. Edison read from *The Detroit Free Press* about current events. Tom listens closely to stories about President Fillmore and Commodore Perry. He is interested in the concept of trade and commerce. Learning things from his father's reading becomes a wonderful tool for Tom!

What we will cover in this chapter:

History and Geography: President Fillmore

History and Geography: Commodore Perry

Science: Tree Identification

Language Arts: Names for Houses

Issues of Human Relationships: Being Neighborly

Lesson Activities

History and Geography: President Fillmore

Tom listens to stories about President Fillmore as his father reads to him from the paper (page 78). Discuss some facts about the 13th president of the United States with your student.

Millard Fillmore (1800-1874) was the second president to assume the position during someone else's term. President Zachary Taylor died in 1850 and Vice-President Fillmore served the balance of Taylor's term. President Fillmore was in office for almost three years, and during that time two things of major significance occurred. First was the signing of an important trade agreement between the United States and Japan. Second, was the Compromise of 1850. The 1850 compromise abolished slave trade in the District of Columbia, admitted California to the Union as the 31st state and established stricter slave trade laws across the Union. If your student is interested in this period of presidential history, find a biography on President Fillmore and continue your research.

History and Geography: Commodore Perry

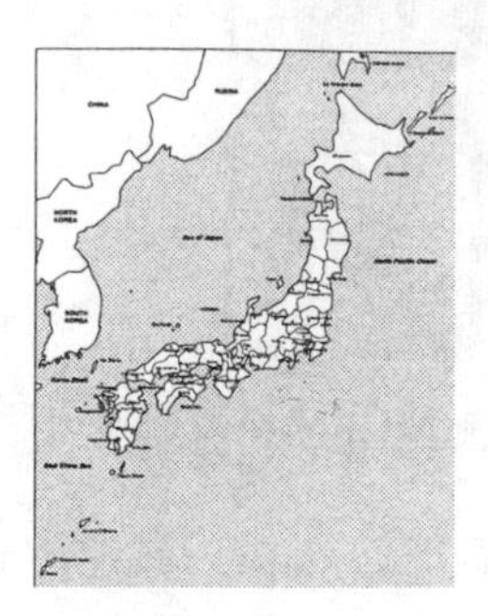

Tom was interested in Commodore Perry and the concept of trade. Ask your student if he has ever heard of Commodore Perry. Matthew Calbraith Perry (1794-1858) first opened world trade ports in Japan. With a signed letter and an appeal from President Fillmore in hand, Perry headed to Tokyo in 1854. Perry refused to speak with anyone other than the highest Japanese leaders. The Japanese eventually agreed to allow trade, and signed the now-famous treaty in Yokohama.

This agreement is considered one of our most significant acts of diplomacy. Talk with your student about what *diplomacy* means. It usually is defined as "the management of relations between two countries." Because of Commodore Perry's diplomacy, Japan and the United States discussed the situation and came to a common understanding. Commodore Perry, under the order of President Fillmore, was practicing what is known as "Foreign Diplomacy." Is your student interested in this concept? Do more research on your own and continue to talk about the importance of foreign diplomacy in an ever-shrinking world. A wonderful topic for additional research might be the Camp David Accords, which helped to bring peace in the Middle East.

Science: Tree Identification

Doesn't Tom's new house sound beautiful? Draw your student's attention to the vivid description of the yard and trees on page 70. What types of trees are in your student's yard or neighborhood? Are they native to the region or were they planted? Have your student collect leaves from each different species and document the types of trees he finds. Are there any oaks, like in Tom's yard? Find a good tree identification reference at your library or bookstore and help your student learn to use it.

Language Arts: Names for Houses

Monticello

Tom decides his new home needs a name. He chooses The House in the Grove. Share with your student some other famous names for homes. Thomas Jefferson's beautiful mansion was named Monticello. George Washington's home was known as Mount Vernon. The classic American film *Gone with the Wind* included both Tara and Twelve Oaks. Most western ranches have names. Often these ranch names are associated with a cattle brand, i.e., the Circle C, the Rocking K, the T Bar J, etc. Does your student think naming a house is an interesting idea? Have him come up with a list of creative names for his own home. Perhaps your student could sit down with his family and decide on a name for his house! Naming an inanimate object, like a house or car, gives it extra character! Have fun!

Issues of Human Relationships: Being Neighborly

Mrs. Edison didn't have to work as hard when she arrived at her house because her neighbors had already cleaned out the rooms for her (page 72). Being a good neighbor is an important part of being a good citizen. Encourage your student to think of things he can do for his neighbors. Raking leaves for an older neighbor, baking cookies for a new neighborhood family or helping someone carry in groceries are wonderful ways to be a good neighbor. Challenge your student to be on the lookout for neighborly acts he can do to serve others!

Writing and Discussion Question

On page 71 Tom is excited about the size of his new home's hallway. He says it is "so wide he can play games up there." What kind of games would you want to play in a large, upstairs hall?

Internet Connections

To view current suggested links relating to this chapter's lessons, see www.fiveinarow.com/connections.

Chapter 7–First Day of School

Parent Summary

Tom's first day of school arrives. With Pitt and his mother by his side, Tom sets out for the one-half mile walk to his new schoolhouse. Tom has heard bad stories about his new schoolmaster, Mr. Crawford, but he tries to be optimistic. When Tom arrives, Mr. Crawford tells him that even though he is seven, Tom must be in the first grade since he has had no formal schooling. The rest of Tom's day doesn't go much better. He is sent to the corner for drawing pictures instead of doing his penmanship, and his lunch is stolen by the biggest boy in class. That boy, Michael Oates, however, decides to befriend Tom and the lunch hour becomes the best part of the day.

What we will cover in this chapter:

History and Geography: One-Room Schoolhouses

Science: One-Half Mile—How Far Is That?

Language Arts: Penmanship Review

Issues of Human Relationships: Focusing Our Attention

Lesson Activities

History and Geography: One-Room Schoolhouses

Tom's school was a one-room schoolhouse. All the grades from kindergarten up were in the same classroom. Ask your student if he has ever seen such a school. This convention of education was popular in the past, primarily in small towns where the community couldn't afford to pay more than one teacher. This type of school is still found in a few very small towns in the United States, but for the most part is now extinct.

One-room schoolhouses are still alive today in homes where parents homeschool their children. In this setting, several siblings in different grades may all be taught by the same teacher. Discuss with your student the many other types of schools: private, public, parochial, boarding, military, etc. Broadening our horizons and learning how other schools operate allows us to appreciate the world! Have your student pick one type of school and research his subject before writing a paper explaining the advantages and disadvantages.

Science: One-Half Mile—How Far Is That?

On page 80 we see Tom walking one-half mile to school. Does your student think that is far? If you wish, it might be fun to go outside and walk one-half mile with your student. What would your student think of walking to school? Tom was fortunate to live less than a mile from school. In years past, many children walked five miles or more to get to school each day. If this is of interest to your student, continue your discussion by talking about how many feet are in a mile (5,280). How many inches? How many yards? Now challenge your student by calculating the distance in metric units. (Hint: 1 meter equals approximately 39 inches.)

Language Arts: Penmanship Review

Tom was supposed to be working on his penmanship, instead of drawing a picture of the House in the Grove. Review with your student the importance of good penmanship. In Tom's day, penmanship was considered a very important subject of study. Both the quality of the handwriting and the discipline it required reflected on the person's character. Encourage your student to continue refining his penmanship. Perhaps your student would enjoy trying something more elaborate. Calligraphy is the beautiful art of embellished penmanship. If your student is interested, find a good book on calligraphy at the library and buy an inexpensive, calligraphy marker. Have fun and focus on the discipline of fine penmanship!

Issues of Human Relationships: Focusing Our Attention

On page 86 Tom is drawing on his slate instead of listening to Mr. Crawford. Talk with your student about Tom's lack of attention in class. Why didn't Tom pay attention? Drawing is a wonderful, creative outlet, but all things have a proper time and place. When we are in class, our focus must be on the topic and we should respect someone by listening when they speak. We owe our elders and teachers our full attention, even if they're less than kind like Mr. Crawford. Encourage your student to pay attention with a special, surprise reward. Perhaps a special lunch or a field trip could be an incentive to remember that listening is often more important than talking. Catch your child in the act of paying close attention and then surprise him with a treat!

Writing and Discussion Question

On page 81 Tom overhears the children saying Mr. Crawford "isn't fair." What is involved in being a "fair" person? What does the word "fair" mean to you?

Internet Connections

To view current suggested links relating to this chapter's lessons, see www.fiveinarow.com/connections.

Chapter 8–The Basement Laboratory

Parent Summary

Tom's schooling continues to be a trial. Tom makes friends easily, but Mr. Crawford becomes increasingly negative toward Tom. One day, after Tom asks a question, the schoolmaster yells at Tom and calls him "addled." Tom runs home weeping, and his mother promises he does not have to return to school again. Mrs. Edison understands that questions and curiosity are the way children learn. She decides to teach Tom at home.

Michael Oates, the boy who had stolen Tom's lunch box, comes to work for the Edison family. He and Tom become good friends. Michael and the other children wish they could be taught by Mrs. Edison, too. Tom always seems to be having a good time.

One day Mrs. Edison teaches Tom about a branch of science called chemistry. Tom is fascinated by this and studies a book in which he sees a picture of a "laboratory." Tom decides he wants his own laboratory so he and Michael Oates set out to collect various bottles. Then Tom makes labels for them and fills them with a variety of items (feathers, dried corn, flour, etc.). It's just pretend, but Tom thinks his laboratory is wonderful! Mrs. Edison lets Tom set his bottles on a table in the basement and Tom is thrilled!

What we will cover in this chapter:

Science: The Different Branches of Science

Science: Warning Symbols

Science: Setting Up Your Own Laboratory

Issues of Human Relationships: Differences and Assumptions

Lesson Activities

Science: The Different Branches of Science

Tom was learning about an area of Physical Science called Chemistry. Discuss with your student the other branches of science. If your student is younger, discuss this lesson briefly, concentrating on becoming familiar with the concepts only. If your student is more advanced or older, challenge him to define each section more extensively. To begin with, there are four main divisions of science: Mathematics and Logic, Physical Science, Life Science and Social Science. It might be helpful in this discussion to have your student chart or outline each section as you talk about it.

The first branch, *Math* and *Logic*, is made up of six different areas.

Arithmetic is the study of numbers and simple calculations like addition, subtraction, multiplication and division.

Algebra is the study of equations and unknown quantities represented by letters.

Geometry is the study of the mathematical relationship of solid shapes, angles, line and points.

Calculus is similar to algebra but deals with changing quantities.

Probability is the study of events and the likelihood of their occurrence.

Statistics is the study of analyzing trends or similarities in large mathematical calculations.

The second branch of science is called *Physical Science*. There are five primary areas that make up Physical Science.

Chemistry is the study of the composition, structure and reaction of elements and compounds, both natural and artificial.

Geology is the study of the earth and its makeup.

Meteorology is the study of the earth's atmosphere and weather.

Astronomy is the study of outer space, planets and stars.

Physics is the study of all matter and energy.

The third branch of science is called *Life Science* or *Biology*, and is organized into two separate sections:

Botany is the study of plants.

Zoology is the study of humans and animals.

Finally, there is the section of science called *Social Science*. This area of science deals with humans and society. It is made up of five subdivisions.

Anthropology is the study of origin and development of humans and society.

Economics is the study of production, distribution and uses of goods produced by a society.

Political Science is the study of a society's government and laws.

Psychology is the study of human beings' thought processes and behaviors.

Sociology is the study of human communities and the relationships among various individuals and groups in societies.

Encourage your student to begin identifying the different sections of science when he notices them. It is important to remember science is a comprehensive and expanding subject. Ask your student what areas he enjoys studying. There are so many occupations and jobs in each area of science (zoologist, geologist, statistician, psychologist, etc.). Challenge your student to research one or more of those occupations and discuss them. Science is an exciting subject—filled with fascinating and eye-opening wonders! (It might be fun to use the list above and apply it to lessons in *Beyond Five in a Row*. For instance, the lesson on Dew Point would be Meteorology, Eggs—Zoology, a lesson on Budgeting—Economics, etc. This is an advanced concept, so keep it fun.)

Science: Warning Symbols

Tom carefully makes little labels for his "chemicals" which bear the symbol of a skull and crossbones (page 98). This symbol is the universal (internationally recognized) picture representing a *poisonous* substance. If you have one, show your student an example of this picture on a household cleaning bottle or medicine bottle. Explain the importance of this symbol to your student. It is there for our safety and protection. There are several other important universal symbols to learn as well. Talk about where you find them and remind your student to leave substances with these markings alone.

Science: Setting Up Your Own Laboratory

Wasn't Tom's idea for his own laboratory delightful? Would your student enjoy having his own little laboratory? Feed your student's interest by letting him set up his own lab, using baby food jars or other bottles he finds. Here is a list of common household compounds and their chemical names that can be collected for your student's chemistry set: white vinegar (acetic acid), household ammonia (ammonium hydroxide), Epsom salts (magnesium sulfate), baking soda (sodium bicarbonate), washing soda (sodium carbonate), table salt (sodium chloride), instant tea (tannic acid), borax (sodium borate), fruit juice (ascorbic acid), and soda water (carbonic acid).

Before filling the bottles, your student can create labels just like Tom (with or without the sign for poison) and paste them on the front of each bottle. Then, encourage your student to label each chemical with the scientific name in large print and the common name below it.

There are many excellent resources for home science experiments available. One great series, which includes experiments using the chemicals your student has already gathered, is called the *Backyard Science* series by Jane Hoffman. Available in most homeschool reference catalogs, this series includes many wonderful titles. Another delightful resource is a book/kit entitled *Kitchen Science*. This book includes a few supplies and is a part of the series, *Adventures in Science*. In the meantime, here are a couple of simple, yet fun experiments your student can conduct with his new "chemistry" set and laboratory.

Invisible Writing—The Salt Water Script

Gather the following items:

sheet of white paper
drinking glass
small paint brush
sodium chloride (table salt)
soft lead pencil

Fill the drinking glass with 1/4 cup water. Add 4 tablespoons sodium chloride (salt) and dissolve by stirring. Dip the paintbrush into the solution. Paint a design or your name on the piece of paper. Let it dry. Then, with the pencil, rub the lead across the design/name lightly. The painted areas will suddenly appear in black.

Bouncing Balls—Perpetual Motion

Gather the following items:

tall glass
3 mothballs
sodium bicarbonate (baking soda)
acetic acid (white vinegar)

Fill the glass 3/4 full of water. Add 1/2 teaspoon sodium bicarbonate and 1 tablespoon of acetic acid. Drop in the three mothballs. After a few seconds add another tablespoon of acetic acid. Soon bubbles of carbon dioxide from the sodium bicarbonate and acetic acid will collect on the mothballs and bring them up to the surface. As they float on the surface, some of the carbon dioxide will escape into the air, and the mothballs will sink again. They may continue to rise and sink for several hours.

Tom would have loved these experiments! Encourage your student to view science as exciting, understandable and applicable! It can be all of those things and more!

Issues of Human Relationships: Differences and Assumptions

Why did Mr. Crawford call Tom "addled?" (page 93) *Addled* means confused or muddled. Ask your student why he thinks Mr. Crawford would assume Tom was confused. Maybe Mr. Crawford thought Tom's questions weren't intelligent. Perhaps Mr. Crawford thought that because Tom was different from the other students he wasn't smart. Or maybe Mr. Crawford didn't want to take the time to answer Tom's questions and so he tried to eliminate the problem by calling Tom addled.

Unfortunately, people sometimes assume when someone is different they aren't as intelligent. When we *assume* something, it means we are pretending to understand something without gathering the facts. Assumptions lead to misunderstandings and often mean we lose out on really knowing someone. Discuss with your student examples of assumptions. Ask your student what he thinks about Mr. Crawford's assumptions about Tom.

Just because someone is different from us, does not mean they are less intelligent or capable. For example, someone from a different country might just nod and smile when we speak to them. If someone assumed they were not intelligent, they would be wrong! More likely, the foreigner doesn't understand a word you're saying because of the language barrier! Always give people the benefit of the doubt! In that way, we increase our respect of others and at the same time we grow in personal character! Next time you find yourself assuming something about someone, take some time to get to know them. There's an excellent chance you'll be quite surprised by the person you meet.

Internet Connections

To view current suggested links relating to this chapter's lessons, see www.fiveinarow.com/connections.

Chapter 9–Tom Tries An Experiment

Parent Summary

Michael and Tom have worked all summer long on a garden. They harvest the vegetables and fruits and sell them in Port Huron. Tom has saved nearly all his earnings to spend on chemicals for his laboratory. September arrives and after Tom and Michael sell their last load of apples, Tom goes to the chemist's shop and buys a bottle of mercury. It is the final addition he has been needing for his set of chemicals. On the way back to the House in the Grove, Michael notices some birds flying in the sky. Tom suggests that if the human body were filled with gas (making it lighter than air) we could fly as well! Tom is excited by his hypothesis and convinces Michael to drink a gaseous liquid he mixes together when they arrive home. Michael drinks it and promptly gets sick. Mrs. Edison is very angry with Tom's foolish experiment and threatens to make Tom destroy his laboratory. Tom offers an alternative suggestion (a lock on his chemicals and a promise not to ever experiment on people again) and so his mother relents, simply punishing Tom by sending him to bed without dinner.

What we will cover in this chapter:

Science: Periodic Table of Elements—A First Look

Science: Mercury

Science: Economics—The Two Ways to Make Money

Science: Economics—Savings, Budgets and the 8th Wonder of the World

Fine Arts: Advertising—Creating A "Look" For Your Business

Issues of Human Relationships: How We Respond to Discipline

Lesson Activities

Science: Periodic Table of Elements—A First Look

Although your student is too young to tackle a full study of the Periodic Table of Elements, he might be interested in a beginning look at this important scientific tool. Begin by looking at the complete table, which you can find in an encyclopedia or science book. Ask your student what he notices? To scale the topic down to a more manageable size, draw your student's attention to the specific square showing sulphur (in the margin). Without going into great detail, talk a little about what each of the notations signify. You will find the following basic information symbolized on each square: the chemical symbol (S), atomic number (16), element name, and the atomic weight (32). If your student is older and more advanced in science, perhaps finding more information on this subject at the library is appropriate. For most *Beyond Five in a Row* students, this simple introduction is sufficient.

Science: Mercury

Tom bought some mercury for his laboratory from Mr. Stevenson (page 107). Ask your student if he knows what mercury is? Begin the discussion with a simple explanation. Mercury is a shiny, silver metal element. It is the only metal in the world that is a liquid when it is room temperature. Other metals—iron, for example—can be liquid when heated to a very high temperature but are always solid at room temperature. Mercury is liquid without this additional heat added. Share with your student the many important properties of mercury. It expands and contracts evenly when heated or cooled, remaining in liquid form over a wide range of temperatures. For this reason, mercury is used in thermometers.

Mercury is found in the earth as an ore (a natural combination of mineral deposits from which a metal can be extracted) called cinnabar. Cinnabar deposits are found in Chile, China, Czechoslovakia and Iran. Alaska, California and Nevada have the largest deposits of cinnabar in the United States.

Be sure to warn your student that mercury is highly poisonous! You should never play with a ball of mercury! The metal can actually seep into your skin and carry with it toxins which can damage brain cells. Mercury is also potentially dangerous to the environment, poisoning our fish and waterways. Industrial wastes have been dumped into rivers, lakes, oceans and bays all over the world. In many regions native fish now carry dangerous levels of mercury. The United States has made substantial progress in reducing mercury contamination during the past twenty years, although a few areas are still dangerously affected—a dramatic reminder of our continuing need to research and respect the dangers of our industrial waste.

Look at a thermometer and show your student the actual shiny mercury inside and then continue your own research on mercury and its uses.

Science: Economics—The Two Ways to Make Money

Tom and Michael were financially successful in their truck farming business. On page 104, Tom convinced Michael they could make more from truck farming than by working at odd jobs in town. Take this opportunity to talk with your student about beginning economics.

There are two main ways people make money. One is to provide labor for another person. For example, Tom could have cleaned stables for the neighbors or run errands for a shopkeeper in town. We can also make money by being an owner. This is what Tom did! He and Michael ran their own business and sold their own goods. Remind your student of this classic economic idiom—the greater the risk, the greater the potential reward. This is an important principle of economics. If Tom had chosen to run errands for a shopkeeper in town he would have been guaranteed a certain wage for a certain amount of labor. But instead, he chose to take some risks (crop damage, weather variabilities, no demand for product, etc.) by starting his own truck farming business and reaped greater rewards by doing so.

A person who starts his own business is called an *entrepreneur*. Tom was an entrepreneur. Choosing to work for wages is never wrong. Make sure your student understands the relative risks and potentials of being an employee or owning your own business. Being an entrepreneur always carries greater risks but offers greater potential rewards.

Would your student like to own his own business someday? Why not start the creative ideas flowing now? To come up with a realistic business plan, your student will need to examine several issues. Use the example of a lemonade stand to explain the questions he'll need to answer.

First, what will he produce or sell? (Lemonade.) Second, who will he sell his product to? (Neighbors.) Third, what raw materials (ingredients) will he need to produce his product? (Lemons, sugar, water and ice.) Fourth, what other equipment will be necessary for production and marketing? (Table, sign, spoon, pitcher, cups, chair and money box.) Fifth, how much will his product cost? (10 cents a glass.) Finally, how will he obtain each of these items and what will each cost? Perhaps the table, spoon, pitcher, chair, cups, water and ice can be borrowed from mom and dad. He'll have to spend several dollars on lemons and sugar. Then he'll have to buy some poster board and draw his sign.

Once you've finished the "business plan" you can begin the production and distribution of your product. If your student seems interested in this ownership and business venture discussion, have him come up with three viable business ideas he could operate right now. (Possible ideas might include: lemonade stand, snow shoveling, window washing, lawn mowing business, walking neighbors dogs, etc.) This project might last for weeks. For more information on this subject, look at the Fine Arts lesson in this chapter.

Science:
Economics—Savings, Budgets and the Eighth Wonder of the World

Tom and Michael made a great deal of money in their truck garden business. Tom, we know (page 106), saved most of his earnings. Using Tom as an example, talk with your student about the importance of saving money and living within a budget. Even young children with small amounts of income can learn to budget their resources and save some of their money. By choosing a specific amount or percentage of their allowance/earnings, begin to set up some guidelines for savings. Allow your student to come up with his own suggestions and guidelines too.

The decision to put off purchases and save our money instead is often difficult. Perhaps sharing the power of compound interest may help motivate your student to begin saving.

The compounding of interest is sometimes referred to as the "8th Wonder of the World."

[**Teacher's Note**: If you mention the term "8th Wonder of the World," be prepared to get into a long discussion about the other 7 wonders—The Pyramids of Egypt at Giza, The Hanging Gardens of Babylon, The Temple of Artemis at Ephesus, The Statue of Zeus, The Mausoleum at Halicarnassus, The Colossus of Rhodes and the Lighthouse of Alexandria.]

When we save money in a bank or savings account we earn interest on our investment. The interest we earn continues to generate additional income as the money "compounds." One interesting way to calculate how quickly our money will grow is by using the "rule of 72's." We can determine how many years it will take our investment to double in value by dividing the rate of return into 72. For example, if we put our money in a savings account paying 6% annual interest, we know our money will double in 12 years. (72 divided by 6 equals 12.)

Likewise, we can determine what rate of return (or interest) our investment needs to return in a given period by dividing the number of years into 72. For example, if we set aside money for our child's college education and we need for it to double in 10 years, we know we'll need to earn at least 7.2% interest on our investment. (72 divided by 10 equals 7.2)

Here's an interesting experiment for your student. Ask him whether he would rather receive $1,000,000 or have you give him a penny and then double it every day for a month. Sit down together and do the math. You'll discover that the penny grows to two cents on the second day of the month, four cents on the third day, eight cents on day four, etc. By day ten you only have $5.12. By day 20 your compounded investment will have grown to more than $5,000, but still far less than one million dollars. Now look at the 30th day—you have more than $5,000,000 in your savings account. What if it was a 31-day month? No wonder compounding interest is considered the 8th Wonder of the World!

Fine Arts: Advertising—Creating A "Look" For Your Business

Whether your student came up with a real or fantasy idea for his own business, now he can begin designing his advertising. Explain to your student that an advertisement's purpose is to make the public want his service or product. It must appeal to the audience he is selling to and describe what he is selling. If he is interested, perhaps your student would like to create his own business card, making sure to include the name of his business, a phone number where he can be reached, etc. He might also enjoy creating a billboard design. Be sure to use strong colors or pictures to show his product or service. He might want to try thinking up a catchy slogan. Encourage your student to "go wild" with this project and try several different designs before deciding on the final choice. If you have a family computer the possibilities for this project become almost endless with simple clip art and page layout design programs.

If your student is older and interested in film or television, he might even want to write a script and videotape a simple commercial for his product. For example, he could take some exterior shots of the lemonade stand and a person smiling after drinking a glass of lemonade. Then he could direct the person to turn to the camera, lift their glass and say something like, "Mmmm! Leo's Lemonade is the best in town! And at 10 cents a glass you can't beat it. Come on by and try some. It's cold and refreshing!"

If you don't have a video camera, have your student create a radio "commercial" and tape it onto an audio cassette. This project opens up the world of sound effects and more. For ideas and further clarification on radio commercials, listen to the radio with your student through a few commercial breaks and talk about what they hear and how they think the commercial was produced.

Have fun with this project. And if your student decides on a real summer job, he may even be able to use the business cards and signs he has designed!

Issues of Human Relationships: How We Respond to Discipline

Tom should never have conducted an experiment on another human being. Tom's mother told him that as punishment for his actions, he would have to destroy his laboratory (page 113). What would have happened if Tom had responded by screaming and complaining? His mother would probably have stuck by her original punishment. Instead, Tom respectfully offers an alternative. Discuss with your student that how we respond to consequences can sometimes affect the situation. Mrs. Edison did not have to relent and allow Tom to keep his lab. However, she was more apt to consider this option when Tom responded respectfully. Encourage your student to examine his reactions to authority. Does he respond by whining and begging or does he remain calm, respectful and considerate? Continue talking about this topic when it seems appropriate and remind your student of Tom's situation.

Writing and Discussion Question

Tom's punishment for making Michael sick might have ended differently. If Mrs. Edison had stuck by her decision to have Tom destroy his laboratory, what might have been the long-term effects on Tom's life?

Vocabulary Words

cinnabar: a heavy, bright red mineral and the principle source of mercury

entrepreneur: a person who manages his own business, assuming the risk for the sake of the potential profit

Internet Connections

To view current suggested links relating to this chapter's lessons, see www.fiveinarow.com/connections.

Chapter 10–Tom's First Telegraph

Parent Summary

The year is now 1859. Four years have passed and Tom's studies with his mother have continued to serve him well. Port Huron has grown and the House in the Grove has truly become a home. Mr. Edison decides to build a 100-foot tower on their property and charge people 25 cents to see the view. The attraction becomes quite popular and people come from all over. When no one is around, Mrs. Edison and Tom enjoy sitting on the tower and doing their lessons. Standing at the top and looking out, Tom pretends he is Christopher Columbus and the St. Clair River is the great Atlantic. Other things are changing around the Edisons besides the new tower. Fort Gratiot, located across the road from the Edisons' home, has been inactive since the French and Indian war. But with increased worry that the nation might be facing a civil war, soldiers have again taken over the fort. So, people come to see the restored Fort Gratiot and climb Mr. Edison's tower!

Tom, now twelve, makes a new friend, James Clancy. He and James become very interested in a new form of communication they have heard about called a telegraph. Inspired by the thought of wired, coded discussions, Tom decides to rig up a telegraph between the boys' houses. By collecting bottles, wire and nails they build a simple telegraph. Now the boys can "talk" anytime they want from their own homes. Learning the Morse Code is fun and soon Tom and James are tapping away. Even Mr. Edison is interested in the new system and learns the code, too! Tom is having a lot of fun!

What we will cover in this chapter:

History and Geography: Samuel Morse and the Telegraph

History and Geography: Marconi and Wireless Communication

Fine Arts: Drama and Memory Enhancement

Lesson Activities

History and Geography: Samuel Morse and the Telegraph

Tom and James loved using Morse Code. Introduce your student to a brief background of the man behind this famous "language." Born in 1791, Samuel Morse was the son of a minister and began studying art at a very young age. By the time he graduated from Yale College in 1810, he wanted to pursue art full time. Morse attended the Royal Academy of Arts in London the following year, receiving several important honors during his three years there.

Within ten years, Samuel Morse had established himself as a leading American painter of historical portraits. One of his best known works, a portrait of Marquis de Lafayette, still hangs in New York's City Hall. It was not until 1832, while aboard the ship *Sully* on his way back from Europe, that Morse became interested in the electric telegraph. Overhearing a dinner conversation about electric currents through wire, Morse set out to create what would eventually be known as the telegraph. After completing dozens of sketches during his voyage back to America, Morse began to work on the project as soon as he arrived on shore. Morse lived with his brothers in New York City and worked as an art teacher at an area university in order to make money and continue his work on his new invention.

[**Teacher's Note**: Morse was unusual but not alone in his dual giftings of science and art. Another example of such giftedness is the great Leonardo da Vinci. If your student has been interested in this aspect of Samuel Morse's talent, take some time to research da Vinci as well. Brilliant artists and scientists don't come in the same package very often!]

Eleven years and many thousands of dollars later, Samuel Morse strung his wire from the Supreme Court in Washington, D.C. to Baltimore and on May 24, 1844 tapped out on the telegraph his famous line, "What hath God wrought!" Within a few years, Morse became internationally known as the inventor of the telegraph and the Morse Code. Today, people have nearly forgotten his artistic achievements and know him as the father of telegraphy. Samuel Morse died in 1872.

If your student is interested in the Morse Code, examine the charts. With practice, anyone can learn the system of dots and dashes. Have fun experimenting with the codes and look for more books and information on Samuel Morse and his amazing invention!

[**Teacher's Note**: For students who continue to show an unusual interest in Morse Code and telegraphy, encourage them to investigate becoming a ham radio operator. Amateur radio, as it is known, has a long and rich history and has been credited by many of this century's great inventors as being the source of a life-long interest in science. There are no age restrictions on becoming a licensed radio amateur. Computer software, cassette and videotapes all offer lessons in Morse Code and in other licensing requirements.]

History and Geography: Marconi and Wireless Communication

To further spark your student's interest, spend some time discussing the next great historical step in the world of communication—radio. Guglielmo [goo LYEL moh] Marconi [mahr KOH nee] became fascinated by the accomplishments of Samuel Morse. Marconi set out to improve on the system by creating a way to communicate *without wires*. People would be able to communicate across the ocean! It was a daunting and seemingly impossible goal, but Marconi was determined!

Working in the area of electromagnetic waves, Marconi began his journey. Unsupported by his own country, Italy, Marconi moved to Great Britain and gained financial backing for his experiments. After many failed attempts and frustrations, on December 12, 1901, Marconi sent the world's first wireless transatlantic communication! He sent the Morse Code for "S" from England to St. John's, Canada.

Coming only fifty-seven years after Samuel Morse's first telegraph message, it was an incredible feat that changed the face of communication forever! Today, radio and television are direct descendants of Marconi's brilliant invention. It is worth taking some extra time to study Marconi's inventions and life in greater detail, too.

Fine Arts: Drama and Memory Enhancement

Tom liked to pretend he was Christopher Columbus or Commodore Perry (page 118). It helped him remember his lessons. Encourage your student to use drama as a memory tool. Acting out historic scenes and speeches helps us remember things more easily—and it's fun! Perhaps your student will want to re-enact Columbus discovering America, just like Tom did. Or if there is interest, acting out Marconi's first wireless transmission or Samuel Morse's first telegram might be fun. Your student can either write a short "script" of an historical event or make a speech. Consider videotaping your student's presentation, or better yet, invite other homeschoolers or family to see the presentation! There are many ways dramatic arts can make history come alive! Explore this area with your student—maybe you could even "get in on the act"!

Writing and Discussion Questions

1. If Tom and James had lived today, they would have called one another on the telephone instead of using a telegraph. Write a short essay on what your life would be like without the telephone. What would be different?

2. Tom's father builds an incredible tower. Tom likes to imagine he is Columbus, high on a mast. What would you pretend to be if you could be high up on the tower?

Internet Connections

To view current suggested links relating to this chapter's lessons, see www.fiveinarow.com/connections.

Chapter 11–A Job on A Train

Parent Summary

Mr. Edison comes home with important news one day: the Grand Trunk Railway has finally completed the track from Port Huron to Detroit. Tom is elated! After dinner, Tom reads an article about the new railroad completion in *The Detroit Free Press*. The next day there is to be a celebration and unveiling of the new locomotive and coach cars. The Edisons decide to attend.

Wearing their best finery, they arrive and the crowd is already swarming. Tom runs to the front so he can see the shiny new locomotive and coaches. Suddenly, Tom overhears a conversation beside him. An older man is saying to another man that they will need to find "a boy to sell newspapers and candy on the train each day" as it travels from Port Huron to Detroit and back. Tom thinks quickly. He needs a real job to buy more chemicals for his laboratory and he loves trains! He walks bravely over to the men and asks if he can have the job. They ask to see his parents, and Mr. and Mrs. Edison give their permission. Tom can't believe it! He is going to work on that beautiful new train and he will be able to expand his laboratory!

What we will cover in this chapter:

History and Geography: Steam Locomotives—Wood, Coal and Oil

Language Arts: Similes and Metaphors

Issues of Human Relationships: Being Helpful

Issues of Human Relationships: Observation and Opportunities

Issues of Human Relationships: Your First Job

Lesson Activities

History and Geography: Steam Locomotives—Wood, Coal and Oil

Tom was fascinated by the powerful steam engine. Encourage your student to do some research on this important part of American history. Steam engines produced energy by boiling water (carried in the tender) until it produced steam. The steam was used to push simple pistons with large steel rods connected that in turn rotated the locomotives wheels. The fire that heated the water was created by wood, coal or oil. Some locomotives burned cut, split firewood while others burned coal. Still another group of locomotives injected oil into the burner area to produce heat. Regardless of fuel, locomotives carried their source of heat in the tender, along with the water. Steam engines were eventually replaced by modern diesel locomotives, but they remain popular today in many railroad museums and millions of tourists travel behind old-fashioned steam locomotives every year on rail fan excursions. A learning diversion on steam engines can be an enjoyable way to learn a great deal about science, history and Americana.

Language Arts: Similes and Metaphors

Draw your student's attention to page 131. Tom describes the smokestack on the train as a "tall silk hat." If your student isn't sure what a "tall silk hat" looks like, show him the illustration. Does he think Tom's comparison is a good one? Introduce to your student (or review) the language arts devices known as a *similes* and *metaphors*. A simile is the term we use for a comparison using the words "like" or "as." For example, Tom used a simile in his conversation with the man at the train station. He said, "The smokestack looks exactly like a tall silk hat."

A metaphor is the term for a direct comparison, omitting the word "like" or "as." For example, Tom might have said, "The smokestack is a tall silk hat." This device is much more poetic in nature. Both the simile and metaphor add to our writing and give interesting texture to our description. Encourage your student to try to think of similes and metaphors for some everyday objects around your home. Examples might be: "That garden rake is like a bear's claw" (simile), or "My fingers are thin string beans" (metaphor). If your student enjoys this exercise, make up a list of ten objects and have him try to think up at least one simile and one metaphor for each item.

Challenge your student to utilize these literary devices in his writing and to notice similes and metaphors when he hears others use them.

Issues of Human Relationships: Being Helpful

At the very beginning of our chapter, Tom is helping his mother with dinner (page 125). Here is yet another example of Tom's helpful spirit. Ask your student what *he* does to help around the house. Perhaps, helping with the meal preparations, assisting younger siblings get dressed in the morning, or mowing the lawn are things he can do. What we do to help is not as important as our willingness to be of service. When we contribute to our family, we reap the benefit of feeling like we're part of a team and the self-confidence that we can help makes a difference! Encourage your student to help out when he can—just like Tom!

Issues of Human Relationships: Observation and Opportunities

We have discussed in previous lessons the amazing curiosity and observation skills Tom has demonstrated. Once again, in this chapter (page 131), Tom is paying strict attention to all that is going on around him. He "pricks up his ears" and hears the man saying they will need a boy to help on the train. By being observant, Tom learns of a wonderful opportunity! Then, by being brave, Tom seizes the opportunity and inquires about the job. Discuss with your student the importance of being observant in his own life. Encourage him to begin watching all that goes on around him. It is in this way we learn about life and discover opportunities along the way!

Issues of Human Relationships: Your First Job

Tom's first real job has come! Spend some time imagining with your student what he would want to do for a first job. Often, working in a restaurant or a supermarket is a young person's first job. Share with your student what your first job was and what it was like. Everyone in the world at some point begins their first job, but in the United States today, few of us begin as young as Tom! If your student already has specific ideas about what he wants to do for his first job, perhaps researching that industry or position is in order. Have fun dreaming with your student about the future and imagining his first real job!

Writing and Discussion Question

What do you think Tom was thinking when he saw the beautiful new locomotive and coaches? Describe what you think he was feeling as he stood there. Try writing in first person (using words like I, me and my) as you write from Tom's viewpoint.

Internet Connections

To view current suggested links relating to this chapter's lessons, see www.fiveinarow.com/connections.

Chapter 12–The Underground Railway

Parent Summary

The spring of 1860 is passing quickly. Tom gets up early every morning and eats a good breakfast before setting out for his job on the train. After a hurried time of selling candy, newspapers and ham sandwiches, Tom's train arrives in Detroit at ten o'clock. The train that brings him back to Port Huron doesn't leave until four-thirty in the afternoon, so Tom has a lot of spare time in Detroit. He decides to read all the books in the Detroit Library—twelve inches of books off the shelf each week. Then he goes and spends time watching the men work at the Detroit Locomotive Works. Tom is always interested in how things are made!

For lunch, Tom finds a great hotel. There, Tom meets many interesting men. The men seem to like Tom too, even though he is young. They like Tom's intelligent, mature attitude and how he is always learning. During the lunch period at Finney's, Tom eats his lunch and watches the people around him. He notices there are many Negroes (African-Americans) eating in a back room. Tom knows about the Underground Railroad from listening to conversations and reading the newspaper. He guesses that most of these people are runaway slaves and Finney's is a stop on their Underground Railroad. Tom is glad the slaves are finding a way out. The days pass quickly and Tom invests more earnings into his laboratory—he now has 200 bottles of chemicals!

What we will cover in this chapter:

History and Geography: Canada—The Provinces and Territories

History and Geography: Canada—A Brief History of Its Beginning

History and Geography: The Underground Railroad

History and Geography: The President *Before* Lincoln—Buchanan

Language Arts: Creative Writing

Issues of Human Relationships: Organizing Your Personal Study

Lesson Activities:

History and Geography: Canada—The Provinces and Territories

Every morning at six-fifteen, Tom's train blows its whistle on the Canadian side of the river (page 134). Take this opportunity to introduce your student to the fascinating geography of the United States' northern neighbor, Canada. By looking at the map in the Appendix, point out to your student the different regions that make up Canada.

Canada is divided into ten regions called provinces and two regions known as territories. The provinces are, from west to east: British Columbia (capital—Victoria), Alberta (capital—Edmonton), Saskatchewan (capital—Regina), Manitoba (capital—Winnipeg), Ontario (capital—Toronto), Quebec (capital—Quebec City), New Brunswick, (capital—Fredricton), Prince Edward Island (capital—Charlottetown), Nova Scotia (capital—Halifax) and Newfoundland (capital—St. John's).

[**Teacher's Note**: Remind your student of the term Maritime Provinces which you learned in *The Boxcar Children* lesson (chapter 4). New Brunswick, Nova Scotia and Prince Edward Island as a group are considered the Maritime Provinces.]

Besides the Canadian provinces, there are three more regions known as "territories." These are the Yukon Territory (capital—Whitehorse), the Northwest Territories (capital—Yellowknife), and Nunavut (capital—Iqaluit). Although these last three regions make up more than one-third of Canada's land mass, they represent only 1% of the total population of Canada. This is because much of the terrain in the territories is frozen year-round.

By no means should your student be expected to fully understand the economic and cultural differences of each region in Canada, but do encourage him to do further research into this fascinating geographic area if the interest is present.

History and Geography: Canada—A Brief History of Its Beginning

In conjunction with your lesson on Canada's geography, continue your studies by sharing with your student a brief introduction to the history of Canada. Canada's name comes from an Iroquois Indian word *kanata*, meaning village or community. This country has been forced to live up to its name—fighting for unity and community ties has been a constant goal for Canada since its inception.

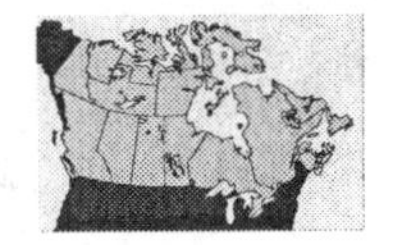

In approximately 1000 A.D. the Vikings, led by Lief Ericson, were the first known Europeans to land on North America. Ericson settled a region called Vinland, on what is believed to be Newfoundland. By the early 1500s French traders began to set up fishing ports and fur trading posts on the eastern coast of Canada. Their region became known as New France, and this influx of culture became the backbone of the now-established French-Canadian heritage.

By 1690, many British colonists were immigrating to Canada and from this time to 1763, the struggle for dominance between the British and French resulted in four separate wars which Great Britain eventually won, conquering New France. Following the war of 1812, Canada's population soared and the immigration of colonists caused an ever-increasing demand for more democratic-like governments. This struggle between the French-Canadian segment of the population and the British/Nouveau Canadians is still an issue of great importance today.

If your student is interested, it is *highly recommended* that you do additional research and topical study on your own regarding Canada's history and culture. It is so vital your student has a beginning understanding of this northern U.S. neighbor and ally. If you have friends or relatives who live, or have lived in Canada, encourage your student to interview them. If you live in a northern state, perhaps a field trip to Canada is appropriate. Even a day trip can be greatly beneficial. Broadening our horizons is part of the learning process!

History and Geography—The Underground Railroad

On page 139, Tom is thinking about the Underground Railroad and slavery. Is your student familiar with the Underground Railroad? Let this be an introduction or review for your student on this important part of United States history.

The "Underground Railroad" was the secret code name for the way in which slaves made their trek across the country from south to north—away from slavery, toward freedom. Many people helped the slaves escape from their masters' ownership. Other people, known as "slave catchers" worked to capture the runaway slaves and bring them back to the South. One anonymous writer described the Underground Railroad saying, "It was a network of people, from all walks of life, who worked, often illegally, for the freedom of slaves in pre-Civil War America."

Branching off from this subject, explore with your student other related topics of importance including: The Abolitionist Movement, *Uncle Tom's Cabin* by Harriet Beecher Stowe, Harriet Tubman and Sojourner Truth.

[**Teacher's Note**: Two excellent sources are *If You Lived At The Time of the Civil War* by Kay Moore (Copyright 1994, Scholastic Inc., ISBN 0590454226) and for older students, the biography *Sojourner Truth—Ain't I A Woman?* by Patricia C. and Fredrick McKissack (Copyright 1992, Scholastic Inc., ISBN 0590446916).]

The history of slavery in America can be confusing and frightening to children. Share as much with your student as you feel is appropriate. Share from your own experience and thoughts too! Your student must come to his own conclusions about the Civil War, the Underground Railroad and American slavery. For now, it is important for him to read and learn what others thought and did about it. Challenge yourself and your student to take an adventure in history and study this emotionally-charged issue more closely!

History and Geography: The President *Before* Lincoln—Buchanan

Point out to your student the following sentence on page 140: "They hoped Abraham Lincoln would be the next President of the United States." Tom is anxious for Mr. Lincoln to step into the role of President, but who is President at this time? Remember, the year is 1860. The current leader is the United States' 15th president, James Buchanan. Share with your student an introduction to this leader of our country.

President James Buchanan was born on April 23, 1791 at Cove Gap, Pennsylvania. He was affiliated with the Democratic Party and was the only U.S. president never to marry. Buchanan was appointed Secretary of State in 1844 by President James Polk. During Polk's administration, war broke out between the United States and Mexico. It was under Secretary Buchanan's leadership the Treaty of Guadalupe Hidalgo (a peace treaty) was signed in 1848. In this treaty, the United States purchased from Mexico the region extending west from Texas to the Pacific Ocean.

Following Polk's presidency, Buchanan left politics. Retreating to his famous mansion, "Wheatland," in Pennsylvania he lived the life of a country gentleman. However, the attraction to political life remained. In 1852 he was nominated for president. He was defeated by Franklin Pierce, a little known candidate from New Hampshire. Under Pierce's administration, Buchanan was appointed Minister to Great Britain. He served in this position for four more years, and in 1856 when the Democrats sought a new candidate for president, they nominated James Buchanan once more. At last, Buchanan was elected president!

It has been said that Buchanan was a president sitting atop a volcano, for during the four years he served as president, the United States was edging closer and closer to the War Between the States. Buchanan was influential in stemming the tide of war for a season, but perhaps no one could have prevented the war entirely. By December of 1860, during the final days of Buchanan's presidency, several states began seceding from the Union, setting the stage for the Civil War.

Draw your student's attention to several of the interesting occurrences that happened during Buchanan's presidency. First, it was during these four years the Pony Express was inaugurated. Also, the watershed decision of Dredd Scott occurred in 1857.

If there is time and interest, encourage your student to do further research on this landmark event. Finally, in 1859 John Brown was seized at Harper's Ferry and hanged for his attempt to start a slave revolt. In light of the volatile circumstances, it is understandable that Buchanan did not seek renomination. Buchanan supported his vice-president John C. Breckinridge's nomination for president, but Breckinridge was defeated by the tall man from Illinois, Abraham Lincoln.

As you continue to discuss this chapter of Edison's life, encourage your student to locate additional information on our 15th president.

Language Arts: Creative Writing

Your student may want to write an essay on the issue of slavery. It can be based on his research of the Underground Railroad, etc. Or it can be an opinion essay where he can state his arguments and reach conclusions. Another idea is to write a short fictitious story utilizing an interesting plot and good characterization that includes the subject of slavery.

Issues of Human Relationships: Organizing Your Personal Study

Wasn't Tom organized? He looked at the library and decided on a foot of books per week (page 136). Then he modified his plan to read only the science books. In this way, Tom could keep track of what he was learning and follow a specific goal (to read every book in the library). Encourage your student to begin organizing his study time like Tom did. By setting goals for ourselves, we can better focus on what we're studying at the moment.

Remember, not all students are as gifted in this area as others. The point of this lesson is not to create "organized little robots." Instead, gently share with your student new ways to learn and structure his studies. Good organization skills and study habits are essential to academic success.

An essential resource for students and teachers alike is a book entitled *The Everything Study Book* by Steven Frank (Copyright 1996, Adams Media Corporation, ISBN 1558506152). Offering great insight into reading comprehension, taking notes, writing essays, and much more, this book is not only enlightening and helpful, but is also a delight to read as well! Order it from your library and it will soon be on your "must purchase" list.

Internet Connections

To view current suggested links relating to this chapter's lessons, see www.fiveinarow.com/connections.

Chapter 13–The Laboratory on Wheels

Parent Summary

Tom now has a business partner! James Clancy, Tom's good friend, rides with Tom, helping sell newspapers on the train. Recently, the Grand Trunk Railway has added two new cars onto Tom's train—a new coach and a baggage/mail car. Tom decides, since there is never much mail and because he doesn't have enough time to work on his experiments at home, to ask permission to move his laboratory into the second new car. Tom and James quickly move the laboratory onto the train. Now Tom will have more time to work on his experiments and a friend to help pass the time in Detroit. Tom shows James the library and the Detroit Locomotive Works, and they eat lunch at Finney's Hotel. Tom is happy about all of it!

What we will cover in this chapter:

History and Geography: The Railway Post Office System

Science: A New Element—Phosphorus

Language Arts: Sherlock Holmes and *The Hound of the Baskervilles*

Issues of Human Relationships: Problem Solving

Lesson Activities

History and Geography: The Railway Post Office System

On page 143 we read the Grand Trunk Railway adds a mail car to Tom's train. Why did trains have mail cars? Who was the mail for? When did the recipient get his mail? Take this opportunity to share with your student the story of the Railway Post Office.

Trains were used in the mail service to speed up delivery. The train would stop at towns and pick up the bags of outgoing mail. Then, while the train moved across the country, men sorted the mail by town and date. In smaller towns where the train didn't stop, a device called a "catching arm" was employed. The town postmaster would put their bag of outbound mail on a tall pole. When the train rolled by, the catching arm would snag the bag of mail and pull it back to the train. Likewise, for those same towns, the train postmaster would throw the sorted mail in bags onto the platforms while the train sped down the track.

This method of mail delivery was by far the fastest and most reliable known at this point. By 1869, when the Golden Spike was driven (connecting the Pacific and Atlantic coasts), mail could be delivered from the west coast to New York in only five days!

[**Teacher's Note**: The Golden Spike and its place in railroad history was covered in chapter 3 of *The Boxcar Children* lessons.]

In today's world, how fast can a letter be delivered in the United States? The Postal Service can now deliver letters in one day! This is called "Next Day" service! By using planes instead of trains for delivery, this amazing feat can be accomplished. The Post Office Department first began experimenting with the use of airplanes in the delivery process in 1918. By 1927, airplane carriers had contract routes as delivery operators for the Post Office.

If your student is interested, take a field trip to your local post office. You can point out the different stamps and packaging materials. He can also see the mailbags and sorting bins. Ask if tours are available.

Another related topic of interest is stamps. Ask your student if he would be willing to take a letter from his house across the country and personally deliver it for less than fifty cents—probably not. Even today, with increased stamp prices, the cost still seems like a bargain considering the magnitude of the task!

The next time your student sends or receives a letter, have him think of all the hard work put into the delivery. Then remember how it was done in Tom's day!

Science: A New Element—Phosphorus

Tom's laboratory is getting huge! Tom has to be particularly careful with his chemical called phosphorus (page 147). Ask your student if he can remember why? Phosphorus is highly flammable (catches on fire easily) and Tom has to keep it wet. Take this opportunity to introduce your student to this new chemical.

[**Teacher's Note**: If you already covered the Periodic Table of Elements in chapter 9, continue this discussion with your student by introducing Phosphorus. If you did not do that lesson, go back and use the pictures and explanations listed in chapter 9 to assist you at this time.]

Phosphorus was discovered in 1669 by a German scientist, Hennig Brand. The chemical symbol for Phosphorus is P. Show your student the atomic weights and number located on the Element square.

Phosphorus is essential for healthy bodies! A small amount of phosphorous is found in egg yolks, milk, fish and peas. Phosphorus helps build strong bones and strengthens our brain and nervous system.

Tom was right about phosphorus being dangerous! Because it burns so easily, match tips (the part that strikes the strip) are covered in phosphorus.

Tell your student to watch and see if phosphorous is mentioned again in our story (chapter 15).

Language Arts: Sherlock Holmes and *The Hound of the Baskervilles*

Enriching your student's literary awareness is essential to providing him with a complete education! If you covered the lesson in this chapter on phosphorus, an interesting literary note on this chemical is found in the classic tale, *The Hound of the Baskervilles* by Sir Arthur Conan Doyle.

[**Teacher's Note**: If your student is older and interested in mysteries, all the stories by Sir Arthur Conan Doyle are great reads and will stretch your student's reading comprehension and vocabulary. If your student is younger, these stories also make excellent read-alouds. These texts are really more on the junior high level, but your student may be ready for a stretch.]

In *The Hound of the Baskervilles*, phosphorus is the chemical used to create the glowing, fiery eyes of the hound, which frightens the people. The inimitable Holmes, of course, discovers this and solves the mystery of the mysterious hound.

Issues of Human Relationships: Problem Solving

In this chapter, we see another excellent example of Tom Edison's problem solving skills. Tom doesn't have enough time to work in his laboratory at home. Instead of quitting his job or giving up his laboratory, he comes up with a plan (page 143). Why not move his laboratory onto the train? What a creative thought process!

[**Teacher's Note**: In the end, as you will see in chapter 15, this plan was perhaps not the wisest decision. But, the end result does not negate Tom's creative thinking!]

Draw your student's attention to this incident as another way Tom solved a problem. This skill of looking at difficult situations and coming up with solutions is a tremendous life skill. Problem solving takes creativity, intelligence and hard work. The next time your student faces a difficult situation, encourage him to look for creative solutions to his problem, rather than giving up or growing frustrated.

Writing and Discussion Question

What could Tom have done to prevent the fire on the train?

Internet Connections

To view current suggested links relating to this chapter's lessons, see www.fiveinarow.com/connections.

Chapter 14–Tom's Own Newspaper

Parent Summary

It is now the fall of 1861. The Civil War is underway and people are hungry for the news. The papers Tom and James are selling on the train are more popular than ever! But Tom notices a problem. The telegraph operators get the latest news, but by the time the printers of *The Detroit Free Press* and other papers get the information and print it, the news is already old. Tom decides to solve the problem. He finds an old second-hand printing press for sale and buys it, along with some ink and metal type. Then, he buys some paper from his friend at the *Free Press* office. Now he is ready to print his *own* newspaper!

Tom decides he can stop by the telegraph office in Port Huron each morning, gather the latest news reports on the war and then print his paper on the way to Detroit. Tom decides to call his paper *The Weekly Herald* and sell it for 3 cents a copy. Tom knows what the people want to read. He includes the latest news of the war, names of the fathers and sons who have joined the Union Army, the market prices of things like eggs and chickens each week, and much more. Tom's *Weekly Herald* is a success! Some people even want to buy it in a year subscription!

One day, Tom is so busy selling his papers with the latest news of the Battle of Shiloh, that he doesn't hear the train pulling out. The conductor reaches down to pull Tom up onto the train, and grabs Tom by his ears. Tom hears a popping sound but doesn't stop to notice. From then on, however, Tom Edison was always partially deaf. The popping sound he'd heard was something being injured in his ear canal.

What we will cover in this chapter:

History and Geography: Gutenberg and the Printing Press

History and Geography: Market Prices Today

Science: Human Anatomy—The Ear

Language Arts: Different Styles of Writing

Language Arts: Subscriptions

Fine Arts: Making Your Own Newspaper Printing Block

Issues of Human Relationships: Learning to Communicate with the Deaf

Lesson Activities

History and Geography: Gutenberg and the Printing Press

Tom buys an old printing press to use for his newspaper (page 150). The press was antiquated, but still functional. Does your student know who invented the first printing press? A man named Johannes Gutenberg from Mainz, Germany invented it!

Gutenberg's birth date and the date of his death are unknown. Along with that mystery, no known portraits of Gutenberg were ever painted during his lifetime. Hailed as one of the most important inventions in all of history, Gutenberg made it possible to print a block of text using uniform, even letters and a technology which allowed the text to be replicated identically as many times as the operator wanted. What did people do before the printing press? Everything was hand written! Imagine the cost of a manuscript or book written by hand!

In 1454, the book Gutenberg chose to use to showcase his great invention was the Bible. This printed text, known around the world as the Gutenberg Bible, is still considered a masterpiece!

If your student is interested in the process of *typography* (the art of printing texts mechanically), look for more books on the topic at your local library. (Also, be sure to take note of the Fine Arts lesson in this chapter.) A fantastic book on this topic is called *Gutenberg* by Leonard Everett Fisher (Copyright 1993, Macmillan Publishing Co., ISBN 0027352382). Including timeliness maps, award-winning illustrations and truly inspired text, this book is a must for everyone who wishes to learn more about history—particularly those interested in typography. Take a little time and discuss what our world would be like today without Gutenberg's invention.

History and Geography: Market Prices Today

Tom knows just what the people buying his paper want to read about. One thing he is careful to include is the "market prices" (page 154). Isn't that interesting? He prints the prices for eggs, butter, chickens and potatoes each week. Does your student know how we learn about market prices today? Use this opportunity to introduce both the commodities market and local advertising.

Market prices for things wholesale (large quantities for resale to consumers) can be studied by using the futures market on the commodity exchange. Weekly, daily, even hourly prices for things like wheat, oats, chickens, cattle, frozen orange juice and pork bellies are posted on the commodities market. Reading commodity prices and understanding how the market works is an extremely complicated lesson. However, you may want to introduce your student to this concept. If your student shows interest in this topic, find some beginner books on the commodity market at your local library. Allow him to look at commodity prices on the financial page of a major newspaper while you're at the library!

On a more understandable, yet practical level, your student can check market prices for his area each week by looking through the grocery advertisements in a local paper! Just like Tom, papers today print the going price for food and other goods weekly. Because of competition between stores, these prices may vary but they are always similar.

By examining several stores' advertisements and recording the market prices for a certain item over a period of time, your student can record his findings and create a graph that indicates the rise, or fall, in food costs.

Just like Tom's customers, knowing what things cost is an important bit of news for us today!

Science: Human Anatomy—The Ear

Thomas Edison became partially deaf as the result of his accident on the train (page 158). This is a good opportunity to study the ear and how it works. Get a book that explains the parts of the ear and has excellent pictures. Have your student make a study sheet explaining the way an ear works. Let him label the parts and color it.

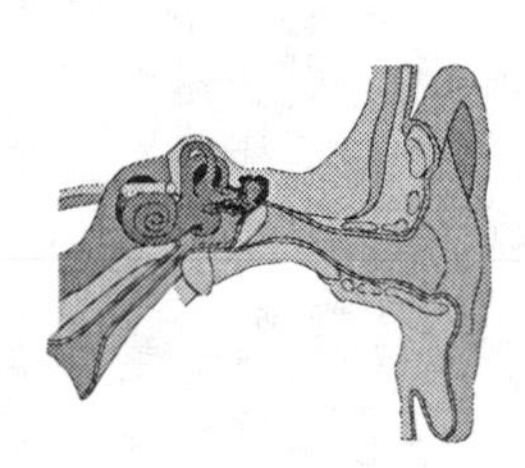

[**Teacher's Note**: Make a teacher's file folder for Anatomy. List what you have covered in this lesson. By keeping a teacher's list you will know what you have studied and in what depth. You can then add to it whenever the subject of Anatomy comes up in your unit study lessons. (While studying the subject of hearing impairment, you might also want to research Helen Keller and Ludwig van Beethoven.)]

Language Arts: Different Styles of Writing

Tom wrote all the articles in his newspaper. What makes writing a news article different from other styles of writing? What should you include? How should you say it? All of these questions can be answered by a lesson in different styles of writing.

Share with your student the classic line, "Just the facts, Ma'am." This statement embodies what a news reporter's goal is when writing an article—to include all the important facts. This means no personal opinions or fancy embellishments. An easy way to remember what to include when you're writing news is to think of the four W's—Who, What, When and Where. If you answer these four questions, you are doing great!

To further explore the different styles of writing, challenge your student to write about a specific incident in three different styles—a personal letter, fiction, and a news article. Here is an example:

Incident—The neighbor's cat was hit by a stranger's car.

Personal Letter

You won't believe what happened yesterday! I was standing in my driveway helping my dad wash the van (you did know my family got a new van, didn't you?) and we hear this horrible screeching sound. I told Eddie later that I didn't even hear the cat meow, just the tires of the car. It was so hot I couldn't run very fast, but I went over to see what had happened. I wish I hadn't. It wasn't a pretty sight. Remember last summer when my dog was hit? I sure miss Fido...

Fiction

The sun was beating down on my baseball cap while Sam scrubbed away on the bumper. Water and suds covered his tennis shoes and his hand swatted at mosquitoes. Sam's dad whistled to himself, as Sam lifted the bucket of dirty water and refilled it. Suddenly, they both heard a squeal of tires against pavement and their minds were filled with anxious thoughts. What was going on? Running up the street, Sam and his dad were the first to arrive at the scene. It was awful...

News Report

At approximately four o'clock yesterday, a cat owned by Mrs. Mary Woolsworth, of 1118 Maple, was accidentally hit by a car. The stretch of road on which the incident occurred is at the intersection of 12th and Maple, known to many area residents as a dangerous corner. According to witnesses, the blinding afternoon sun may have played a part in the driver's inability to see properly. Mrs. Woolsworth told police that the cat had been....

The first example (personal letter) is filled with details and comments only a close friend would understand or find interesting. The second example (fictional writing) has many embellishments or extended descriptions, which add great texture to the writing, but aren't really necessary for the reader to understand what happened. The final example (news report) includes just the facts. It answers the questions *Who* (Mrs. Woolsworth's cat), *What* (run over by a car), *When* (about one o'clock) and *Where* (corner of 12th and Maple).

This exercise will truly stretch your student's language art skills! Work together with your student on this activity, and watch as his writing skills increase! You might want to think of a specific incident that has occurred recently in your neighborhood and have your student write about it in the three uniquely different styles discussed. Don't be afraid to repeat this assignment every few weeks with new incidents.

Language Arts: Subscriptions

Tom's *Weekly Herald* is so popular that people want to order by *subscription*. This may be a new word or concept for your student. A subscription means that with a one-time payment, the customer (or subscriber) is promised he will receive something (in Tom's case, a newspaper) for a fixed period of time. In other words, Tom's customers wanted to pay for 52 issues (one full year) of *The Weekly Herald* in one payment. In return for their money, Tom would give them their paper each week for an entire year.

Ask your student what the responsibilities of the publisher of a subscription product are? Tom, just like other publishers, had to make note and list who ordered a subscription. He had to record when each person's subscription began. And most importantly, Tom had to make the money he made on subscriptions last.

Many publishers have gone bankrupt when they spent all their subscription earnings early, and then had to keep producing product through the year. What a lot of responsibility for young Tom Edison!

Show your student an example of a subscription card from a magazine. Generally, the customer can choose between one, two or even three years worth of subscription and can either include payment or be billed by the publisher later.

If there is interest, share with your student all the things people can buy by subscription today—food (fruit monthly or jelly-of-the-month clubs), flowers, music, coffee and even contact lenses. Have your student point out different subscriptions when he sees them. This form of payment has certainly become a popular idea!

Fine Arts: Making Your Own Newspaper Printing Block

Wouldn't it be fun to have your own printing press? Well, here is a very simple way to make one text block. To do this activity you will need a piece of cardboard, bottled glue, a piece of paper and an inkpad. Look at the illustration for further explanation. First, have your student print the word "CAT." Take the bottle of glue and have him write this word on the cardboard. Let the letters dry and then write over them again with the glue. Continue this process several times until the "type block" letters are built up.

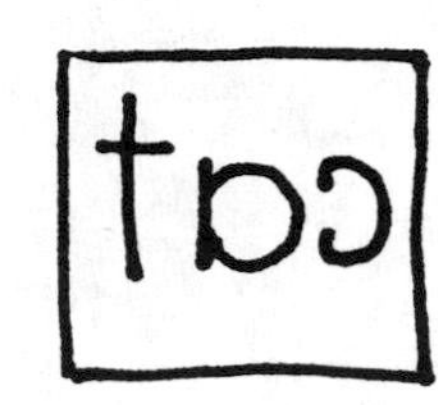

Then, after pressing the fully dried design into the inkpad, press the block down onto paper and you will have printed a bit of text! But what's wrong? The letters are all backwards! Let your student experiment and do it wrong first with this short word, CAT. Then explain to your student that every letter or character that is to be printed on paper must be put on the press blocks backward. The mirrored image of each letter is then correct and readable on the finished product. Now have your student use his own name or an entire headline. Try it again and see the difference! Have fun with this activity and let your student be as creative as he wishes! (Be sure to mention that today's newspapers use photographic plates rather than metal type to print each day.)

Issues of Human Relationships: Learning to Communicate with the Deaf

Thomas Edison was always partially deaf as the result of his accident on the train (page 158). Being deaf makes life more of a challenge, but certainly not impossible! Even for people who are profoundly deaf (can't hear anything), life can be fulfilling and fun! One way deaf people are able to communicate with each other and hearing people is called ASL, or American Sign Language.

[**Teacher's Note**: Be sure to explain the other ways deaf people communicate, as well—lip reading, written communication and sometimes vocal communication.]

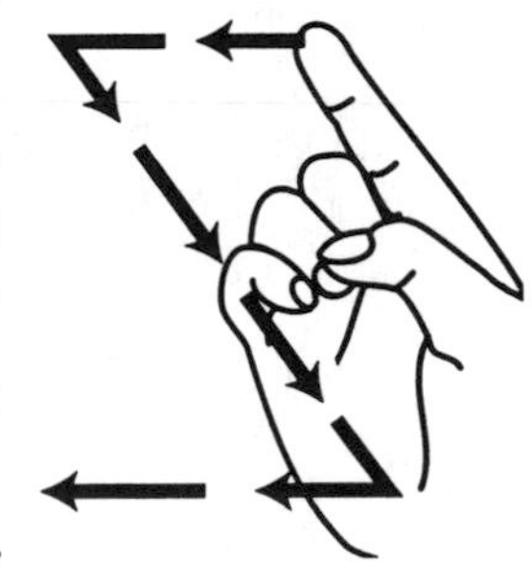

Perhaps your student knows someone who is hearing impaired and is already familiar with ASL. American Sign Language is made up of hand gestures that express ideas rather than words. Since certain words have no direct translation, there is also a language called the American Manual Alphabet. Listed in the Appendix is this alphabet. Using these gestures, ideas or words can be spelled out when a single translation is not available.

Learning sign language is fun because it is both interesting and useful! Even if you just learn the alphabet, you can now communicate with a whole segment of the population you couldn't before. Learning different "languages" is a wonderful way to expand our world.

Even if your student doesn't have any deaf friends or relatives at the moment, learning the finger alphabet is a great way to communicate with family and friends. There are so many times in life when it is impolite to talk (church, funerals, dinner table with guests, etc.) and by using sign language, your student can communicate quick messages without being disruptive.

If for no other reason than cultural enrichment, encourage your student to explore the realm of ASL. It is a creative language form that is both delightful to learn and truly useful!

Writing and Discussion Questions

1. How do you think Tom knew how to print his own paper?

2. How did Tom know what people wanted to see in a newspaper?

Internet Connections

To view current suggested links relating to this chapter's lessons, see www.fiveinarow.com/connections.

Chapter 15–An Explosion

Parent Summary

Tom's *Weekly Herald* is gaining popularity and notoriety. One day the conductor tells Tom he has a visitor. Tom's unexpected visitor is Mr. George Stephenson from England. Mr. Stephenson tells Tom that *The Weekly Herald* is one of the finest papers he has ever seen. He asks Tom if he can take back one thousand copies to sell in England. Tom is pleased by the praise, and works all night long with James to get the papers ready.

Many months later Mr. Stephenson writes to Tom from London and says the people love Tom's paper and that *The London Times* has printed an article on Tom Edison. Along with the letter, Mr. Stephenson includes a copy of the article about Tom. Tom is very proud.

Tom continues to work in his laboratory on the train, but one day a horrible accident occurs. The train hits rough track and bounces back and forth. Tom's chemicals are knocked to the floor of the car and the phosphorus bursts into flame. Tom and the conductor put out the flames, but the conductor is furious with Tom. He throws Tom off the train along with his printing press and the rest of his laboratory bottles. He tells Tom he never wants to see him again. Tom is heartsick. Eventually, however, he is offered his old job back as long as he doesn't bring his laboratory on board.

Later on in the summer, Tom does a brave deed and saves Mr. Mackenzie's (the telegraph operator) little boy from being hit by a train. To repay him, Mr. Mackenzie offers to teach Tom all he knows about telegraphy. Tom is thrilled and soon he has a job working in the telegraph office.

What we will cover in this chapter:

History and Geography: A Newspaper Editor—What He Does

Issues of Human Relationships: Speaking Words of Praise

Issues of Human Relationships: Being Brave

Career Path: Journalism—A World of Possibilities

Lesson Activities

History and Geography: A Newspaper Editor—What He Does

Tom was the editor of his paper, *The Weekly Herald*. What does an editor of a newspaper do? Ask your student what he thinks the job involves. Explore this fascinating occupation with your student.

Many people, doing a vast array of different jobs, make up a newspaper office's staff. The editor is the person in charge of all the writing. Often, if there are many different sections of a newspaper, there will be an editor in charge of each individual section (e.g., food, entertainment, local news, sports, etc.), but there is always a senior editor responsible for the contents of the entire paper. This person's title is usually Editor-in-Chief. This is Tom's job title. Tom has a staff of two. James helps him print and circulate (sell and distribute) the papers, and Tom gathers the news, writes the articles, prints and then sells the papers.

Being the editor-in-chief of a newspaper is an exciting but stressful job. Deadlines for articles, ideas for new articles, gathering facts and verifying quotes, checking the progress of street reporters and giving final approval for the presses to begin the actual printing are just a few of the daily responsibilities of an editor-in-chief.

If you are able, try to arrange a brief tour of a local newspaper office. Small-town newspaper offices are generally receptive to student tours and even large city papers have a public relations office you can contact. If your student is interested in the fast-paced, exciting world of journalism, be sure to read the Career Path lesson in this chapter.

Issues of Human Relationships: Speaking Words of Praise

On page 163 we read about Tom's notoriety in London and the article written about his paper in *The London Times*. Mr. Stephenson tells Tom he is doing an excellent job on his paper! Tom is very proud!

Talk with your student about how words of praise make us feel. When someone values us or values what we have accomplished, it makes us feel warm and confident. When someone says, "What an excellent job!" suddenly you feel like you can do even better!

Challenge your student to look for opportunities to speak words of praise to others. It will enrich the person being spoken to and build up your student's character as well! When we hear words of encouragement and praise it helps us through times of frustration. When we're down or sad, we can remember the encouraging word someone said to us! Learning to praise others with our words instead of tearing them down is a major step toward maturity. Who knows? Perhaps if Tom hadn't been encouraged by Mr. Stephenson, he wouldn't have continued to work on his paper to make it the best it could be!

Issues of Human Relationships: Being Brave

Have your student read pages 167-168 aloud with you. Talk about the frightening incident Tom faces. Imagine seeing a little boy like Jimmie Mackenzie sitting on the railroad tracks and knowing only you could save him! Tom acts heroically.

Ask your student what bravery means to him? Sometimes, being brave means setting aside our own fears in order to help someone in need. But practicing bravery does not mean we must wait for opportunities to "save" a person in distress. Being brave is also facing our own fears.

Learning to swim, playing an instrument in front of an audience at a recital, or telling our parents the truth about something we're nervous about are all examples of acting bravely. Learning to be brave is not a question of age either. Many adults still have fears in their lives they haven't been able to face yet.

If you have a fear you wish to share with your student, perhaps talking about it will encourage both of you. Discuss with your student things he might need to face with bravery. Being brave is a question of strength and confidence—two things that will improve with practice! Challenge your student to look for opportunities to practice being brave—it will get easier every time.

Career Path: Journalism—A World of Possibilities

If your student is interested in writing, advertising, photography, videography, acting, or just in exploring new ideas, the world of journalism encompasses many career paths. Journalism may be a new word for your student. Journalism is the process of gathering, writing, editing, publishing and circulating news in newspapers, magazines, radio or television. There are so many exciting and different jobs in journalism!

Talk with your student about the following jobs and make a list of more you can think of: television news anchor, television news writer, television news producer, weather man, staff newspaper writer, food critic, movie critic, war correspondent, photojournalist, magazine advertising executive, public relations manager, etc.

For most of these jobs, a person needs a degree in journalism. Most colleges offer a Bachelor of Arts degree in this area and the classes include media-related studies and writing courses. However, many journalists will tell you that on-the-job training is what made them great!

Journalism is a field that often requires a year or two of what is known as *internship*. Being an intern requires working in the field (at the news station, advertising office, layout department, etc.) for little or no money. In this way, you get to "learn the business" and gain valuable experience. Then, after you've proven yourself competent, you may be hired on as an assistant reporter or some other entry-level position.

For more information on journalism and career opportunities in the field, go to your local library and do additional research with your student. Being a good journalist requires hard work, dedication, tenacity and a "nose for news." This means knowing what the public wants to hear and where to find that information. Tom Edison had a great nose for news!

Writing and Discussion Question

What do you think Tom was thinking when he saw Jimmie Mackenzie on the train tracks? What would you have done?

Internet Connections

To view current suggested links relating to this chapter's lessons, see www.fiveinarow.com/connections.

Chapter 16–Moving Pictures

Parent Summary

The Wild West Show is in Port Huron! Tom and his friend, James Clancy, are very excited! Before they leave for the show, however, Tom is hard at work on an experiment. By rubbing a glass jar with a piece of silk and then laying cut paper dolls against the glass, Tom can make the dolls 'dance' from the static electricity. Tom tells James he wishes he could harness that electricity to their telegraph. Then they wouldn't need batteries!

The boys leave to go the Wild West Show and when they arrive people are already milling about. The panorama show was great! Tom is amazed that some people scream and act frightened just from the drawings on the huge canvas.

After the show, Tom tells James he wants to invent a device that will show people actually moving, instead of just a drawing. James doesn't understand how Tom plans on accomplishing something so amazing, but by now he is used to his inventive friend, Tom Edison!

What we will cover in this chapter:

[**Teacher's Note**: Due to chapter 16's content, the following lessons include mostly Fine Art activities. Consider this chapter an art unit unto itself and have a wonderful time!]

History and Geography: The Wild West Shows

Science: Electricity

Fine Arts: Paper Dolls—As Wild or Winsome as You Wish

Fine Arts: Create Your Own Panorama

Fine Arts: Moving Pictures—A Flip Book

Fine Arts: Tom's Dream—Your Own Movie

Lesson Activities

History and Geography: The Wild West Shows

The panorama picture show Tom and James watch is called a Wild West show. Has your student ever heard of the Wild West? What does it make him think of? Does he know any of the famous names that are synonymous with the Wild West? And so much history!! Use an encyclopedia or find a book at the library and do additional research on topics like the Pony Express, various Indian tribes, steamships, military forts, famous towns like Tombstone, Arizona, Dodge City, Kansas, or Cheyenne, Wyoming, etc.

Also, Buffalo Bill Cody, Annie Oakley and Sitting Bull are particularity associated with the Wild West shows. If you wish, this would be an excellent time to introduce your student to this very unique part of Americana, known as the Wild West.

Science: Electricity

Tom makes his dolls move, almost like magic! (page 174) James is amazed! Ask your student if he has any idea why rubbing glass with a piece of silk would create electricity? Take this opportunity to give your student a gentle introduction into the world of electricity.

[**Teacher's Note**: For the younger students, this lesson may be beyond their grasp. For your older students, it may be appropriate or you may even wish to do further research with them on this topic.]

Electricity is a form of energy. It is all around us because it is made of tiny particles called electrons. An electron is the smallest unit of electricity—so small, in fact, that not even a microscope can see it! Our bodies, the sky (lightning), everything is made up in part of electrons. The movement of those electrons is what we call electricity.

There are two types of electricity. *Static electricity* is made up of *non-moving* electrons. This is what Tom creates with his paper dolls! If you wish, take a moment and show your student simple examples of static electricity. For instance, when you run a comb through your hair many times your hair will begin to crackle and pop. That is static electricity! If your rub your cat's fur back and forth quickly, you will see the cat's hair stand up on end—static electricity! And, just like Tom demonstrates, rubbing glass with a piece of silk will create static electricity, too!

The second type of electricity is called *current electricity*. Current electricity is created by a generator and consists of moving or flowing electrons. Almost all of the electricity in the world is generated in one of three ways: 1) generators, 2) batteries, or 3) solar cells.

If your student is interested in this topic, a fantastic resource book and kit for interesting experiments and explanations is called *Backyard Science—Electricity*. Available in many educational catalogs, the kit includes equipment, supplies, experiment booklets and more! Another excellent book for further research is the series from Harcourt Brace by Neil Ardley, entitled *The Science Book of Electricity*. This book includes vivid color photographs, explanations and experiments, and follows an easy-to-understand, delightful format!

Enjoy learning along *with* your student about this fascinating wonder of nature!

Fine Arts: Paper Dolls—As Wild or Winsome as You Wish

Tom makes paper dolls (page 172) to prove his experiment in electricity. However, making paper dolls can be a fabulous vehicle for creative design, historical or fanciful recreation, color rendering work and just plain fun!

Your student might wish to begin by cutting the accordion-style dolls just like Tom did. Other options include the more formal version of paper dolls. Begin by creating a cutout cardboard body. Then you can design clothes with little tabs to hold them on. Encourage your student to be as creative as he wishes with these clothed, paper figures. Maybe a doll of Tom Edison would be fun! Perhaps a favorite historic figure or friend! Maybe your student could even create paper replicas of his whole family! Remember, these dolls can be as simple or detailed as your student wishes. Colored pencils, crayons, watercolors, or even tissue paper collage-work can be used to create the doll clothes your student desires!

Relax, smile and watch what your student can do! Perhaps you may even wish to take part in the fun! Making paper dolls can be very therapeutic and inspiring, as well—they're not just for kids anymore!

Fine Arts: Create Your Own Panorama

Has your student ever heard of a panorama picture show? Tom and James go to see one, along with people from all over Port Huron and beyond. What is so alluring? Discuss briefly with your student the amazing evolution of entertainment! In the days of kings people were hired to entertain. Jugglers, mimes, and court jesters were the latest form of entertainment! Later, hand-drawn panoramas like Tom sees became the exciting new form of entertainment.

Imagine, people screaming in fright at an illustration! Today we have movies, television, videos, virtual reality, video games, computer graphics, high definition television, and much, much more! Our world today is a dizzying array of color and movement—coming at us faster every minute!

For this reason, sometimes it is pleasant to relive and recreate quieter moments of entertainment from days gone by. To help your student create his own panorama you will need some long white paper.

[**Teacher's Note**: Here's a great tip for finding long rolls of paper. Often newspaper printing offices will sell spools of unprinted newsprint paper that are nearly used up. They change the rolls of paper regularly so they won't run out in the middle of a job, but there is still a lot of paper left on the bolt. These end spools are a treasure for any kind of art mural or panorama project like this!]

Unprinted newsprint paper, plain shelf paper, or even the white side of old wrapping paper can be used for this project. Now it's time to draw or paint the pictures and scenes on the paper. Your student's imagination is the best idea-generator there could ever be, but here are few suggestions for the panorama to get you started: scenes from Edison's life; from your student's favorite vacation or dream vacation; scenes from the neighborhood or city where you live; a mini-pictorial of your student's childhood up to this point; or even your student's own version of the Wild West!

When the drawings are complete and the paint is dry, tape each end of the panorama to rods or tubes (wrapping paper tubes work great for this!). Then roll all of the paper to one end, leaving the opening scene or title section at the front.

Now, pop some popcorn and watch your student's creation roll by! Perhaps you'd like to invite friends or family for the viewing.

Fine Arts: Moving Pictures—A Flip Book

This lesson illustrates the next stage of entertainment from panorama to the motion picture. Flip books have been around for a long time. Particularly popular in the '20s and '30s, flip books were highly collectible and often featured famous silent film stars of the day. Has your student ever had the pleasure of seeing a flip book? Take this opportunity to help your student create his own.

To be successful, a flip book must have fairly small pages. Four-inch square pages tend to work well. Explain to your student that the flip book's "movement" is created by drawing a series of pictures, one on each piece of paper. On the first piece of paper, have your student draw the scene—a tree, a flower, a person, a car, a dancer, a family, whatever he wishes. Then, on each successive piece of paper, he needs to draw *almost* the same picture with one bit of the illustration changed. An arm waving, a branch blowing a bit, etc. When the complete scene is finished, staple the pages together at the side and flip away! This is an art project Tom would have loved!

This flip book animation is the basis of modern-day cartoons! It is also the way movies and videos work, since each frame of film or videotape is only slightly different from the ones before and after. The tiny amount of movement in each frame creates the illusion of continuous movement when the frames are viewed quickly.

Fire Arts: Tom's Dream—A Movie of Your Own

This activity is the modern culmination of what Tom is wanting—being able to create or record actual moving pictures! (page 181) If your student is older, this may be a project he can work on alone, but even if your student is younger he can still create his own movie with your help!

[**Teacher's Note**: This project requires access to a home video camera. Many people have them, but if you don't, perhaps someone you know would lend you one for a week or two. If you cannot find access to a video camera, don't be afraid to improvise and let your child use a still camera instead. In any of its many forms, photography is a marvelous art form for children and adults!]

Talk to your student about what he needs to think about before he begins filming. There are many types of movies—documentaries, news reports, demonstrative, infomercials and, of course, a filmed screenplay. Let him choose whatever creative form he wishes. Perhaps he would like to try writing his own short script! By involving a friend(s) or family member(s) he can create his own cast and choose his own setting. His "stars" can memorize their lines and he can begin recording!

Another project is filming "*A Day in the Life of...*" his family, his dog, an imaginary friend, whatever! This type of movie can be narrated (telling what is happening, feelings, factual information or the story) by your student while he is taping.

Simple title pages and credits can be drawn on paper and filmed for a short time at the beginning and end of the movie.

This art form, for some children, is an amazing discovery! Certain children who might lack skill in drawing or sculpture, suddenly discover a whole new world through the eye of a camera!

For more information on making movies, look at your local library for books on the topic! Don't forget, your child is never too young to discover a new talent or passion! Stephen Spielberg's mother has said in interviews that she couldn't keep a home movie camera out of her son's hands from the time he was a young boy. He loved making movies! Who knows? Perhaps your student is a future film-maker. If not, this is still a fascinating, vibrant art form that is sure to interest and delight your student!

Writing and Discussion Question

On page 179 we read that Tom and James "weren't a bit afraid" of the panorama picture show. Do you think this is true?

Internet Connections

To view current suggested links relating to this chapter's lessons, see www.fiveinarow.com/connections.

Chapter 17–The Lights Golden Jubilee

Parent Summary

Thomas Alva Edison, at 22, moved to New York City. Working with a group of friends in an electrical engineering firm, Tom saved enough money to build his first "real" laboratory. He moved to Newark, New Jersey and conducted many experiments. After a time, Tom had so many inventions and so much research underway he was forced to build an even larger laboratory in Menlo Park. It was there, in Menlo Park, along with his friend Francis Jehl, that Tom Edison invented the light bulb—one of the greatest inventions of all time.

The inventions did not stop there. Thomas Edison also invented the phonograph, perfected the telephone mouthpiece, the first motion picture camera and much more. In all, Tom Edison patented over 1,200 inventions during his lifetime!

Years later, as a tribute to the now great, Thomas Alva Edison, his friend Henry Ford "recreated" the Menlo Park Laboratory in Greenfield Village. Down to the most intricate details, Edison's laboratory was perfect and it remains there today. On October 21, 1929, fifty years after the invention of the light bulb, many people gathered at Greenfield Village to watch Mr. Edison "re-enact" the famous discovery. All over the United States people listened to the radio broadcast from Greenfield Village by candlelight. When they heard the radio announcer say Edison had turned on his light bulb, Americans everywhere blew out their candles and turned on their lights!

What we will cover in this chapter:

History and Geography: Adding to Our Map

History and Geography: President Herbert Hoover

History and Geography: The Great Depression and 1929

Science: A Light Bulb—How It Works

Lesson Activities

History and Geography: Adding to Our Map

If you have continued to make use of the reproducible map located in the back of the book, there are several more sites to locate in this chapter. The book tells us that when Tom was 22 years of age he moved to New York City. Then Tom moved to Newark, New Jersey. Both of these cities can be marked on your student's map. If your student wishes to, he can also mark Greenfield Village (located outside of Detroit in Michigan) on his map. Your student's map of Edison is now complete!

History and Geography: President Herbert Hoover

The now-famous Thomas Edison sells a paper to President Hoover on the train ride to Greenfield Village (page 188). Imagine having the president of the United States come to your party and ride a train and ask for your paper! Tom Edison had certainly gained respect and honor worldwide.

Ask your student if he has ever heard of President Hoover? Who was he? What did he do? What do we remember him for? Take this opportunity to introduce your student to our 31st president.

Herbert Hoover was born on August 10, 1874, in West Branch, Iowa. Both his parents died by the time he was nine years old. Sent to live with various relatives after that, Hoover worked many part-time jobs to help pay for his education. Working his way through college by delivering newspapers and doing laundry, Herbert Hoover graduated in 1895 from Leland Stanford University in Palo Alto, California with a degree in mining engineering.

For almost 20 years, Hoover worked on engineering projects in Europe, India, South Africa and Egypt. Considered a genius in mining engineering, Hoover worked as a consultant for other miners all over the world and by the time he was 40 years old Hoover had accumulated enough wealth to retire.

Hoover's success as a businessman was due to the fact he was a master with money and people. Hoover served in a variety of posts as both ambassador and secretary throughout World War I and on through President Coolidge's presidency.

When Coolidge chose not to run again for the presidency in 1928, Hoover stepped in as the Republican nominee. A hard battle was fought for the victory, but Hoover won on the basis of his promises. Hoover is known for coining the promise "a chicken in every pot." Although America was more prosperous than at any time in history, people are always eager for more. Hoover won in a landslide victory.

Tragic circumstances, however, beyond Hoover's control, were about to develop. On October 24, 1929 (just under a year after Hoover took office) the most devastating stock market crash in history took place. Known forever as Black Thursday, stock prices began to drop rapidly. By the following week, America was facing its greatest challenge since WWI. The Great Depression continued through Hoover's term and into the 1930s.

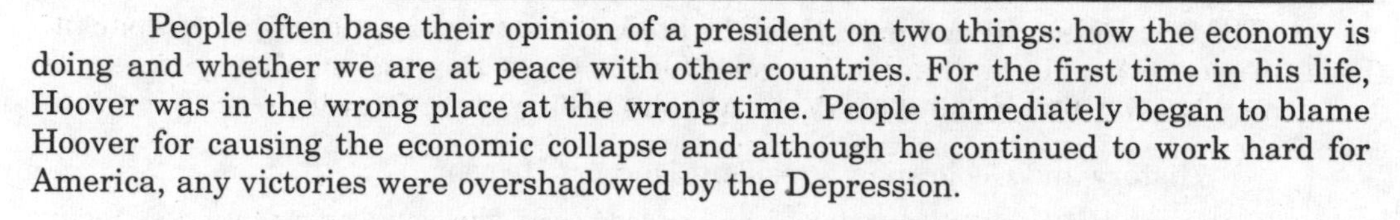

People often base their opinion of a president on two things: how the economy is doing and whether we are at peace with other countries. For the first time in his life, Hoover was in the wrong place at the wrong time. People immediately began to blame Hoover for causing the economic collapse and although he continued to work hard for America, any victories were overshadowed by the Depression.

People were so poor during the Depression, many lived in shanty towns which came to be known as "Hoovervilles." If they were living on the streets, people would use newspapers as blankets and these became known as "Hoover Blankets." The man who had risen to the top was now on his way down. And nothing could stop the fall. In 1932 Franklin Delano Roosevelt defeated the incumbent Hoover in a landslide.

Former President Hoover lived to be 90 years old and wrote several books about his presidency. Respected to this day by many people, Herbert Hoover was an amazing individual.

For more information on President Hoover, go to your local library. If your student is interested in the Great Depression, go through the following lesson.

History and Geography: The Great Depression and 1929

President Hoover buys a paper from the great Tom Edison on October 21, 1929, on his way to a huge party for Edison (page 188). Little did the President know that only three days later, the most tragic economic collapse in history was about to strike the free world. What does your student know about the Great Depression? If you chose to study President Hoover in the previous lesson, you learned that many Americans blamed the president for this nightmare which afflicted the United States for more than a decade.

At this point, it is not necessary for your student to have a full comprehension of the sources and ramifications of the Great Depression. Since many scholars and economists still argue over these points, it is surely too complex for your student at this time. But, do share with your student some beginning concepts surrounding this important period in American and World History.

The Great Depression didn't just happen in one day. Although the huge stock market crash on Black Thursday, October 24, 1929, is considered the beginning of the Depression, many factors occurred leading up to that day, causing the major economic shift. In addition to rapidly falling stock prices, banks became insolvent (unable to pay back depositors) as well. Between January 1930 and March 1933, nearly 9,000 banks went bankrupt and millions of Americans lost all of their savings!

Because of this devastating economic collapse, people began to lose their homes and their possessions and some actually began to starve. People who had a nice home, car and a vacation every year were suddenly on the street. People looked to their president to find an answer.

President Hoover did not move in dramatic government intervention, believing that market forces would quickly solve the struggling economy without direct intervention. It didn't happen. By 1932, Americans chose a new president, Franklin D. Roosevelt, who promised to save America and stop the cycle of the Great Depression. His famous proposal, known as the New Deal, was the exact opposite of what Hoover had suggested.

Roosevelt actively engaged the government in new job and employment mandates, relief for the homeless and starving, and changes in business programs. This is perhaps the most important aspect of the Great Depression—its effects on America long-term. From that day until this, the United States government has played an ever-increasing role in the lives of both business and individuals.

The Social Security Act was passed in 1935, which provides money for retirement. The attitudes of Americans changed forever after the Great Depression. Many people who had gone through that terrible time in our nation's history, were forever preoccupied with obtaining material possessions, food and savings.

Today, at least two generations have passed, and the young generation of today doesn't understand what it was like to live in that type of financial uncertainty and poverty. When people today refer to "the generation gap," this is, in part, what they mean. The ideals held by the generation that survived the depression are radically different from those of subsequent generations.

If your student is interested in further study on this turning point in American history, find additional books and videos on the topic. One way to ease tensions between generations, or cultures, is to study what caused the differences. If your student has grandparents or relatives who lived through the Depression, a visit or interview would be most appropriate and educational. First-hand experiences are always moving and eye opening—particularly for the young. Have your student write a report or "newspaper article" on the basis of his interview.

Science: A Light Bulb—How It Works

As you know, Tom Edison's greatest contribution to modern life was the invention of the light bulb. Take this opportunity to explore with your student how a light bulb works.

[**Teacher's Note**: To observe a light bulb easily, go to the store and buy a "clear" light bulb so that you can see the interior without obstruction.]

Light bulbs convert electricity into light (and heat too, as a by-product). Electricity is applied to the base of the light bulb and forced through the filament. The filament is the thin, coiled metal wire clearly visible in the bulb. The filament is usually made from tungsten metal. As electricity passes through the filament the wire is heated to nearly 5,000 degrees. As the filament heats up it gives off light. Try looking at a variety of light bulbs including automobile headlights, flashlights, etc.

Encourage your student to check out one or more books on electricity and the light bulb from the library. A three-dimensional model made of clay or cardboard or a drawing explaining the way in which light bulbs convert electricity into light makes a wonderful multi-day science project that is unforgettable.

Also, note that the invention of the light bulb was wonderful, but homes had no electricity! Next, Edison worked on ways to make electric power available to buildings! Imagine trying to find ways to generate power and then developing a system to carry it to homes.

Internet Connections

To view current suggested links relating to this chapter's lessons, see www.fiveinarow.com/connections.

HOMER PRICE
BY ROBERT McCLOSKEY

Chapter 1—The Case of the Sensational Scent

Parent Summary

The opening paragraph of Robert McCloskey's book, *Homer Price*, gives the reader a wonderful sense of place through McCloskey's skillful description. We find ourselves in Homer's world. Homer Price lives two miles outside of Centerburg at the junction of Route 56 and Route 56A. His parents own a tourist camp and Homer helps out around the place by pumping gas or helping his mother in the kitchen. In his spare time, Homer enjoys building radios. One night, Homer is busy in his room doing just that. He gets hungry for a snack and heads to the kitchen, being sure to put out a saucer of milk for his cat, Tabby. He feels something brush his skin and reaches down to pet his cat. But it isn't Tabby—it's a skunk! Homer remains very still, knowing skunks can make a terrible stink, and follows the skunk outside. Homer discovers the skunk is living under the house, right beneath his window! Wanting the skunk for a pet, Homer decides to call him Aroma. Homer trains Aroma to listen for a low whistle and climb into Homer's rigged basket pulley system. In this way, Homer can have Aroma in his room each night. Aroma makes his bed in Homer's old suitcase.

One night, Homer finishes a new radio and turns it on. Listening to his radio, Homer hears fabulous news! An area Centerburg resident, Mr. N. W. Blott, has just won $2,000 for writing the best slogan for Dreggs After Shave Lotion. The following week, the radio station is going to broadcast live from Centerburg when they present Mr. Blott with his check and 12 complimentary bottles of after shave lotion. Homer is excited!

The day of the broadcast Homer rides his bicycle to Centerburg to watch the show. Just as Mr. Blott is presented with his prize, four masked men with pistols say, "Put 'em up." Within moments, the four burglars steal all of Mr. Blott's winnings and his after shave lotion! Homer is amazed and that night he tells his parents what happened. The sheriff and his men are unable to apprehend the scoundrels, and Mr. Blott offers half of the money as a reward for finding them.

The next day, Homer and Aroma (in a basket on the bike) go fishing. On their way home, Homer decides to cut through the woods. Suddenly he hears voices and comes upon the four burglars, the money and the after shave lotion! The money and after shave lotion are laying in an open suitcase. While Homer watches the men talk, Aroma spies the suitcase and heads over for a snooze. Curled up in the suitcase, Aroma is immediately seen by one of the burglars. He throws a rock at Aroma, breaking six bottles of after shave lotion and scaring Aroma to death! Emitting a cloud of scent, Aroma permeates everything around him with a foul odor! Homer runs toward his bike and waits for Aroma to catch up.

That evening, Homer is thoughtful. He decides the police will find the burglars and doesn't want to get involved. Later on that night, four men stop and ask Homer for a room. Homer takes them to one of the largest tourist cabins and the men give him a dollar tip. As Homer walks away, he notices the money smells funny—a little like Aroma and a little like the after shave lotion! The burglars!

Homer calls the sheriff in Centerburg, but when no one comes to help Homer takes matter into his own hands. Coming up with a plan, Homer manages to round up the burglars with one of their own guns, and marches them back into town. Homer saves the day! The story of Homer and the smelly money appears in the newspaper and business picks up for Homer's parents' tourist camp, too. Everybody wants to see the famous skunk, Aroma, who helped identify the burglars!

What we will cover in this chapter:

History and Geography: The Famous Homer—A Brief Introduction

History and Geography: The Highways and Roads of America

History and Geography: Motels of the Past—Tourist Camps

History and Geography: The Early Roots of Radio and Television

Science: Simple Machines—Pulley

Language Arts: Different Fictional Story Formats

Language Arts: Headlines—Making Them True and Interesting

Language Arts: Advertising Slogans

Fine Arts: What's Wrong with This Picture?

Issues of Human Relationships: Having Parents Who Understand

Lesson Activities

History and Geography: The Famous Homer—A Brief Introduction

Draw your student's attention to the first illustration located at the beginning of the book. Here we see a drawing of Homer Price chewing on a hayseed. Homer's head is resting on a broken bust of the famous writer "Homer." But our Homer has written "Price" on the pedestal! Does your student understand what this picture means? Has your student ever heard of the Greek writer, Homer? What a wonderful opportunity to introduce your student to the *famous* Homer!

Homer, a Greek writer of ancient times (approximately 800-700 B.C.) is best known for his work on two poems entitled, *The Iliad* and *The Odyssey*. Both of these poems are extremely long and are called epic poems. Epic means the poem involves lengthy, narrative writing, usually covering a subject of great importance, like a war or a historic figure. Homer's two epic poems center on events occurring during the time of the great Trojan War (approximately mid-1200s B.C.) and mix history with mythology or legend.

No one knows what Homer looked like, when he was born or died, or even where he lived. The legend (a fictional tale so ancient it is believed to be true) surrounding Homer is that he was blind and illiterate. He is believed to have composed his poems orally, telling them over and over again while other men wrote them down. However, some experts believe Homer never even existed and that someone *else* wrote these poems!

If your student is interested in learning more about this famous and mysterious man, Homer, he might enjoy reading portions of the poems themselves. They are filled with excitement and adventure. Many excellent abridged and "student" versions of these two tales are available in bookstores and libraries.

History and Geography: The Highways and Roads of America

In our story, Homer's family lived at the *junction* (where two roads meet) of Route 56 and Route 56A (page 10). Pictured on page 8, the sign by Shady Rest Tourist Camp plainly shows U.S. 56. Can your student find the sign? What does your student know about the roads and highways of America? Show your student a road map of the United States. By sharing the basics with your student, they will become more knowledgeable and aware of the streets and roads around them.

There are five main categories of roads in the United States and together (surfaced and unsurfaced) they cover over 4 million miles. The categories are: city streets, county roads, state highways, U.S. highways, and interstate highways. The different categories dictate who maintains the road. City streets are named as well as numbered. Every city sets up its streets in a different way. Some cities have numbered streets running in one direction and named streets running in the other. Some cities, like Lincoln, Nebraska, for example, have their streets lettered in one direction and numbered in the other. A person in Lincoln might have a business located at the intersection of F street and 14th. Cities also often name streets in a common series: Washington, Jefferson, Lincoln, etc., or Oak, Maple, Elm, Walnut, etc., Massachusetts, Alabama, Colorado, etc. What is the name of the street where your student lives? How are your city's streets organized?

The next category of road is the county road. Maintained by the county or parish, these roads are generally located on the outskirts of a city, in a more rural area. State highways, maintained by the state, are numbered and can by located anywhere.

The two roads intersecting (a junction) at Homer's house are U.S. highways. Remind your student that the highway's signs identifying each type of road have specific shapes and colors. Make it a point to watch for the many different types of road and highway signs the next time you're driving.

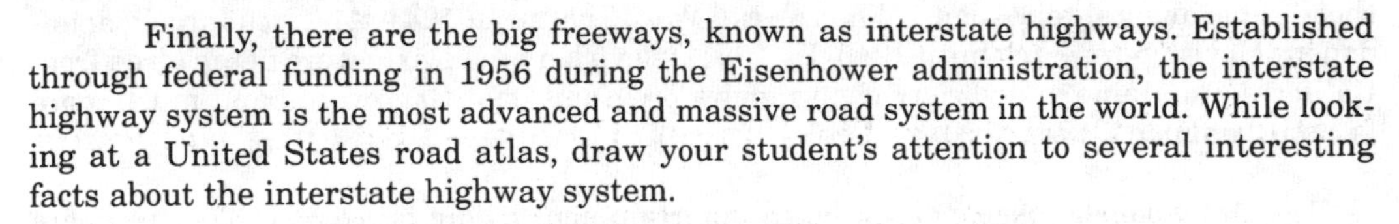
Finally, there are the big freeways, known as interstate highways. Established through federal funding in 1956 during the Eisenhower administration, the interstate highway system is the most advanced and massive road system in the world. While looking at a United States road atlas, draw your student's attention to several interesting facts about the interstate highway system.

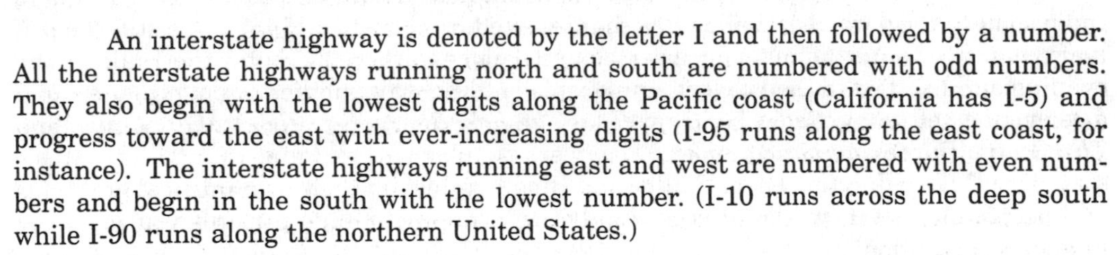
An interstate highway is denoted by the letter I and then followed by a number. All the interstate highways running north and south are numbered with odd numbers. They also begin with the lowest digits along the Pacific coast (California has I-5) and progress toward the east with ever-increasing digits (I-95 runs along the east coast, for instance). The interstate highways running east and west are numbered with even numbers and begin in the south with the lowest number. (I-10 runs across the deep south while I-90 runs along the northern United States.)

Encourage your student to take notice of the different road signs he sees around him! And maybe the next time your student takes a trip, he'll be able to help the driver navigate!

History and Geography: Motels of the Past—Tourist Camps

Draw your student's attention to the picture on the title page of this chapter (pages 8-9). In the picture we see the sign for the Prices' business "Shady Rest Tourists Camp—Running Water." The picture also shows us Homer's gas pump, which he uses to fill guest's cars, and the sign over his mother's lunchroom that says "EAT."

Your student has probably stayed in a hotel at one time or another. If not, he has certainly seen them. Hundreds of motel chains are all over the country. Small tourist camps are largely a thing of the past and the predecessor to today's "motels." Share with your student a little bit about this interesting piece of Americana.

Tourist camps were often composed of a series of little cabins or houses called "bungalows." Each cabin had a bed and bathroom and was decorated, cleaned and maintained by the family who owned the camp. Therefore, every tourist camp was different and no two cabins were alike. The "ma and pa"-owned tourist camps often served food cooked by the family (Homer's mother made fried chicken and hamburgers (page 10)) and often had a gas pump for the motorists' vehicles. Some small towns still have little tourist camps like Shady Rest, but most of these family-owned businesses have given way to the competition of large motel chains.

Does your student think it would be fun to stay in a tourist camp? What would he like better about the tourist camp compared to a large motel? What would he not like as well? Maybe your student would like to come up with a name for his own imaginary Tourist Camp just like the Prices'. He can draw a map or build a model of the cabins. How many will he have? What kind of food will the lunchroom serve? What road will his tourist camp be located on? Have fun sharing and learning with your student about this unique piece of history.

History and Geography: The Early Roots of Radio and Television

Homer likes to build radios (page 10) and learn how they work (page 12). When the money is stolen from Mr. Blott and a reward is offered, Homer tells Aroma, "If we could just catch those robbers we would have enough money to build lots of radios and even a television receiver."

Have your student look at the copyright date of *Homer Price*. Robert McCloskey wrote our tale in 1943. Were there televisions in 1943? Yes, but they were very, very new! Television was in the experimental stage in the 1930s.

The Radio Corporation of America (RCA) installed television receivers in 150 homes in New York City in 1936. A cartoon of *Felix the Cat* was the first program aired on these experimental televisions. When World War II began in 1941, America largely abandoned television research until 1945. By 1951, television broadcasts were being aired from California to Maine and variety shows, news programs, sporting events and much more became common.

But what did people do for home entertainment before television? That is where radio comes in. No wonder Homer was so interested in radios! In 1943 it was still the primary source of entertainment in most homes. People gathered around the radio in the evening and listened to their favorite programs just the way families often gather around a television set today. Radio programs like *The Lone Ranger*, *Little Orphan Annie*, and *The George Burns and Gracie Allen Show* were popular with old and young alike. Music stars like Duke Ellington, Glenn Miller and Bing Crosby had their own musical programs and people loved it. It was a different kind of entertainment—the pictures you saw were in your imagination!

Perhaps the single most famous event in radio occurred on October 30, 1938. Orson Welles' famous book *The War of the Worlds* was being read dramatically over the radio. The book is about Martians coming to earth in their space ship and invading. The radio announcer began the program by saying it was a dramatic reading and it was all fictional, but thousands of people tuned in during the program and thought it was actually happening! People fled their homes and towns, called the police and some suffered such shock they had to be hospitalized! Imagine that!

If your student shows interest, many libraries and bookstores have old-time radio programs on tape. Perhaps your student could talk with a grandparent or older friend about living in the "golden-age" of radio.

In 1943, Homer probably had never seen a television but had certainly heard of one. And coupled with his curiosity and love for electronics, he would certainly have wanted to try to build one for himself!

[**Teacher's Note**: There are wonderful resources available for students who are serious about electronics, like Homer. Many companies have created discovery kits on inventions, building your own radio, having fun with electronics, etc. The age level and price differ on every kit, but check your educational resource guides or catalogs for these! Most are under $25 and include all the equipment!]

Science: Simple Machines—Pulley

Homer used a pulley system to get Aroma into his room each night. A pulley is one of the six "simple machines," and is made up of a wheel with a groove around its rim so a rope (or other cord) can lay in the groove. When we want to lift a heavy object, it can be attached to one end of the rope. As we pull on the other end, while the rope runs through the pulley, this simple machine enables the weighted object to be moved up or down more easily than if a person just tried to lift it.

[**Teacher's Note**: The other five simple machines are as follows: lever, wedge, inclined plane, wheel and axle, and screw (which is really a spiral inclined plane).]

Challenge your student to utilize a pulley in an invention of his own. A great "first" pulley invention is an "egg cracking machine." There are an infinite number of possible designs. Here is just one list of possible materials that could be used. By gathering a wooden platform, string, a small metal pulley, some fishing weights (or other heavy metal pieces), small pieces of wood for a frame, and the egg, have your student try to invent his own egg-cracking device.

Encourage him to "think" through his plan and even draw his designs on paper before he begins to build his invention. If his first few attempts are unsuccessful, challenge him to keep trying until it works!

Once his egg-cracking device is "operational," perhaps he would enjoy demonstrating it to family and friends. Encourage him to watch for other ways in which pulleys are used.

Language Arts: Different Fictional Story Formats

The first fictional book we read in *Beyond Five in a Row,* Volume 1, was *The Boxcar Children*. Remind your student of how it was organized with each chapter leading into the next. It was clearly necessary to read each chapter completely in order to understand the following chapter. Now look at the contents of *Homer Price* and think about how the author organized this first chapter. Instead of tying each chapter together, McCloskey chose to write each chapter as an individual story. You can read the chapters in any order and the story will still make sense!

If your student has enjoyed the creative writing portions of *Beyond Five in a Row* and is working on a short story or has an idea for one, perhaps he would enjoy writing a story in this format—each chapter (it could be as short as a page) containing a complete tale with a beginning, middle and ending.

Language Arts: Headlines—Making Them True and Interesting

Wasn't it amazing that Aroma and Homer made the headlines in the paper (page 28)? Have your student look at the headline again, "Boy and Pet Skunk Trap Shaving Lotion Robbers By Smell."

What should a good headline do? What should it include? What should it avoid? These are all questions to ask your student as you begin to study and observe various headlines in the paper. The headline about Homer is great because it tells what happens briefly, it makes the reader want to read the article, and it doesn't exaggerate the facts or make false claims.

A newspaper headline is intended to catch the reader's eye and make him want to read the article. It should always briefly explain what the article is about. But a headline should never tell an untruth or be *sensationalistic* in nature. This means to exaggerate the truth. A journalist's job is to portray accurate, factual stories, not imaginary tales.

Have your student write two or three headlines for the same story—Homer and Aroma saving the day. As you look at the newspaper headlines, have your student tell you what he thinks about each one. Does it tell the truth? Does it make him want to read the article? Is it sensationalistic?

For additional work, have your student take the front page of the newspaper (watch for any articles you may not want him to read) and then write new headlines for each of the major articles. Discuss the differences between his headlines and the headline the paper's editor chose. Which does he think is better? Why?

Language Arts: Advertising Slogans

Mr. N. W. Blott won $2,000 and a dozen bottles of lotion when he came up with a slogan for Dreggs After Shave Lotion (page 12). That is a lot of money for thinking up one sentence! Advertising, however, is important business and the Dreggs Company knew they would make back all the prize money and more if they had a great slogan!

The word *slogan* may be a new word for your student. A slogan is a specific, short phrase or sentence used to sell a product. It must be "catchy" or memorable so people will like it or remember it and then buy the item you're trying to sell. Mr. N. W. Blott came up with the slogan, "The after shave lotion with the distinctive invigorating smell that keeps you on your toes."

[**Teacher's Note**: Because *Homer Price* is a book intended to be humorous, Mr. Blott's slogan may not be the best example of a catchy, short phrase that is memorable. However, share with your student successful slogans that are common today. For example: McDonald's®—Have You Had Your Break Today?; Always Coca-Cola®; Pizza Hut®—Makin' It Great!, etc. Or perhaps you have a few favorite or memorable slogans from your childhood. Share these with your student!]

Companies pay a great deal of money to professional advertising agencies to come up with great slogans or commercials for their products. It takes a lot of creative spark and hard work to come up with a catchy phrase. Remind your student of the three S's of advertising: Short, Specific, and Saucy. The slogan should be to the point (short), about the product or what it can do for you (specific) and have a musical jingle or catchy lilt to the phrase (saucy).

Look with your student at some magazine advertisements and watch some commercials on television. Talk with your student about what he likes and doesn't like and what he thinks is successful. Does it make him want the product? Does he remember the ad? Is the ad convincing? Now, if your student is interested, have him try his hand at the advertising business. See if he can come up with two or three advertisements for the Dreggs After Shave Lotion. Can he do better than Mr. Blott? If he enjoys this exercise, let him think up additional advertising slogans for a variety of other products.

Fine Arts: What's Wrong with This Picture?

The burglars are funny! They all mistrust one another so much that they end up sleeping in the same bed in order to keep an eye on one another. Have your student study the picture of this scene on page 25. What does he notice? The author tells us there are *four* burglars. How many men are in the bed? What's wrong with this picture? There are *five* people in the drawing! What happened?

Sometimes illustrations are wrong. In the printing process, things get overlooked. And in this case, perhaps McCloskey drew his illustrations a long time before or after he *wrote* the book. Maybe he was *planning* on having five burglars at first, and then later changed to four. Share with your student how interesting it is that even professional, award-winning illustrators might make mistakes sometimes. And encourage your student to double-check the consistency of his own texts and illustrations when he is working on a story. Who knows? This famous author/illustrator might even have made the picture this way on purpose as a humorous touch for his unusually observant readers!

Issues of Human Relationships: Having Parents Who Understand

Homer is thinking hard about what to do with the burglars. He finally decides he will need to take matters into his own hands and take responsibility. Homer tells his mother he has some important business to take care of and asks her if she can take care of things for awhile (page 23). Homer's mother answers, "Well, I think so Homer, but don't stay away too long."

Homer's mother was very understanding. She recognized Homer's need for some time alone and respected his polite request. It's nice to have parents who understand you when you're young. Sometimes, adults forget that children can have plans and feelings of their own. Talk with your student about the importance of understanding each other. Parent-to-child and child-to-parent.

When our parents understand us, it makes us feel validated. To validate someone means we make them feel valued, important and worth listening to. Everyone wants to feel like that! Challenge your student and yourself to look for more ways to validate one another.

Writing and Discussion Questions

On page 22 Homer is trying to decide what to do with the robbers. He decides to call the sheriff! The book tells us, "Homer knew that the sheriff would be down at the barber shop in Centerburg playing checkers and talking politics." How does Homer know what the sheriff is doing?

Vocabulary Words

Homer: Greek epic poet from approximately the 8th century B.C., who wrote *The Illiad* and *The Odyssey*

junction: a place or point of crossing, as two highways

tourist camp: an old-time motel, usually family owned and operated

bungalow: a small house or cottage

sensationalism: the use of exaggerated language intended to shock

slogan: a catch phrase used to sell or advertise a product

validate: to make someone feel worthy or important

Internet Connections

To view current suggested links relating to this chapter's lessons, see www.fiveinarow.com/connections.

Chapter 2—The Case of the Cosmic Comic

Parent Summary

Homer and Freddy like to look at the Super-Duper comic books. They are exciting and the boys think the Super-Duper is powerful and very cool! One day, Freddy calls Homer's house with exciting news. The real Super-Duper is coming to Centerburg! A new Super-Duper film is premiering and the actual, "real, honest-to-goodness" Super-Duper will be there! The boys plan a day-trip to Centerburg for the following Saturday. Freddy's horse, Lucy, pulls the boys by wagon to Centerburg. Homer, Freddy, and Freddy's little brother Louis, are all very excited!

The Super-Duper's car is parked outside the movie theater. Long, shiny and red, the boys think it is the best car ever! They see the real Super-Duper, shake his hand and get his autograph. Freddy asks Mr. Super-Duper if he can please fly for them, but the Super-Duper says "not today."

After the movie, the boys head home. As the wagon rounds a corner, they hear a car honking and suddenly see a red and silver "SWOOSH!" go by them. The Super-Duper! Then they hear a loud crash. Freddy thinks perhaps an electric ray got the Super-Duper. They round the corner and see the car smashed against the fence. The boys are thrilled! Now they're going to get to see the Super-Duper pry the bumper off the fence with his little finger! Or lift the entire car back onto the road with one hand! But, the unexpected happens.

The boys hear, "Ouch!" The Super-Duper is hurt! Freddy and Homer help the Super-Duper pull his car back onto the road with the wagon and Lucy. The boys are disappointed in the Super-Duper. He in only human after all!

What we will cover in this chapter:

Science: Another Element—Chromium

Science: Horsepower—Does That Really Mean a Horse?

Language Arts: Formula Fiction

Language Arts: A New Vocabulary Word—Monogram

Fine Arts: Cartooning—A "Funny" Way to Communicate

Fine Arts: The Art of Melodrama

Issues of Human Relationships:
Dealing with Disillusionment by Developing Discernment

Lesson Activities

Science: Another Element—Chromium

The Super-Duper's car was long and red, with chromium trimmings (page 39). What a cool car! But what is chromium? If you have introduced your student to the Periodic Table of Elements, here is another new element!

Chromium is a chemical element. It is a strong, hard, gray metal which gets very shiny when polished. For this reason, it is used to cover or coat other metals to give them a durable, glistening finish. The Super-Duper's car had very sparkling trim! Today, shiny metal bumpers on some cars are made of chromium, and we have shortened the name of the metal to "chrome."

A French chemist, Louis Nicolas Vauquelin, discovered and named Chromium in 1797. Take a look at the chemical symbol for Chromium (Cr), along with its atomic number and weight. Can your student find this element on the Periodic Table? Your student is gaining more knowledge of the elements every time you cover a lesson like this!

Science: Horsepower—Does That Really Mean a Horse?

Homer and Freddy have to get an early start for Centerburg. Freddy says, "...it takes old Lucy about an hour to go as far as Centerburg."

Does your student remember how far away Homer's house is from Centerburg? (About two miles, page 10) Imagine, traveling at two miles per hour! Lucy, the horse, does not go very fast, does she?

Ask your student if he has ever heard the word "*horsepower*." Does this unit of power really refer to a horse? Well, a famous Scottish engineer named James Watt (1736-1819) was the man to coin (to make up a new word or phrase) the phrase "horsepower." He used it to *loosely* define the power of the new steam engines by comparing them to horses. In other words, he compared the power it took a horse to lift or pull something to the power it took his steam engines to do the same job. One horsepower is defined as "550 foot-pounds of work per second." For this age level, let's simplify the calculation by eliminating the "per second" part of the equation and simply define *foot-pound* as the work required to raise one pound twelve inches.

[**Teacher's Note**: Obviously at this point in the lesson, your younger students may get lost. If this is beyond them, simply introduce them to the term and leave it at that. For your older students, the scientific calculations may be challenging and fun.]

If an engine lifts a 550 pound object three feet in the air, it is expending 1,650 foot-pounds of energy (550(pounds) x 3(feet) = 1,650). How many horsepower were required? (Three; 1,650 divided by 550 = 3.) Try to come up with your own calculations using this equation.

You can also calculate the horsepower of a human at work. How much does the person weigh? How high is he climbing? If a 110-pound student is climbing up Thomas Edison's 100-foot boyhood tower, how many horsepower did he use? (110 (pounds) X 100 (feet) = 11,000 foot-pounds. 11,000 divided by 550 = 20 horsepower.)

Therefore, in answer to our initial question, "Does horsepower really mean a horse?", the answer is yes and no. Lucy was pulling the wagon carrying Homer and Freddy at approximately one horsepower. However, this old Scottish phrase now defines a much more specific unit of power.

Language Arts: Formula Fiction

Homer notices the Super-Duper stories all seem alike (page 37). Freddy disagrees. "No, they're not! Sometimes the Super-Duper smashes airships and sometimes he smashes ocean liners. Then, other times he just breaks up mountains."

Does your student think Freddy's argument is valid? It sounds like all the Super-Duper stories are alike, just like Homer said. Take this opportunity to introduce your student to a type of writing called *formula fiction*.

Just because the Super-Duper stories are all alike doesn't mean they're not exciting and fun to read! In fact, predictability in stories is sometimes relaxing. You know what's going to happen. No shocking surprises, no scary cliffhanger endings.

The name *formula fiction* is somewhat self-explanatory. A formula is a predictable way of doing something—ending up with the same result every time. Perhaps the most classic formula fiction series are the *Nancy Drew* and *Hardy Boys* books. Written by Carolyn Keene/Franklin W. Dixon, these stories have become synonymous with formula plots and predictable endings. But, they are also two of the most well-loved, well-known children's mystery series in the world. Critics may argue that the *Nancy Drew* and *Hardy Boys* books are not of the greatest literary quality, but they have survived despite such criticism.

Formula fiction is a *literary device*—a way of writing. If your student enjoys creative writing, perhaps he would like to develop a set of characters and a formula plot of his own. By writing even a few short installments, he can get a first-hand look at formula fiction.

[**Teacher's Note**: If you get in a discussion with your student about the *Nancy Drew* and *Hardy Boys* books (perhaps you loved them as a child), it may be interesting to note that the creator and author of both series is one and the same. Both names, Carolyn Keene and Franklin W. Dixon, were the pen names of a man named Edward Stratemeyer. Aided by a staff of ghostwriters who actually wrote the texts and remain to this day anonymous, Stratemeyer developed the characters and plots for all the *Hardy Boys* books and several of the *Nancy Drew* books before his death in 1930. Ghostwriters have continued to develop the formula plots and books that are still being published today in both series, but Stratemeyer's pen names continue to appear on the books. Perhaps your student would like to come up with a pen name! It certainly helps to create anonymity and mystery—and it's fun, too!]

Language Arts: A New Vocabulary Word—Monogram

On page 39 we read a wonderful description of the Super-Duper car. "It was long and red, with chromium trimmings, and it had the Super-Duper's monogram on the side." Does your student know what a *monogram* is? A monogram is the combination of the first letters of a person's name into a design. A person's monogram is often designed with the first letter from the first name, middle letter (slightly enlarged) from the last name, and the third letter from the middle name. For example, a woman named Sara Lou Brown would have the monogram—SBL. Have your student create his own monogram.

Monograms can be found everywhere: embroidered on towels, handkerchiefs, shirt pockets, etched on drinking glasses, silverware, stationery, and on anything else someone wants personalized.

If your student thinks this is fun, experiment with adding his monogram to something. A pillowcase can be personalized with a monogram and some fabric paint. If your student likes sewing, a simple pillow or handkerchief can be embellished with a monogram. Have fun and encourage your student to be creative!

Fine Arts: Cartooning: A "Funny" Way to Communicate

Homer, Freddy, and little Louis love the Super-Duper comic books! Comic books are less popular today than in years past, but a similar story form that is still extremely popular is the cartoon strip, sometimes called the 'funny papers.' Cartooning utilizes several specific artistic devices to create its trademark look.

First, the figures are usually only "sketched" out and not in full detail. Often the artist will exaggerate a specific feature to make the figure more humorous. Secondly, the spoken words of the characters are often located in what are known as 'balloons.' Next, cartoons are separated by *panels*.

Cartooning is actually two things—an art form and a communication form. Sometimes the best way to express an idea or feeling is by making it funny, and what better way to do that than through the medium of a cartoon? Classic cartoon strips include

Peanuts, Beetle Bailey and *Blondie*. Cartoons have also been used for many years for political satire (making fun of policies and politicians).

To learn more about cartooning, begin by looking at comic strips in your local newspaper. You may also want to look at political cartoons, generally located on the opinion/editorial page of your paper. What does your student notice about them? What is the same in each? What is different?

An excellent source for learning the art of cartooning is called *The Big Yellow Drawing Book—A Workbook Emphasizing the Basic Principles of Learning, Teaching, and Drawing Through Cartooning* by Dan, Marian and Hugh O'Neill (Copyright 1974, M.S. Offset Co.). The format is easy enough for the youngest student to enjoy and is set up like a workbook, with panels of examples and then blank panels to try various techniques yourself. A fabulous book!

Have a great time exploring the world of cartooning with your student and think about the Super-Duper while you're at it!

Fine Arts: The Art of Melodrama

On page 38 Homer and Freddy discuss the plots in the Super-Duper comic books. Homer makes the observation that Super-Duper "always rescues the pretty girl and catches the villain on the last page." "Of course," says Freddy, "That's to show that crime doesn't pay." In a nutshell, Freddy and Homer have just described a classic form of theater—the melodrama. Introduce your student to this recognizable dramatic form and familiar term.

Melodrama became a highly popular form of theater in the 1800s, involving a predictable (or formula) plot which always included a hero (a person of high moral character who is brave, strong and handsome), a villain (a person of low moral character who is evil, smart but physically weak, dressed in black and ugly), and a beautiful woman (the damsel in distress who is in love with the hero but imprisoned by the villain and too weak to escape by herself).

Melodrama was loved by the public! They shrieked in terror at the villain's evil laugh while he twirled his long mustache. They swooned at the handsome young hero, and always sighed during the kiss at the end. Happy endings are a must in melodrama, for just the reason Freddy mentioned. Melodramas always prove that crime doesn't pay, the righteous always win and love is the most powerful thing in the world.

Exaggerated as it is, melodrama is still played in theaters all across the United States and the term 'melodramatic' is used to define someone who is being overly dramatic. If your student is interested in acting, perhaps he would like to write or stage his own melodrama. Tinny piano playing is usually the background music for melodramas and in this theater form, you can never over-act!

Issues of Human Relationships: Dealing with Disillusionment By Developing Discernment

Homer, Freddy and little Louis think a ray-gun or a villain must have hurt the Super-Duper (page 45). They are waiting to see him lift the car up with his little finger. They are sure all they have read about him is true. But what do they hear him say? "Ouch!" The Super-Duper is human! He isn't really a super hero at all. And in fact, they have to help him get untangled. Homer and his friends are disappointed!

Sometimes people fail us. They don't meet our expectations and we can feel *disillusioned*. Disillusionment means we lose our false ideas or illusions and become aware of reality—and become disappointed! Disillusionment affects adults and children alike. It is a very real feeling. Discuss with your student times in your life when you've felt disillusioned. Has he ever felt that way?

If you are a human being, there is really no way to escape feeling disillusioned sometimes. But there is a way to reduce the number of times we are disillusioned. We need to develop *discernment*. Discernment is the ability to see clearly and to show good judgment. Discernment can be a learned skill. When we begin to exercise good discernment we are much less likely to be disillusioned or disappointed.

For example, when we have a friend who has a habit of not telling the truth and exaggerating stories and he tells us that he's going to take all of his friends to Disneyland for his birthday next summer, should we believe him? If we get our hopes up, convinced that we're going to have a wonderful time on this once-in-a-lifetime birthday trip, there's a very good chance we'll be disappointed. But good discernment would suggest that this boy has often failed to tell the truth in the past and this is probably another one of those times. We probably shouldn't count on going to Disneyland if we have good discernment.

Encourage your student to develop good discernment and wisdom and he will avoid many of life's disappointments.

Writing and Discussion Question

What do you think was going through Homer's mind when he heard the crash of the Super-Duper's car and then saw the situation?

Vocabulary Words

chromium: a grayish-white, hard, metallic chemical element

horsepower: a unit for measuring the power of motors or engines, equal to 550 foot-pounds of work per second

to coin: to make up or invent a new word or phrase

foot-pound: a unit of energy equal to lifting one pound a distance of one foot

monogram: the first letters of a name combined into a single design

melodrama: a drama concerned with exaggerated conflicts and emotions and stereotyped characters

disillusionment: to be freed from illusion that can disappoint us

Internet Connections

To view current suggested links relating to this chapter's lessons, see www.fiveinarow.com/connections.

Chapter 3—The Doughnuts

Parent Summary

Homer's Uncle Ulysses owns an up-and-coming lunchroom, updated with all the newest labor saving devices! One day, Homer's mother goes with his Aunt Agnes to sew and knit for the Red Cross. Homer decides to go along and spend some time with his Uncle Ulysses in the lunchroom while the ladies are gone.

When Homer arrives, Uncle Ulysses is shining and cleaning his favorite labor saving device—his automatic doughnut machine. Uncle Ulysses decides to head over to the barbershop for a little while, and asks Homer if he would mind taking care of the customers and making a batch of doughnuts while he is gone. The first customer in the store after Uncle Ulysses leaves is a nice, traveling, advertising man named Mr. Gabby. He decides to stay and wait for the fresh doughnuts Homer is about to make. Then a rich lady in a shiny, black car comes in. Homer tells her the doughnuts aren't made yet, and she insists on helping him mix up the batter. The rich lady tells Homer she has a very special recipe and takes over! Homer is amazed at how much batter the lady makes, but doesn't say anything.

When the first few doughnuts come out of the hot oil, everyone says they are delicious! The lady buys some doughnuts and leaves. Homer decides the automatic machine has made enough doughnuts and tries to turn the stop lever. Nothing happens! The doughnuts keep rolling down the chute into the hot fat! Homer tries the start lever without results. He calls Uncle Ulysses and asks him to come back to the lunchroom. Then he and Mr. Gabby work on stacking the doughnuts everywhere they can find. They put a sale sign out saying, "2 Doughnuts for 5¢," but people aren't buying them fast enough! Uncle Ulysses arrives on the scene and is shocked! What is he going to do with all those doughnuts?

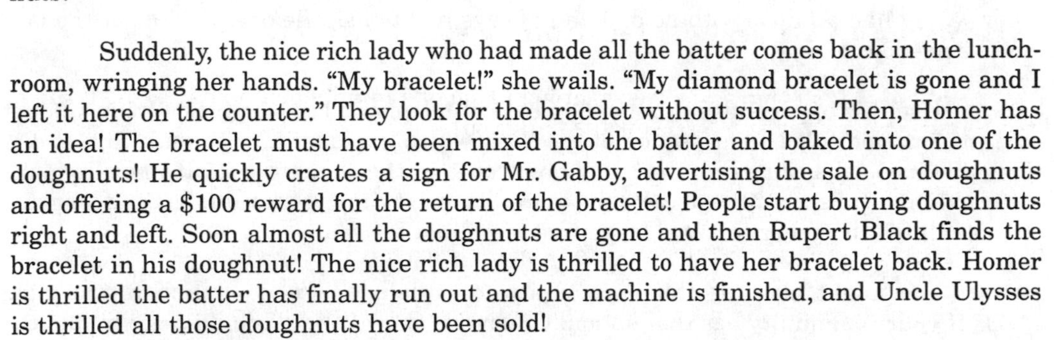

Suddenly, the nice rich lady who had made all the batter comes back in the lunchroom, wringing her hands. "My bracelet!" she wails. "My diamond bracelet is gone and I left it here on the counter." They look for the bracelet without success. Then, Homer has an idea! The bracelet must have been mixed into the batter and baked into one of the doughnuts! He quickly creates a sign for Mr. Gabby, advertising the sale on doughnuts and offering a $100 reward for the return of the bracelet! People start buying doughnuts right and left. Soon almost all the doughnuts are gone and then Rupert Black finds the bracelet in his doughnut! The nice rich lady is thrilled to have her bracelet back. Homer is thrilled the batter has finally run out and the machine is finished, and Uncle Ulysses is thrilled all those doughnuts have been sold!

What we will cover in this chapter:

History and Geography: Telephones and Operators in the Past

History and Geography: The Red Cross—People Helping in a Personal Way

Science: New Technology—Labor Saving Devices Today

Science: Economics—Supply and Demand

Language Arts: Literary Enrichment—Thematic Stories

Fine Arts: Design Your Own Sandwich Board

Fine Arts: Cooking—Make Your Own Doughnuts

Fine Arts: Illustrating Movement

Lesson Activities

History and Geography: Telephones and Operators in the Past

Homer needs Uncle Ulysses' help right away! That automatic doughnut machine won't stop! Homer decides to call his Uncle down at the barbershop. Draw your student's attention to page 58. The book tells us Homer "gave the number" and then waited for someone to answer. What does it mean to "give the number?" Take this opportunity to share with your student the way in which calls were placed in the past.

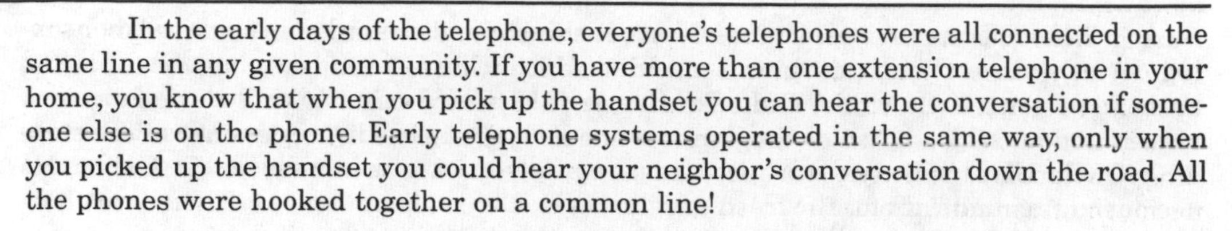

In the early days of the telephone, everyone's telephones were all connected on the same line in any given community. If you have more than one extension telephone in your home, you know that when you pick up the handset you can hear the conversation if someone else is on the phone. Early telephone systems operated in the same way, only when you picked up the handset you could hear your neighbor's conversation down the road. All the phones were hooked together on a common line!

The operator (sometimes called "central") would ring each individual family with their own unique ring pattern. For instance, your phone pattern might be "two longs and one short" ring. Everyone in the community could hear the two long and one short phone rings, but you knew that whoever was calling wanted your house. If your phone rang with one long and one short ring, you knew that was for your neighbor down the road and so you didn't answer.

Later, as phone systems grew more complex, each phone had a unique phone number, but the operator still placed your call for you. Rather than dialing the barbershop, Homer asked the operator to dial the barbershop for him. Today, of course, each phone has it's own unique phone number and we can dial our own telephone calls directly anywhere in the world. When you see phones in books, on TV and in movies, notice if they have a dialer or if the caller needed "central" to place the call. In an old Andy Griffith show, Andy had a phone with no dial and always had to ask the operator to get the person he needed.

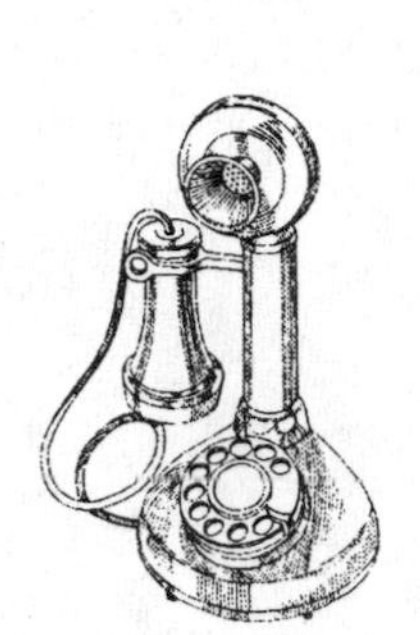

Use this opportunity to get out your local telephone book and show your student the information-filled front section of the book which explains how to make direct-dial long distance calls, shows all the many area codes in the country, explains how to make international calls, credit card calls and more. The next time you need to make a long distance call to a friend or relative, let your student dial for you!

You might also use this opportunity to explain emergency numbers including "911" if your community has that option. Otherwise show your student where to find the number for the fire department, sheriff's office, etc.

History and Geography: The Red Cross—People Helping in a Personal Way

Homer's mother and Aunt Agnes help the Red Cross (page 50). What does your student know about the Red Cross? Take this opportunity to share with your student the touching story behind this organization of peace and healing. A Swiss philanthropist, Jean Henri Dunant, founded the Red Cross in 1863.

[**Teacher's Note**: You may wish to review the lesson on philanthropy found in *The Boxcar Children*, chapter 10 lessons.]

A few years before (1859) Dunant was in Italy during the Austro-Sardinian War. To his horror, he saw the field at Solferino the day after nearly 41,000 people had been killed or wounded. He didn't allow himself to be overwhelmed by the vast number of wounded, but instead chose to help in whatever way he was able. Organizing a band of volunteers, Dunant and his group tended to as many of the injured as they could.

This incident changed Dunant's way of thinking. He became driven to find a way to help in other situations like Solferino. In 1862 he published a small booklet entitled *Un Souvenir de Solferino (Recollections of Solferino)*. The last line in the text read "Would it not be possible to found and organize in all civilized countries permanent societies of volunteers who in time of war would give help to the wounded without regard of their nationality?"

He succeeded in doing just that! His heart-rending plea was looked upon with favor and on October 26, 1863, delegates from 16 countries met to discuss Dunant's plan.

During these meetings, the Red Cross symbol was chosen (the red cross on a white background in honor of Dunant's homeland, Switzerland) and the basic plans for the Red Cross were written out. In the United States, in 1881, Clara Barton founded the American Association of the Red Cross. (You might want to find a good biography of Clara Barton. This now famous, dedicated worker was extremely shy as a child and was homeschooled for much of her education.)

Today, the Red Cross' efforts go beyond war relief. Natural disaster relief (floods, volcanoes, tornadoes, fires, etc.), public health services and organizing blood drives are just a few ways the Red Cross maintains an active and helping hand in all aspects of life, worldwide. The Junior Red Cross was founded in 1917 and gives school children a chance to help.

From the late 1800s to around 1950, the citizens of the United States (people like Homer's mother and Aunt Agnes) helped the Red Cross in a *personal* way. Knitting scarves for the soldiers, ripping cloth for bandages, baking tins of cookies, and other things of this nature were ways people could serve their country and the soldiers directly. As late as the 1950s schools and junior organizations had children putting together care packages (washcloth, toothbrush, toothpaste, books, etc.) for the soldiers stationed all over the world.

People can now serve the Red Cross by other means. Whoever is motivated by concern for human life can become active in the Red Cross at the local, national or international level. For more information on how your student can become involved or the number for your local chapter, call the Red Cross National Office at (202) 737-8300.

Science: New Technology—Labor Saving Devices Today

Uncle Ulysses is fascinated by labor saving devices! (page 51) Newer, faster means of doing things are invented every day! Trying to keep up with the latest technology is difficult.

Discuss with your student what types of labor saving devices (sometimes called "time-savers") we have today—things Uncle Ulysses would have loved!

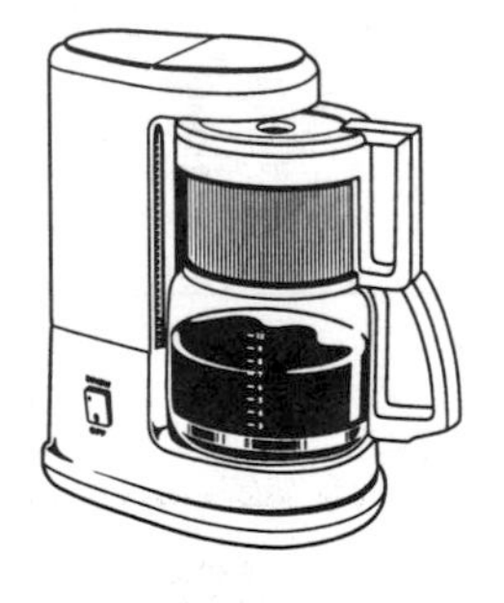

We have answering machines, bread machines, snow blowers, weed eaters, food processors, personal computers, fax machines, cellular phones, programmable VCR's, redial buttons on our phones, personal pagers, the Internet, e-mail, rice cookers, dishwashers, microwave ovens, and much more! How many labor saving devices can your student come up with? Keep a running list. Anyone can add to it and see who can come up with the most unusual or silly labor saving device! You can call the device an "Uncle Ulysses Special." Have fun!

Labor saving devices, however, are more than just fun. They have dramatically changed the face of our culture in the 21st century. Jobs that used to take many hours can now be accomplished in only a few minutes. Imagine handwriting a copy of a newspaper article that you wanted to share with a friend, compared to using a photocopy machine. Imagine cutting a large lawn with a push-type mower compared to using a modern riding mower. As more and more laborsaving devices have found their way into American culture, most of us have had more free time for recreational use. We no longer spend all day mowing on Saturday, but instead we can finish mowing by 10:00 a.m., and then decide between playing golf, bowling, etc. Uncle Ulysses would have been delighted.

Science: Economics—Supply and Demand

The doughnuts in Uncle Ulysses lunchroom are out of control! Mr. Gabby, the traveling sandwich man, has a great idea! By advertising a sale on doughnuts, they can sell a lot more (page 62). Mr. Gabby tells Homer, "You got the doughnuts, ya gotta create a market. ...Understand? ...It's balancing the demand with the supply. ...That sort of thing."

What a wonderful opportunity to share a beginning lesson in economics with your student! The concept of supply and demand is so fundamental to all discussions of economics that it is essential to begin sharing the idea with your student. Even the youngest student can understand the idea of supply and demand.

If you wish, begin with a simple example. In fact, the illustration from our story is perfect! Whether or not you have a product you wish to sell by accident (such as Uncle Ulysses' doughnuts) or you've purposely created a product (such as lemonade for your lemonade stand), you have to make people want it! (Create demand.) Advertising is one common way in which manufacturers increase the demand for their product.

When you have lots of product to sell, you have supply. You have an incentive to keep your price as low as possible to increase demand. In other words, the lower your price, the more people will want to buy of your product. Sometimes there is very little supply. Perhaps you have a very rare Honus Wagner baseball card and there are only a few known to exist. Many people would like to own that baseball card (demand) but there are only a few available (supply). Prices will be very high because of the law of supply and demand. You could sell many of your Honus Wagner baseball cards for $50 each, less of them at $500 each and far fewer still at $5,000 each. As the price goes up, the demand goes down. Less people want them.

If you have thousands of the same, identical baseball card to sell, you may have to begin lowering your price in order to convince many, many people to purchase one from you. (This is what Homer had to do—lower the price on his doughnuts in order to convince many, many people to buy them.)

Prices are also controlled by the demand "side" of the equation. If your baseball card is of someone famous, many, many people will want to own one—big demand. They will compete with one another to purchase a limited supply and force the price to rise. On the other hand, very few people may be interested in buying a baseball card of a rookie who never played in a big league game and is now selling used cars in Arkansas. The low demand for his card means prices will have to be awfully cheap to convince anyone to buy one of his cards.

High prices result from either limited supply or high demand. Low prices result from excess supply or limited demand. This simple economic "law" is the primary force behind most western economies. Whenever you see a sale table with items marked down, you know that either nobody wants that item anymore, or the store has a huge supply they need to sell. Likewise, when you see something selling at a high price, you know that either everybody wants one, or there are just very few available for anyone.

For more information on supply and demand, an *excellent* and popular book is *Whatever Happened to Penny Candy*? by Richard J. Maybury (Copyright 1992, Bluestocking Press, ISBN 0942617150), available through bookstores and homeschool supply catalogs.

Language Arts: Literary Enrichment—Thematic Stories

This chapter in Homer Price is a wonderful tale of treasure lost and found. Many other stories have a similar theme, and an instructional exercise in literary enrichment is to conduct a thematic study (comparing and contrasting two similar books).

A wonderful book to use for comparative analysis with this third chapter of Homer Price is entitled *Too Many Tamales* by Gary Soto (Copyright 1993, G.P. Putnam's Sons, ISBN 0399221468).

Too Many Tamales is the delightful story of a Mexican-American family's get-together during the Christmas season. Maria, the daughter, helps her mother make a steaming platter of fresh tamales. While her mother steps away for a moment, Maria decides to slip on the diamond ring her mother took off while she was mixing the dough. Later in the evening after the cousins arrive and the presents are piling up under the tree, Maria remembers the ring. She can't remember where she put it and the cousins run downstairs behind her. Staring in dismay at the mound of hot tamales, Maria decides the ring must be in one of them. The cousins begin eating, and soon the floor is littered with paper-thin cornhusks and every one of the tamales has been devoured. But no ring! The story ends with a sweet moment between Maria and her mother, Rosa. Rosa tells Maria that she had found the ring and put it back on. All is well and the family makes up another batch of tamales.

The reason this book is such a nice choice for a thematic study is two-fold. First, the story shares the same story line as Uncle Ulysses' doughnut machine disaster. Second, *Too Many Tamales* is a wonderful snap-shot of another culture and life. At first, don't tell your student that the story has similarities. Just begin reading the story aloud and see if he comments on the similarities.

For your young student, simply reading the story and discussing the similarities is a great exercise. For your older student, even though *Too Many Tamales* is a picture book, the exercise can be made more difficult by assigning a formal written paper. He can develop his paper by comparing and contrasting the two stories, and perhaps discussing differences in the illustrations.

Fine Arts: Design Your Own Sandwich Board

Mr. Gabby wore a sign called a sandwich board (picture pages 64-65). What an interesting way to advertise! Sandwich boards are more a thing of the past, but your student might have fun designing and making one today. Perhaps, your student could take a slogan he wrote in the last chapter for Dreggs After Shave Lotion and use that, along with a picture or two and create his own sandwich board.

By using poster board, cardboard or even a paper grocery bag cut in half, your student can design the back and front. Then add a couple of straps made from fabric or string and you have it! Be creative and have a ball!

Fine Arts: Cooking—Make Your Own Doughnuts

Reading this chapter makes you hungry for some fresh doughnuts, doesn't it? Why not take this opportunity to cook something with your student! Beyond the delight and bonding time this activity offers, take some time to talk with your student about where a few of the ingredients used in the recipe are grown or gathered. Work on dry and liquid measure. Discuss the fractions involved in the cooking, etc.

Here is a recipe for doughnuts that you can make at home *without* using hot oil; safer and *healthier*!

2 (1/4 oz.) pkgs. dry yeast
1/4 cup warm water
1 1/2 cups warm milk
1/2 cup sugar
1 tsp. salt
1 tsp. nutmeg
1/4 tsp. cinnamon
2 eggs
1/3 cup shortening
4 1/2 cups flour
1/4 cup butter, melted
sugar to decorate

In a large mixing bowl, dissolve the yeast in warm water. Add milk, sugar, salt, nutmeg, cinnamon, eggs, shortening and 2 cups flour (hold the rest of the flour in reserve).

Blend for 30 seconds with a mixer on low speed as you add the remaining flour. Cover the bowl and allow the mixture to rise until doubled in volume (approximately 60 minutes). Turn dough out onto a well-floured surface and roll with a rolling pin until your dough is 1/2" thick. Using a well-floured doughnut cutter (or a large and small drinking glass) cut dough into doughnut shapes. Place your doughnuts on a well-greased baking sheet. Preheat oven to 425° F. Brush the tops with melted butter and allow to rise until the volume of each doughnut has doubled once again (approximately 20 minutes). Bake your doughnuts for 8-10 minutes. Brush once more with melted butter and sprinkle sugar on top. Now enjoy! (Makes 1 1/2 to 2 dozen doughnuts.)

Fine Arts: Illustrating Movement

Robert McCloskey is an award winning author and illustrator! His illustrations for Homer Price are delightful! Filled with gentle, sweet faces and pleasing lines, the artwork in this book is exceptional. There are many techniques worth studying (we will be covering more in future lessons), but one of McCloskey's most interesting techniques is the way he illustrates movement.

Show your student the title illustration for this chapter (pages 48-49). Homer is mopping the floor. Uncle Ulysses is proudly standing by the automatic doughnut machine, and a Centerburg resident is eating at the counter. Draw your student's attention to the multi-slice toaster behind Uncle Ulysses. How does McCloskey make the toast look like it is actually popping up? (He uses lines drawn in the direction he wants the toast to move.) Isn't that interesting?

Now, look with your student at the illustration of the rich lady mixing up the doughnut batter (page 55). Take a moment and look at her jewelry sitting next to the bowl. Notice how the same type of lines can make an object look like it is glittering. What is different between the "moving lines" McCloskey used to bring the toast to "life" and the "glitter lines" he uses on the jewelry? Talk with your student about the differences and then have him try these simple techniques! Learning drawing methods by studying the work of wonderful artists like Robert McCloskey is a great way to improve your own drawings!

Encourage your student to try using McCloskey's techniques to bring *movement* or *sparkle* to a variety of drawings, using either pencil, crayon, colored pencils or markers.

Writing and Discussion Question

What do you think Rupert Black did with his $100 reward? What would you have done with such a large reward?

Internet Connections

To view current suggested links relating to this chapter's lessons, see www.fiveinarow.com/connections.

Chapter 4—Mystery Yarn

Parent Summary

The town of Centerburg is all in a flutter! The annual county fair is coming and instead of trotting races, this year there will be a new kind of contest. Area residents will compete to determine who has the biggest ball of saved string! Homer's Uncle Telemachus, the sheriff, and the woman both men have their heart set on, Miss Terwilliger, agree to unroll their collected string balls and set the record straight once and for all. Since both men, Uncle Telemachus and the sheriff, want to marry Miss Terwilliger, they decide the winner will get her hand in marriage. For some time Miss Terwilliger has invited Uncle Telemachus over for fried chicken every Sunday, and the sheriff over for fried chicken every Thursday. She can't seem to make up her mind which one to marry, and the two men figure this contest will put the question to rest once and for all. But as the story turns out, we find Miss Terwilliger with a plan of her own.

The day for the big contest arrives and the rules are explained. Every day of the week-long county fair, from two o'clock till four o'clock, the balls of string will be unrolled around the horserace track. Whoever has the longest piece of string wins the contest and the title of World's Champion String Saver!

The first day of the contest arrives. After the two hours of unrolling, Miss Terwilliger's ball measures 5'9"; the sheriff's measures 5'8" and Uncle Telly's measures 5'8" in diameter. Each day, after unrolling the balls of string for the allotted two hours, the contestants measure the string ball remaining. By the end of the week, it seems obvious Miss Terwilliger is going to lose. The town is electric with excitement! What's going to happen?

On the final day of the unrolling, we find out that the sheriff's ball of string has a core of a walnut. Uncle Telemachus' ball is string clear to the center! He's going to win! Suddenly, in a very mysterious way, Miss Terwilliger turns up the winner! Nobody is quite sure how, but Miss Terwilliger wins the title of World's Champion String Saver!

Later, the next week, Miss Terwilliger decides to marry Homer's Uncle Telemachus. It is a beautiful wedding and the best man is the sheriff! A beautiful ending to a wonderful day!

What we will cover in this chapter:

History and Geography: County Fairs

Science: Birds' Eggs

Fine Arts: Collections

Fine Arts: Trees and Leaves—Art Mediums

Issues of Human Relationships: Frugality

Issues of Human Relationships: Special Occasions—Sunday Dinner

Lesson Activities

History and Geography: County Fairs

The time has come for the county fair in Centerburg (page 72). What fun! Has your student ever been to a county fair? There are so many things to see and do! Generally, a county fair includes exhibits and contests for the best livestock (chickens, calves, horses, pigs), vegetables, pies, etc. Often there are rides like Ferris wheels and carousels and lots of yummy things to eat!

One way children can become involved in county and state fairs is through a group called 4-H. 4-H is a national organization supported by county extension offices. It is for both boys and girls. Adults and parents act as volunteer leaders. The children can learn about many subjects including food, art, sports, animals and livestock, sewing, camping, etc. After a child has worked on a specific project, county fairs provide exhibition arenas, divided by age group, for the children to display their work. Awards and ribbons are given out and the whole experience can be a positive, confidence-building vehicle for exposing children to many new things.

4-H is the largest youth development program in the United States. For more information on a chapter in your area, contact your local county extension office (located under county government numbers in your directory).

Whether or not you choose to participate in an organization like 4-H, county fairs are so much fun! If you have the opportunity to attend one, take your student and have a great time!

Science: Birds' Eggs

Mrs. Terwilliger's special occasion dress was robin's egg blue. Take a moment to find an encyclopedia or other reference material and look at a robin's egg. What kind of blue is it? Look at other bird's eggs. There is such a variety of color, size and markings! It is amazing! Can your student point out a robin's egg and note its difference from a sparrow's egg?

Did you know that some egg designs (especially those in nests on the ground) are colored so as to be camouflaged? Did you know that the unusual and incredible markings on bird's eggs are pigments absorbed by the porous eggshell as it travels through the female bird's oviduct?

There is a great deal to be learned about eggs besides their color. How often does a bird lay eggs? When do birds begin incubating—after the first egg is laid or the entire "clutch?" These questions and many more vary with different birds. Follow this learning trail as far as you would like. There are beautiful and informative books on birds' eggs in your library in both the juvenile and adult sections. Or plan a visit to a wildlife sanctuary and learn from the guides as much as you can about the birds there.

Fine Arts: Collections

Miss Terwilliger, Uncle Telly and the sheriff are serious string collectors! What does your student collect? Does he have any collections? Talk with your student about some of the things people collect: stamps, quilts, old coins, baseball cards, lamps, political pins, ball caps, tea cups, antique cars, dolls, etc. Whatever you can think of, someone probably collects it.

What is the attraction to collecting? You learn a lot about a topic you're interested in and you can become an "expert" in your field. Many people begin an interest in their topic casually, by simply owning a few of something. As the interest grows the real collecting begins. Even children can have entire collections of their own—bird nests, paper clips, pine cones—anything can grow into a collection. Encourage your student to become a collector of something, just like Uncle Telly. It is delightful and rewarding!

Begin by exploring subjects that interest your student. What does he like? He may choose to collect something that is already popular with collectors, such as baseball cards or stamps. Or, he may prefer to collect something unique such as famous quotes, different types of canning jars, belt buckles or soda pop cans from around the world. The point of collecting is to find an enjoyable avocation and learn about a subject.

Fine Arts: Trees and Leaves—Art Mediums

At the beginning of our chapter, Homer is busy raking the leaves in his yard. Has your student ever helped rake leaves? Do you live in an area where you have deciduous trees (trees which shed their leaves)? If you are doing this lesson in the fall and live in an appropriate region, perhaps you can go with your student to rake some leaves in the yard. Smelling the fresh air and listening to the crunch of leaves underfoot are some of the enjoyable activities of autumn.

To help capture this time of year and for a fun art project, have your student gather several leaves he especially likes. If you live in a region with maples or oaks, colored leaves are wonderful for this project. If not, pine needles, green leaves, interesting dry vines, etc., work well, too. The important part is to let your student pick the leaves he finds interesting. Encourage him to look at the shapes, edges, stems, veins, colors, etc., when making his selection. Have him close his eyes and feel the leaves.

After the leaf selections have been made, have your student arrange them in whatever pattern he chooses. He may wish to "frame" a poem he has written or a picture he has drawn with the leaves. When the leaves and whatever else he has chosen to include are laid out in the pattern he has designed, take two pieces of clear contact paper, laying one sticky-side-up. Begin moving the leaves and picture or poem onto the sticky side of the contact paper, pressing down each leaf. When the design is complete, lay the other piece of contact paper on top, being sure to match up the edges and press out any air bubbles. (Use a straight pin to puncture any remaining air bubbles and squeeze the air out.)

Now, your student has either a wall hanging or placemat made from his own gathered leaves! A great gift for a grandparent or neighbor—or you can keep it for yourself! If your student enjoys this project, he may want to work on improving his design and consider making a set as a gift for grandparents or friends.

Issues of Human Relationships: Frugality

Miss Terwilliger wears the same dress for every special occasion—Sunday church, holidays, and social functions. She wears a simple, knitted, robin's-egg-blue dress. When fashion dictates a short skirt, she simply unravels a few inches off the bottom and then saves the yarn for the next time long skirts are in style. Then she knits the yarn back into her skirt and lengthens it once more!

Discuss with your student the concept of *frugality*. Being frugal means you don't spend money unnecessarily or wastefully. When someone is frugal, he is sometimes called "thrifty." Miss Terwilliger may seem too extreme in her frugality, (having only one good dress), but she is, at least, an excellent example of not living an excessive lifestyle.

Look for this recycling symbol on various recyclable items and at recycling stations.

Encourage your student to find ways to be thrifty. Today, we rarely save things like string or yarn, but we can recycle! This is an exceptional way to be thrifty, help the planet and reduce wastefulness. Glass, plastics and aluminum can all be recycled. Challenge your student to recycle when possible and to be on the lookout for other ways he can practice a more "frugal" lifestyle. Being wasteful and spending beyond your means shows a lack of wisdom. Miss Terwilliger was a clever woman and had learned to make do with what she had! We can all learn a few things from Miss Terwilliger!

Issues of Human Relationships: Special Occasions—Sunday Dinner

Miss Terwilliger makes her famous fried chicken every Sunday for Uncle Telemachus and every Thursday for the sheriff. You can create a special occasion with your student and prepare a fried chicken dinner with all the fixin's including mashed potatoes or potato salad, green beans, rolls, and whatever else you want. You might begin by looking in your newspaper for shopping ads from the grocery store and noting the price of chicken. You can explain the different ways that chickens are packaged: whole fryers, legs and thighs, breasts only, etc., and talk about the differences in price. Then buy the chicken, bring it home and prepare it for frying. If weather permits, taking your fried chicken dinner on a picnic is a delightful way to enjoy the fresh air—and food always tastes better outside!

You can take this concept a step further by developing your own unique weekly traditions. Just as Miss Terwilliger was known for fixing her famous fried chicken on Sundays and Thursdays, you can think up your own traditions. Perhaps you'd like to always serve waffles on Saturday morning, or always rent a movie on Saturday night. Maybe you'd enjoy always going out for ice cream on Sunday evening or always going out for hamburgers on Friday evening. The tradition you choose isn't important. What matters is developing your own, unique family traditions that build security for children and provide everyone with something special to look forward to each week—just the way Uncle Telly looked forward to dinner with Miss Terwilliger on Sundays!

Writing and Discussion Question

Miss Terwilliger's ball of yarn had to be removed through the opened side of her house! Imagine a ball of yarn that large! How would *you* have moved the ball of yarn? Write a description of at least three ways.

Miss Terwilliger won the contest! It seemed impossible! Homer knows how she did it, but the clues are very vague. Do you know how she won? Discuss some of your ideas.

Internet Connections

To view current suggested links relating to this chapter's lessons, see www.fiveinarow.com/connections.

Chapter 5–Nothing New Under the Sun (Hardly)

Parent Summary

Not much is happening in Centerburg. The county fair is over and election time hasn't quite arrived. Homer decides to go down to Uncle Ulysses' lunchroom one day and help him serve up blue-plate specials. Suddenly an unusual thing is seen in Centerburg. A stranger in a strange truck is coming down the street, rattling and banging with a huge canvas tarp covering whatever is in the back, and pulls up right in front of Uncle Ulysses' lunchroom! Who is the stranger? What is in his truck? Why are his clothes so tattered? Why is his beard so long? Before long everyone in Centerburg has heard of the strange man. They say he reminds them of Rip Van Winkle, a fictional storybook character. The man seems very shy around adults, but likes children.

Finally, the sheriff and Uncle Ulysses come up with a plan. They send Homer to get to know the fellow and find out what his intentions are in Centerburg—AND to find out what is in his truck!

Homer comes back from his investigation with interesting news. The man's name is Michael Murphy and under his canvas is his invention. It's taken him 30 years to make, but he has finally built a better mousetrap—a real mousetrap! Mr. Murphy's mousetrap plays music and entices the mice into the trap. No harm comes to the mice. As soon as Mr. Murphy is able, he releases them somewhere else.

Centerburg thinks this is a fine plan! The mayor strikes a deal with Mr. Murphy to remove all the mice in Centerburg using his musical mousetrap for only $30. The big day arrives and everyone in Centerburg shows up for the grand mouse evacuation. The children are the most enthralled with the entire spectacle! Soon all the mice in Centerburg are in Mr. Murphy's musical mousetrap and he is starting for the outskirts of town. The children, whistling along with the music, follow the truck. Suddenly, Centerburg's librarian comes running to the mayor and sheriff in a panic!

"We guessed the wrong book…not *Rip Van Winkle*, but another book, *The Pied Piper of Hamelin*!" The librarian is frantic!

Suddenly, everyone is frantic! Uncle Ulysses, the sheriff, the mayor and the librarian all jump into the sheriff's car and zoom off after the procession, screaming out the windows for the children to come back. The sheriff yells, "Let 'em go!" And that is just what Mr. Murphy does. He pulls a lever and all the mice run out of the musical mousetrap, down the ramps and back to their holes in Centerburg. Meanwhile, Homer shows the sheriff and his uncle that he and all the children had cotton in their ears so the music couldn't woo them. All is well and everyone is glad!

What we will cover in this chapter:

History and Geography: Political Parties

Language Arts: Famous Sayings—A New Phrase to Learn

Language Arts: Washington Irving and *Rip Van Winkle*

Issues of Human Relationships: Making a Good Appearance

Issues of Human Relationships: Making People Feel Comfortable

Career Paths: Law Enforcement

Lesson Activities

History and Geography: Political Parties

After the county fair, election time is nearing for Centerburg (page 94). Draw your student's attention to the line, "election time, still being a month away, the Democrats and the Republicans are still speaking to one another."

Take this opportunity to discuss with your student the two main political parties in the United States. As background, it is interesting to note that, at the founding of the United States, our forefathers made no mention of any specific parties. In fact, George Washington himself seemed opposed to such definitions, thinking they would bring division to the new country. However, as people are apt to do, different groups began to coalesce based on similar moral beliefs, economic realities and political feelings. These natural polarizations began only three years after the Constitution was written in 1787.

Thomas Jefferson led what first became known as the Democratic-Republican Party (later known as the Democrat Party), supporting a weak central government. Alexander Hamilton was at the forefront of the Federalist Party, supporting strong, influential government. These two parties were the first known political divisions within America. By 1854, the new Republican Party gained momentum over the issue of anti-slavery, and those who had been affiliated with the Federalists began to align themselves with the Republican Party. By the time Abraham Lincoln was elected in 1860, he was known as the first Republican President.

[**Teacher's Note**: Your student is probably familiar with these two political parties. If you choose, you may continue the discussion by analyzing the concept of third parties in the United States. Parties such as the Libertarians, Socialists, and Naturalists are present and vocal but have never won a presidential election. Perhaps the most significant move by any third party was led by Ross Perot in 1992 against former Presidents George Bush and Bill Clinton. Perot's Independent Party didn't win the election, but caused a tremendous dialogue nationwide and gained more respect than any third party in modern history. Perot made use of the television medium in a powerful way and hosted many "infomercials" on his policies and beliefs. Ross Perot is perhaps best remembered for his pie charts that he used to illustrate what he considered to be the country's problems. (Find some examples of pie charts in news magazines or newspapers and show them to your student. Pie charts can communicate difficult information in a visual way that is easier to understand.)

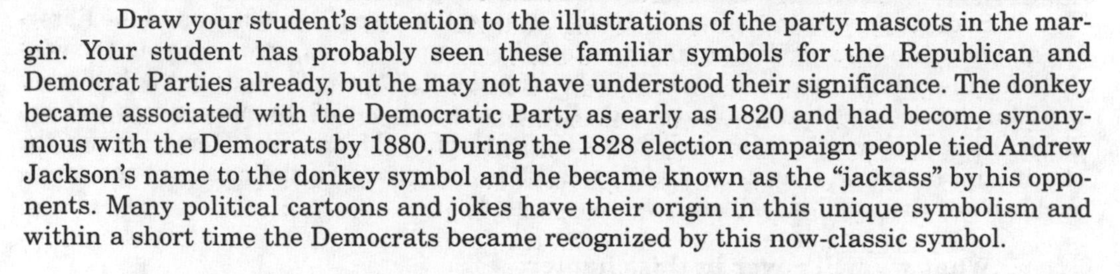

Draw your student's attention to the illustrations of the party mascots in the margin. Your student has probably seen these familiar symbols for the Republican and Democrat Parties already, but he may not have understood their significance. The donkey became associated with the Democratic Party as early as 1820 and had become synonymous with the Democrats by 1880. During the 1828 election campaign people tied Andrew Jackson's name to the donkey symbol and he became known as the "jackass" by his opponents. Many political cartoons and jokes have their origin in this unique symbolism and within a short time the Democrats became recognized by this now-classic symbol.

The Republican Party (also known as the G.O.P., "grand old party"–a self-proclaimed nickname) is recognized by the symbol of an elephant. Interestingly enough, the same political cartoonist who drew a nationally-accepted picture of the Democrat's donkey in 1880, Thomas Nast, also drew the first popular rendering of an elephant in relation to the Republican Party in 1874. Nast's first cartoon to feature this symbol showed a gigantic, obese elephant with the sign "Republican Vote" on its side. All the other animals in the picture had the names of other parties and were uncharacteristically small. It made people laugh and quickly became widely associated with the Republican Party. (For fascinating reading on America's symbols and traditions find *Fireworks, Picnics and Flags* by James Cross Giblin (Copyright 1983, Houghton Mifflin Co, ISBN 0899191746). There is a section on Thomas Nast and many other interesting bits of information, written in an enjoyable style.)

To the extent you choose, discuss with your student the differences between the two major political parties in the United States. Beyond the emotionally charged issues and family-history affiliations, the Democrats and Republicans differ over one specific, fundamental issue—government involvement. The question both parties consistently struggle with is to what extent should the government (and by extension, taxpayer dollars) be in control of individual lives? This question is a fluid, evolving concept that changes with every presidential administration.

Traditionally, the Democratic Party has believed that government should play a significant role in public and private lives, helping protect individual rights and becoming the final source to which every American can look for personal well-being. The Republicans, on the other hand, have traditionally held that government is essentially a cumbersome but necessary entity that often unnecessarily complicates the lives of individuals and that in general, "less government is better."

No one party has all the answers, and an important point to remember is that unlike other governments, the United States keeps no formal record of affiliation or membership with political parties. Thus, people can vote for a Republican president in one election and a Democratic president in the next. This freedom of political choice allows what is known as *split-ticket* voting where an individual can even vote for both parties within the same ballot.

If your student's family is actively involved in a political party, perhaps contacting the local campaign office and allowing your student to watch what goes into preparing for an election would be great. If your student is older he can help with campaigns, even before he is old enough to vote. Handing out buttons, putting up posters, and helping with mailings are all things your student can do to make a difference and allow him to become an active participant in his country's political life! Becoming involved with politics at an early age can be instrumental in developing a full understanding of America's government and our political system.

Language Arts: Famous Sayings—A New Phrase To Learn

This chapter offers a wonderful new phrase to teach you student. Famous sayings or idioms are delightful to learn and enable your student to understand more of the world around him.

On page 95, Homer is busy helping Aunt Aggie and Uncle Ulysses serve up the blue-plate specials. A blue-plate special is the term for an inexpensive restaurant meal served at a fixed price on a plate (originally it was blue). In most restaurants the blue-plate special generally changes daily, but the menu is set for the week. For example, every Monday the blue-plate special might be meatloaf with mashed potatoes and fruit salad. Every Tuesday the blue-plate special might consist of baked chicken with green beans and Jell-O®. Every Wednesday the blue-plate special might be spaghetti and meatballs with green salad and garlic toast, and so forth. Watch at diners or country restaurants in your area for blue-plate specials being offered.

[**Teacher's Note**: If your student worked on the lesson in chapter 1 of *The Boxcar Children* and designed his own imaginary restaurant and menu, encourage him to go back and add a list of blue-plate specials. What would he serve? How much would he charge?

Language Arts: Washington Irving and *Rip Van Winkle*

Everyone in Centerburg calls Michael Murphy, "Old Rip." He does seem to be a "Rip-Van-Winklish" sort of character, doesn't he? Does your student know the story of Rip Van Winkle? Does he know who wrote it?

Published in 1819 within a book of short stories entitled *The Sketch Book*, "Rip Van Winkle" is now considered a classic. Written by Washington Irving, the story is an impressionistic journey of one man's unusual experience in a small town. Irving is considered in most literary circles to be the first successful, professional American author. Born in New York City on April 3, 1783, he was the son of a wealthy merchant. Destined for a career in law, Irving soon found he was more proficient at writing.

There are dozens of adaptations and juvenile versions of *Rip Van Winkle*. If your student has the patience for more difficult literature, you might suggest that he read the original work. A scant ten pages long, the story is written in formal English and although the descriptions and narrative are stunning, they can be challenging for even the best readers.

A more practical approach might be to obtain a copy of the original text and read aloud a small paragraph to your student, so he can get a feel for Irving's style and an appreciation for his use of description. Here is a paragraph example from the original text by Washington Irving:

He now hurried forth and hastened to his old resort, the village inn—but it too was gone. A large, rickety, wooden building in its place, with great gaping windows, some of them broken and mended with old hats and petticoats, and over the door was painted, "the Union Hotel, by Jonathan Doolittle." Instead of the great tree that used to shelter the quiet little Dutch inn of yore, there now was reared a tall, naked pole, with which was singular assemblage of stars and stripes—all this was strange and incomprehensible. He recognized on the sign, however, the ruby face of King George, under which he had smoked so many a peaceful pipe; but even this was singularly metamorphosed. The red coat was changed for one of blue and buff, a sword was held in a hand instead of a scepter, the head was decorated with a cocked hat, and underneath was painted in large characters, GENERAL WASHINGTON.

Have your student pick out what he considers the most descriptive words (examples might include: rickety, naked, metamorphosed (meaning to change from one thing to another), ruby, etc.). Does he like this type of writing? After you have studied an easier version of this text, reading the original may be more enjoyable!

Interestingly enough, *Rip Van Winkle* goes far beyond being a fairy tale with witty twists and turns. It is Washington Irving's social statement on the Dutch settlers and their early roots in the New York area. Including descriptions of the Catskills, the Hudson River, the Appalachian Mountains and the early Dutch governors, it is a fascinating peek at the background of Irving himself, since this was his early childhood home.

Take some time and study Washington Irving. It will be worthwhile and interesting to both you and your student!

Issues of Human Relationships: Making a Good Appearance

Mr. Michael Murphy is making the town of Centerburg nervous with his appearance. His ripped clothes, patched jacket, uncut hair and beard are all unusual. Even his money is dirty! (page 101) The citizens begin to make judgments about Mr. Murphy based on his appearance. Talk with your student about the importance of wearing clean, decent clothes and maintaining proper personal hygiene.

It isn't important to keep up with every trend of fashion and look "picture perfect" all the time. But it is important to make a good impression when you meet people, and not be offensive in your appearance. Discuss with your student how different events dictate different clothing choices. For example, tennis shorts, shirt and sneakers would be perfect at the park or tennis courts, but would be inappropriate at a funeral!

Being aware of your appearance doesn't mean you have to be vain. Encourage your student to dress in a way that makes him, as well as those he is with, feel comfortable. In this way, people won't be offended and your student will have a more pleasant life with those around him. Perhaps your student has heard the saying, "Always make a good first impression." Wearing clean, appropriate clothing and attending to our personal hygiene is one important way to make sure our first impressions are positive.

If you think your student would enjoy it, write down three or four different "situations" (church, picnic, swimming, etc.) on slips of paper. Now have your student select a folded slip of paper. Give him three minutes to go and select an appropriate wardrobe for the event. You can even have him put the clothes on just for fun, if you'd like! Now discuss his choice. If he is enjoying this activity, allow him to select several additional situations and dress appropriately.

Issues of Human Relationships: Making People Feel Comfortable

Mr. Michael Murphy is very shy (page 99). He has no friends in Centerburg, and he knows he looks different from everyone else. Uncle Ulysses tries to talk to him, but doesn't want to make him feel uncomfortable. Everyone else in town just stares at Mr. Murphy. What does your student do when he is around someone who is very shy? Or perhaps your student is shy himself.

Learning to make people feel comfortable is an important life skill. When we are around someone who is shy, being able to ask interesting questions and approach them in a quiet manner can make all the difference in the world. Learning to make jokes on ourselves can sometimes be a simple way to ease tension and bring someone else out of their shell.

Talk with your student about times he has been the shy one and times when he has been the bold one. Coming to the realization that we all feel bashful sometimes can be an encouraging discovery! Everyone has been shy at one time or another and it's just a question of how we handle it in ourselves and with others.

If you wish, do some role-playing games with this issue. Acting out scenarios often helps us realize what we're doing right with people and what we need to work on. Have your student play the shy person and approach him in several different ways—staring, making fun, pointing, ignoring, talking, smiling, introducing yourself, including him in an activity, etc. It will become very apparent what is pleasant and what is not when you're shy. Now switch roles with your student and have him try it.

If your student is shy himself, this may encourage him to become bolder. Relating to others and learning kind, appropriate behavior is vital to making and maintaining friendships throughout life!

Challenge your student to work on this issue in his own relationships and get updates on how it's going! Developing interpersonal skills like this takes practice, but the result is very rewarding!

Career Paths: Law Enforcement

The sheriff in Centerburg works hard at his job. Does your student think being a sheriff would be an interesting job? Why or why not? Law enforcement is a difficult but rewarding career. Talk with your student about the different job options in this interesting field.

Share with your student the two most common ways a person can become a police officer—civil law enforcement and military law enforcement. If a person goes through the military police (MP) program, his education and training are paid for in exchange for military service. You can also become a police officer by going through a civil police academy program. Ranging in duration from six months tofour years, such courses are offered by hundreds of colleges in criminology, psychology, forensics, criminal intelligence and sociology. There are also courses on how to handle a wide variety of weapons.

Within civil law enforcement there are four main divisions. City police departments patrol and maintain order within a city's limits. County sheriffs (just like the sheriff in Centerburg) protect and guard anything within their county lines. State police (called state troopers) have the responsibility for an entire state. Generally, state troopers work on cases involving criminals at large (the criminal might be located anywhere, beyond county jurisdiction) and enforce traffic laws on the major highways (highway patrol). Interestingly, Hawaii is the only state in the United States which does not have a state police department.

Perhaps the most elite police forces in the United States are the federal law enforcement agencies. The two most prestigious federal groups are the Federal Bureau of Investigation (FBI) which enforces federal law, and the Secret Service, which protects the president, the president's family, former presidents and their families, and other government officials.

In order to be a police officer, candidates must be physically fit and have great stamina. The working hours are long and often irregular. A person wanting to be a police officer should have a thorough understanding of the law, be methodical in his personal work habits, be courageous and have a strong sense of compassion tempered with justice.

Encourage your student to try to arrange a visit with an area police station. An interview or conversation with an officer who is actually "on the beat" is a great way to get a first-hand look at what the job actually entails. Some agencies will give tours of their facilities. Encourage your student to write a full report on his studies about this interesting career field. If you successfully arrange a tour, as always, try to come up with several specific questions you'd like to have answered.

Writing and Discussion Question

We've discussed the fact that it's important to be kind to strangers like Mr. Murphy. But we also need to be cautious around strangers. What are some of the things that you *shouldn't* do with strangers?

Internet Connections

To view current suggested links relating to this chapter's lessons, see www.fiveinarow.com/connections.

Chapter 6–Wheels of Progress

Parent Summary

Miss Naomi Enders, the nice, rich lady who helped make all those doughnuts, is helping Centerburg once again. Only this time, she truly is being helpful! Along with Uncle Ulysses' help (a lover of all labor-saving devices), Miss Enders has decided to share her wealth with Centerburg by building a new suburb called Enders Heights. The suburb will feature nice homes at affordable prices. Miss Enders wants everyone in Centerburg to have a home. But this won't just be any suburb. Uncle Ulysses convinces Miss Enders to build all the houses identically. In this way each home, street and the entire neighborhood can be built in a systematic, time-saving fashion. He tells her it is the "modern" way to build homes—mass production! Miss Enders loves the idea and the building soon begins.

Each house in Enders Heights is just alike, complete with the same yard design, fireplace, painting *over* the fireplace and more. Every Enders Heights home is identical.

With a few mishaps along the way, the neighborhood is soon finished and all of Centerburg turns out for the "One Hundred and Fifty Years of Centerburg Progress Week" celebration!

What we will cover in this chapter:

History and Geography: Women's Suffrage—A Brief Introduction

History and Geography: People's Signature Trademarks

Language Arts: Famous Sayings—Two New Phrases to Learn

Language Arts: New Vocabulary Words—Ideas for Application

Fine Arts: Design and Make Your Own Checkerboard

Fine Arts: *Whistler's Mother* and James Abbott McNeill Whistler

Issues of Human Relationships: Habitat for Humanity and HUD

Career Paths: Landscape Architecture

Lesson Activities

History and Geography: Women's Suffrage—A Brief Introduction

"Uncle Ulysses' pet theories had broken up as many pinochle and checker games as arguing about the World Series and Woman Suffrage put together" (page 130). Does your student know about Women's Suffrage? This chapter of *Homer Price* presents an opportunity to introduce this important historical subject.

If you wish, begin with a definition of suffrage. *Suffrage* means the right to vote. A person who works for this goal is called a suffragist. There was a time in America's history when women were not allowed the fundamental right of voting. Two women, Elizabeth Cady Stanton and Susan B. Anthony, were at the forefront of the women's fight for the right to vote. Along with thousands of other women, these two courageous females led the way to the signing of the 19th amendment.

The women handed out flyers, gave lectures and picketed each election in which they were not allowed to vote. The opposition to women's voting was great. Men believed women didn't have the intelligence or responsibility to handle voting for important government officials. Men also felt that the husband should represent the wife in all legal matters—that a woman couldn't make her own decisions.

Two organizations were formed to fight these myths and beliefs. The National Woman Suffrage Association (led by Susan B. Anthony and Elizabeth Cady Stanton) was a radical group, focused on achieving a national amendment to the constitution. Another organization, the American Woman Suffrage Association, was led by Lucy Stone and her husband Henry Blackwell. This group shared similar beliefs with that of the National Association, but felt the goals would be better reached through a more conservative state-by-state approach. The fight for freedom was not without a price. Women suffragists were beaten, starved, jailed and taken from their families for "illegal" activity. And yet, the bravery of these women was finally realized through the victory of the 19th Amendment. Passed August 18, 1920, the amendment states: *The right of citizens of the United States to vote shall not be denied or abridged by the United States or by any state because of gender.* To this day, the 19th Amendment is known as the Susan B. Anthony Amendment.

Unfortunately several nations still deny women the right to vote. All located in the Middle East, these nations govern without the representation of *all* of their citizens.

For more information on this fascinating part of our history as a people, go to your local library and locate more books on the topic.

All students, both male and female, should have an understanding of this important milestone in our nation's history.

History and Geography: People's Signature Trademarks

Does your student remember what Thomas Edison's personal trademark was? Right! He pulled at his eyebrow (*Beyond Five in a Row,* Volume 1, *Thomas Edison*, chapter 5 lessons). Can your student tell you from this chapter what Uncle Ulysses' is? Stroking his chin! If you did not do the lesson on Edison, go back and read through it. If you did, just mention to your student this is yet another example of someone's signature trademark.

Language Arts: Famous Sayings—Two New Phrases to Learn

Freddy wants to help in the lunchroom (page 126). Homer says, "Uncle Ulysses would like it. He always says the more help the merrier, but Aunt Aggie is a 'Too many cooks spoil the soup' sort of person." Ask your student if he knows what Homer means? Take this opportunity to share two new famous idioms with your student.

The first, "the more the merrier," is a common saying and it means just what it says. The more people we have involved in the project, the more fun it is! That does sound like Uncle Ulysses, doesn't it?

Homer uses the second phrase to describe Aunt Aggie. "Too many cooks spoil the soup" means the more people who are involved, the more chaotic and messed up things become.

What kind of a person is your student? Is he a "more the merrier" person who enjoys working in groups, or is he a "too many cooks spoil the soup" kind of personality who works best when left alone? What kind of person are you? Talk with your student about issues of flexibility and how both philosophies can be correct in different situations.

Encourage your student to be listening for these common sayings in future conversations. And now that he knows them, he can use them himself!

Language Arts: New Vocabulary Words—Ideas for Application

This chapter is unusually rich with new vocabulary words for your student. Take notice of the word list at the end of this lesson and use them for both spelling exercise and definition comprehension. To give your student more learning retention, be looking for ways to use the words in sentences throughout the day. Encourage your student to try to use them in *his* conversation as well! If you wish, you might have your student write a sentence for each word, using it in context. Learning a new word apart from usage and context is of no value. Challenge your student to broaden his vocabulary and to try using a few "fifty-cent words" to enrich his vocabulary.

Fine Arts: Design and Make Your Own Checkerboard

Uncle Ulysses and the sheriff sure do play checkers a lot, don't they? Even this chapter makes reference to them (page 130). Why not have your student make his own checkerboard? This game is entertaining and can be as simple or complex as your ability and learning level allows.

The basic board, regardless of how it's made, must involve 64 alternating colored squares.

Each player must have 12 playing pieces. Traditionally red and black discs, these pieces can actually be whatever your student wishes. Oreos and vanilla wafers, pennies and dimes, different colored jelly beans, different colored pieces of paper, stones—whatever he chooses!

To make the actual board, your options for construction are endless! If your student enjoys working with wood, perhaps he would like to make an actual board and wooden checkers. Your student can paint the squares with fabric paint on canvas and make a "roll-away, travel" checkers set. With that type of board, your student could even make cloth playing pieces. By laying sticks or twigs in a grid pattern on a piece of cardboard and forming 64 squares, your student could make an "au naturel" playing board. Stones or seedpods would make great playing pieces for that set.

Let your student's creative juices flow with this activity! And the great part is, after the board is complete the real fun begins—playing checkers! Your student will love the game, and remind him to think of Uncle Ulysses and the barbershop when he plays.

Fine Arts: *Whistler's Mother* and James Abbott McNeill Whistler

On page 136, there is a description of the décor in the new houses in Enders Heights. The book tells us that every house has a print of *Whistler's Mother* over every fireplace. Is your student familiar with *Whistler's Mother*? Does he know who painted it?

Take this opportunity to share with your student about one of the most famous paintings in the world. Artist James Abbott McNeill Whistler (1834-1903) was an American artist, but spent most of his life in Europe. Known for his talent in art, quick wit in conversation, and fearless nature, Whistler took on celebrity status quickly.

Look in your encyclopedia or an art history book you've obtained from the library, and show your student the painting everyone talks about.

Commonly called *Whistler's Mother*, the painting's real name is *Arrangement in Gray and Black No. 1: Portrait of the Artist's Mother*. Finished in 1872, the painting features extremely matte, non-dimensional forms and is off-center. His mother is featured sitting in a stiff, wooden chair, with her feet up on a little stool. Hands laid in lap, the woman appears to be extremely controlled—almost corpse-like. The etched strokes and dull colors became synonymous with Whistler's style.

Does your student like this painting? Why or why not? As an interesting side note, Whistler, in his day, became as well known for his interior design projects as his paintings.

Your student will hear *Whistler's Mother* mentioned many times throughout his life. The name has become not only well known in relation to the painting, but has evolved into an idiom used to describe someone who is acting extremely stiff and reserved. For example, "Well, you're sure acting like Whistler's Mother."

Encourage your student to research more of John Abbott McNeill Whistler's work if he is interested.

Issues of Human Relationships: Habitat for Humanity and HUD

Miss Naomi Enders is certainly generous, isn't she? Her desire is to provide people with homes (page 28). Miss Enders tells Uncle Ulysses, "I could rent them reasonably to deserving families." Does your student think this is unusual? Actually, there are several programs with the same motive as Miss Enders. The two primary organizations are called Habitat for Humanity and HUD (Housing and Urban Development).

Habitat for Humanity (HFH) is a wonderful outreach program! Organized by chapter, HFH if located in every state in the union. There is even an international branch of Habitat for Humanity (HFHI). HFH workers are almost 100% volunteers. HFH invites anyone from children to the elderly to help them help others. Volunteers need a heart to serve and a willingness to work hard, and get dirty.

Habitat's goal is to provide decent, clean, well-built homes to low-income families. This goal is accomplished both by finding homes that are run-down or condemned and fixing them up, and by building new homes.

Another similar organization in terms of goal, is the U.S. Department for Housing and Urban Development, known as HUD. Unlike HFH, HUD is a government program and is thus funded primarily by tax dollars. HUD identifies low-income neighborhoods and renovates houses available for sale. Then, because of the taxpayer assistance, they are able to provide the homes for an extremely reasonable rate to needy families.

This may all seem unconnected and far away to your student. Help him put it into perspective for a moment. Have him imagine never having a yard to play in—never having the option to have a garden—never being able to have a pet, etc. Many options are only possible when you own your home. For children who grow up in housing projects (government funded mass apartment complexes) and unsafe homes, the option of having a freshly painted, sturdy, safe home of their own is a miracle.

If you or your student is interested, investigate local Habitat for Humanity chapters in your area and see what you can do to help make a difference. If nothing else, introducing your student to these humanitarian efforts will birth within him a greater sense of compassion and community-awareness. Miss Enders had the right idea!

Career Paths: Landscape Architecture

Enders Heights is constructed so quickly! "Each front yard had its own climbing rose bush, two dwarf cedars, and maple trees, all planted and sodded round about" (page 136). Who decides where the trees go? Who designs the yards?

Sometimes the person who owns the house does these types of "home improvements," but often a person called a *landscape architect* is called in to do the design work.

Ask your student if he has ever heard of a landscape architect? Landscape architecture is a growing field and holds many career opportunities.

In general, a landscape architect plans and designs outdoor areas. He might design a city park, a walking path, a municipal fountain or a residential neighborhood. The difference between an *architect* and a *landscape architect* is this—the architect designs the actual buildings and a landscape architect designs the outdoor areas surrounding the building and helps determine what effect the building will have on the environment.

Landscape architects go to college where they work toward a B.L.A. (Bachelor of Landscape Architecture) degree. Master's degrees are also available for those who wish to attend graduate school. Courses you would be required to take include art (drawing, drafting, and sculpting), environmental science, architectural technology, botany, human behavior and media communications. Landscape architecture encompasses a wide variety of academic disciplines.

Have your student draw a simple plan for your home or perhaps an imaginary home. Now have him develop a landscape plan to compliment the building. Encourage him to explore the use of trees, shrubberies, flowers, walkways, ponds, fountains and more. More advanced students can research individual species for their plant material. They might even be interested in building a three-dimensional model of their landscape design.

If your student enjoys being outside, knows and enjoys plants, likes working with people, is concerned about the environment and has a talent for drawing, this career might be worth further exploration!

Writing and Discussion Questions

Everyone in Enders Heights lived in a house just like the next one. What would that be like? Would you like to live in a "cookie-cutter" home like that? Why or why not? Discuss some of the advantages and disadvantages of living in a house identical to your neighbor.

Vocabulary Words

suffrage: the right to vote

suburb: a residential district on or near the outskirts of a city

urban: constituting or comprising a city or town

rural: constituting or comprising the country life

receptive: able or ready to receive new things and ideas

imperative: absolutely necessary; urgent; compelling

arbitrate: a decision based on judgment not rules (an arbitrator)

architect: a person who designs and draws plans for buildings

landscape architect: the art and profession of planning or changing the natural scenery of a place for a desired purpose

[**Teacher's Note**: Did you or your student notice that there are other famous names included in the characters of the story of *Homer Price*? We talked about Homer's name being the name of a famous Greek poet but there are two other names that are significant if you know your Greek writings: Ulysses and Telemachus. Ulysses (in Latin, Odysses in Greek) was a brave hero during the Trojan Wars according to Greek mythology. His son was named Telemachus. So, Robert McCloskey borrowed heavily from these famous Greek myths to find the names for his characters. Your student will appreciate how authors use both imagination *and* appropriation in writing their stories! It also shows why learning about the Greek and Roman myths helps clarify literary allusions and adds fun to reading.]

Internet Connections

To view current suggested links relating to this chapter's lessons, see www.fiveinarow.com/connections.

BETSY ROSS
DESIGNER OF OUR FLAG
BY ANN WEIL

Chapter 1–The Choice

Parent Summary

Our story of Betsy Griscom (Ross) begins in 1758. Betsy was born in 1752, so our first chapter takes place when she is six years old. Betsy is sitting at the dinner table with her mother, her father and her seven brothers and sisters. Two more siblings are still too young to sit at the table. Soon there will be twelve people. Whew! Betsy wonders how they will all fit. Her father says he will have to build another, larger table. Betsy offers to help her father when the time comes, but her brother George exclaims, "Thee is a girl and thee is too little." Betsy is hurt and confused. Why can't she work with wood and tools? She decides to prove to George that she is old enough and she can do "boy's work."

Going to the woodshed, Betsy decides to build a doll table. Using her father's saw, Betsy soon becomes frustrated and ends up cutting her finger! Running to the house, Betsy shows her mother her injured finger. While Mrs. Griscom bandages the finger, she talks with Betsy about the dangers of working with saws and tools. "A saw is not for a little girl to play with," says Betsy's mother. Now Betsy feels truly awful. It was bad enough for George to tell her she couldn't do something, but her mother too?

Mrs. Griscom recognizes Betsy's angst and gets a beautiful silver thimble. She places the thimble on Betsy's other hand. Then she talks with Betsy about the importance of being true to yourself and not doing things just to prove others (like George) wrong. Betsy decides she likes building doll furniture, but she likes sewing just as much. Now, she knows to listen to her own heart!

What we will cover in this chapter:

History and Geography: Thee and Thou

Language Arts: Personification

Language Arts: Different Literary Voices

Fine Arts: Increasing Sensory Awareness

Issues of Human Relationships: Parental Decisions

Issues of Human Relationships: Learning How to Respond to Judgments

Lesson Activities

History and Geography: Thee and Thou

The first thing your student probably noticed when reading this chapter is the use of thee and thou in the Griscom's conversations. This form of speech is often referred to as "King James English" and was used by the people who were a part of the religious group known as Quakers. At this point, simply explain to your student that the Griscom family talks differently because of the cultural and religious beliefs. Later, in chapter 3, Quakers are covered in greater detail.

Language Arts: Personification

"Betsy thought of the whining old saw that had hit her over the head and bitten her finger" (page 21). Have your student look at this sentence. Can a saw whine? Can a saw hit someone over the head? Can a saw bite a person? No.

The author, Ann Weil, is making use of a literary device called *personification*. Share with your student this term and discuss its meaning. Personification is the term for giving an inanimate (non-living) thing, idea or quality the characteristics of a person. Used many times in poetry, personification also gives life and spark to ordinary *prose*. Without the use of personification, Betsy's saw only made a funny sound, fell off the shelf and then accidentally cut her finger (which was her fault). But isn't it more interesting the way the author describes it?

Encourage your student to try to implement this device in his own writing. To begin, have him write several single sentences using personification. For example: 1) The car *howled* as it came to a stop, 2) The sponge *drank up* all the spilled milk, 3) The radio *chattered* happily throughout the afternoon.

Your student's writing and conversation will come to life as he begins to use literary devices like personification!

Language Arts: Different Literary Voices

On page 20 Mrs. Griscom is talking to Betsy. She says, "I'm talking about a little girl named Betsy. Does she want to use a saw?"

That's an interesting use of personal pronouns, isn't it? Why didn't Mrs. Griscom say, "Does thee want to use a saw?" (Or, in contemporary English, why didn't she say, "Do you want to use a saw?")

We can write in *first person, second person* or *third person*. First person writing always uses the personal pronoun *I*. Autobiographies, diaries and eye-witness accounts are commonly written in first person. "*I* went to the baseball game last night and *I* had a wonderful time."

Second person uses the personal pronoun *you*. We use second person primarily in writing dialogue, giving directions or in personal letters. "*You* keep going south for one mile. Then *you* turn left."

Third person uses the personal pronouns *he, she, it, them* or *they*. Most narrative prose is written in third person. "After dinner, *they* all went out for a walk. *They* walked until well after dark."

Normally, when we ask someone a direct question we would use second person: "Do you want to use a saw?" But Mrs. Griscom changes to third person, referring to Betsy as if she were someone else standing nearby watching, "Does she want to use a saw?" It's not clear why the author chose to change person from second to third for Mrs. Griscom's question, but it's an interesting variation in speech, isn't it?

As an exercise, have your student try writing a simple story (1-3 paragraphs) about the topic of your choice. First have him write it in first person, perhaps as a diary. "The first time *I* ever went camping *I*..." Then have him rewrite the same story in second person, perhaps as a personal letter to a friend. "The first time *you* ever went camping *you*..." Finally, have him write it a third time in third person, perhaps as a short story. "The first time *he* ever went camping *he*..."

Fine Arts: Drama Exercise: Increasing Sensory Awareness

Betsy could hear her mother walk down the hall, into the bedroom, open a drawer, close the drawer, walk down the stairs, through the hall again and then through the kitchen (page 21).

Betsy is using her sense of *hearing*. What are the five senses? (Seeing, hearing, touching, tasting and smelling.) How did Betsy know her mother was in the hall? Or on the stairs? Perhaps the floor creaks in the Griscom's hall and her mother's heels make a click on each wooden step. Ask your student if he can think of other ways Betsy might have been able to decipher where her mother was in the house.

Learning to increase our sense of "awareness" can be interesting, informative and entertaining. Help your student learn more about his sense of hearing by doing a simple exercise used in many drama classes.

[**Teacher's Note**: This lesson works best during a time of year when the windows can be open.]

Begin by having your student lie on the floor. Spend a few moments in silence and then instruct your student to listen and see what he can hear within the limits of the room. Then have him "stretch" his ears and see what he can hear within the *building*. Have him "strain" his hearing a little further and see what he can hear immediately *outside* the house or building. Finally, what can he hear farther down the street? How far away can he hear specific things? Then have him filter his hearing back to immediately outside the house or building, then inside the building, and finally back inside the room.

Each of these steps should be separated by approximately 30-60 seconds of silence so your student can listen. What could he hear? By concentrating and being quiet, your student was probably aware of many more sounds than he is generally accustomed to hearing. Now, if you wish, pose a hypothetical question to your student. What different sounds would he have heard if he lived somewhere else? In the innercity? On a farm? By the ocean? In China? In the wilderness? What would other children in different parts of the world hear if they did the same exercise? Interesting, isn't it?

If your student enjoys this sensory awareness exercise, you can develop more activities to help sharpen the other four senses. For example, blindfold your student and have him taste different things and tell you what they are. Can he decipher the difference between lemon, lime, orange and grapefruit? Another activity could be to provide him with objects of differing textures and see if he can tell you what they are while blindfolded. In this case, stretch his imagination by asking him to develop more intricate descriptions of what he is feeling.

For example, if you lay a square of carpet in front of him, he'll probably say, "That's carpet." Encourage him to describe exactly what it feels like on his fingertips, like, "I'm feeling soft, moveable fibers. When I run my fingers one way it feels smooth, but the other direction feels like little "hooks" catching on my fingernails. When I run my fingers back and forth quickly, the friction makes my fingertips hot."

This type of observation in your student will increase as you do these exercises more frequently. Encourage your student to use his senses to the best of his ability!

Issues of Human Relationships: Parental Decisions

Mrs. Griscom tells her daughter that cutting saws are not things for little girls to play with. Later in the chapter, it becomes obvious Mrs. Griscom's statement doesn't reflect feminine stereotyping, but instead is based on Betsy's age. She is too young to use a cutting saw.

Explain to your student that it is part of a parent's job (not a sibling's, like George) to decide when things are appropriate and at what age. It is important to learn to respect our parents' decisions and understand that they come from a love for us and a concern for our welfare.

Does your student think it's appropriate for Betsy (at age six) to be using a cutting saw? Challenge your student to be mindful of his parents' concerns and respect the decisions and boundaries they place on him.

Issues of Human Relationships: Learning How to Respond to Judgments

Betsy's brother George is wrong to tell his sister she can't make a table, because she is too little and a girl (page 14). People often make judgments about us. Whether those judgements are justified or not, it is *how we respond* to them that is important.

Draw your student's attention to the passage that describes Betsy's response (page 14). She stamps her foot and says, in a petulant manner, "I can make a table or anything else I want." Ask your student if this response was right?

If we think about it, Betsy's response is the way we wish we could respond sometimes, but it isn't a gracious or appropriate way to act. It would have been better for Betsy to have said, "I think I'm pretty good at making things, George."

Encourage your student to monitor his responses to difficult situations and other people's judgments. When our parents tell us to do something, it is as important to respond respectfully as it is to fulfill the request. Becoming aware of how we feel emotionally and how we respond verbally is an important life skill. Challenge your student to think about this topic more and perhaps discuss with him situations when you have responded poorly as well. Knowing adults wrestle with these same issues helps young people acknowledge them in themselves.

Writing and Discussion Question

Betsy decided that she was "glad she was herself." What are some of the things about yourself that you're glad about?

Internet Connections

To view current suggested links relating to this chapter's lessons, see www.fiveinarow.com/connections.

Chapter 2–The Sour Dough

Parent Summary

Baking day has arrived! Betsy is thrilled to help her mother make the family's bread. George, the younger brother, wants to help too, but baking is Betsy's special time with her mother. To make the bread rise, the Griscoms use a special sourdough starter, which dates back several generations to Mrs. Griscom's grandmother. When Betsy's mother married, she took some of the starter, just as her mother had before her. And someday, Betsy will take some of the sourdough with her, linking hundreds of years and thousands of loaves together. A very special thing!

Just as the bread begins to rise, the baby starts to cry and Mrs. Griscom asks Betsy to finish up. Betsy is happy to do it and after an added admonition from her mother, remembers to set aside some of the sourdough for next time. As the bread continues to rise, Betsy plays with George for awhile. Later on, Mrs. Griscom cannot find the sourdough Betsy set aside for next time. Where is it? Betsy is sure she took some out. Does George have it? No. Did it fall on the floor? No. Betsy is panic stricken. If they cannot find the starter, the link to her family's past will be forever broken. Just as she is about to give up, they find the little piece of dough under a bowl on the table. Laughing and thankful, the Griscoms' bread is saved!

What we will cover in this chapter:

History and Geography: Building a Heritage

History and Geography: Sourdough and the Pioneers

Fine Arts: Sourdough Bread Baking

Fine Arts: Making Your Own Corncob Doll

Issues of Human Relationships: Finishing What You Start

Lesson Activities

History and Geography: Building a Heritage

The Griscoms have a meaningful (and delicious) link to their ancestors (page 32). Betsy is aware of how irreplaceable the sourdough starter would be if it were ever lost. This leavening legacy is a wonderful example for your student of a heritage.

Every family has a heritage, including the country they're from, the traditional food they eat, the places they've shopped for years, the neighborhood they've always lived in and so forth. Sometimes families live in the same house for generations. Farms are often handed down to children and frequently a family's heritage is "the family business." For example, a family may run a restaurant and then hand the business down to the children and their children's children.

What is your family's heritage? Why not work on developing a more clearly defined heritage? Sourdough starter can certainly be something used today, if you love baking. Flowers can be a special legacy by saving bulbs or seeds harvested each year for the next. Writing songs together as a family or working for a specific charity year after year. Whatever you choose to begin or already recognize as a part of your family's heritage, encourage your student to appreciate the heart-warming feelings it can instill. And remind your student, someday he will be able to share the heritage with his children and grandchildren!

If your student seems interested, many projects can branch off of this discussion—mapping out your family tree, discovering or designing your family's crest, making a cookbook of your family's favorite recipes, making a scrapbook of your family for a grandparent, or assembling a time capsule of your family's favorite things to be opened at a later date (the time capsule can include poems, recipes, favorite music on cassette, a video tape of the family, letters, photos, a newspaper of the day, etc.).

It is never too late to begin building a family heritage—start today!

History and Geography: Sourdough and the Pioneers

The use of sourdough starters as the leavening agent in bread making has existed since ancient history. In more recent times, the pioneers in America relied on this type of leavening carrying precious bowls of sourdough starter cushioned in quilts or bags of flour, or even snuggled inside one's coat for warmth! Sourdough leavening is not the same as the type of packaged yeast we use today. It is a *wild* yeast made from differing ingredients, but basically flour (of some kind), a sweetener (such as sugar, sorghum, or honey), and liquid (such as water or milk). This mixture is left open to the air and wild yeast spores, which float in the air, fall on the ingredients and begin to grow. After a time, a small amount of this mixture, when added to bread ingredients, will cause the bread to rise. Loaves of sourdough bread are chewier and crustier than bread made with packaged commercial yeast. Each time a baker uses a portion of the sourdough starter, he replenishes the ingredients and allows it to continue growing so there will be more for the next loaf. If a family lost their starter, they would have to borrow some or begin the process of creating a starter over again. Because it took up to eight days for the starter to be ready, losing or killing your starter was a sad situation! That meant the family had no fresh bread, pancakes, biscuits, etc., for a week or more! That's one of the reasons why Betsy and her mother were so upset at the prospect of losing their starter.

Fine Arts: Sourdough Bread Baking

If you would like to try making some sourdough bread, you are in for an adventure! The wild yeast in sourdough is not as reliable as commercial yeast. Each loaf may turn out a bit different. But as you work with it, find books at your library with additional information and learn about its rich history and chemistry. You will have a great time. Find a good bread baking book and try making your own starter as well as using your starter in a good sourdough bread recipe. The learning opportunities are amazing! Even if you do not choose to try making sourdough bread, find a loaf in the bread or bakery section of your grocery. Try it out with your student. Sourdough is good toasted, too!

Fine Arts: Making Your Own Corncob Doll

While busily looking for the sourdough, Betsy comes across a *corncob doll* that has been missing for nearly a week. Does your student know what a corncob doll is? Throughout history, unique things have been used to make toys and dolls for children. In pioneer days in America, people used corncobs as an inexpensive base for a homemade doll. Children often made their own dolls and designed outfits, faces and names for each one. Why not help your student make his own corncob doll? The doll can be a cowboy, an Indian, a fancy city doll, an alien, anything your student wishes! Clothing can be made from felt or cloth. Your student can draw "designs" for the doll before you begin construction. One of the best parts of this project is eating the corn on the cob. Now, let the cobs dry for a few days while you work on designs. Have fun!

Issues of Human Relationships: Finishing What You Start

Betsy certainly enjoys baking day! She loves the feel of the dough and the time spent with her mother. She also likes to play and George waits for her on baking days so that she can play with him! After Betsy helps her mother by finishing up the bread, she leaves to play with her brother (page 29). Her mother organizes the kitchen again and washes the dishes, sweeps the floor and scrapes down the worktable. When we begin any project (building a model, cooking, planting a garden, drawing, practicing an instrument) it is important to finish what we start. Cleaning up, reorganizing and putting things back in their proper place are all part of the "finishing" process. Knowing to "clean up what you mess up" is a sign of maturity. Challenge your student to practice this principle in his own life and he will feel better about his projects and himself!

Writing and Discussion Question

What are some of the things that you think are a heritage in your family? Are there some new traditions that you would like to start in order to enrich your family's heritage?

Internet Connections

To view current suggested links relating to this chapter's lessons, see www.fiveinarow.com/connections.

Chapter 3–Peppermint Stick Candy

Parent Summary

Betsy's first day of school has finally arrived! She is so excited! Betsy stops and tells the owner of the neighborhood grocery market, Mr. Grant, how exciting it is to go to school for the very first time. He tells her if she'll stop by his store on the way to school, he'll give her a peppermint stick. Betsy is filled with joy. New school clothes made just for her, her first day of school and a peppermint stick!

As Betsy and her other sisters get ready for school, George is sad that he is too young to go as well. Betsy rushes off with the girls, quickly saying goodbye to George, and heads off to see Mr. Grant and get her promised candy. The red and white glistening sugar candy is so beautiful and Betsy can't wait to bite into it. After all, the Griscom children don't get candy often. But suddenly, her little brother's face in the window flashes into Betsy's mind. Without saying a word, Betsy turns and runs back to her house and thrusts the candy into George's hand.

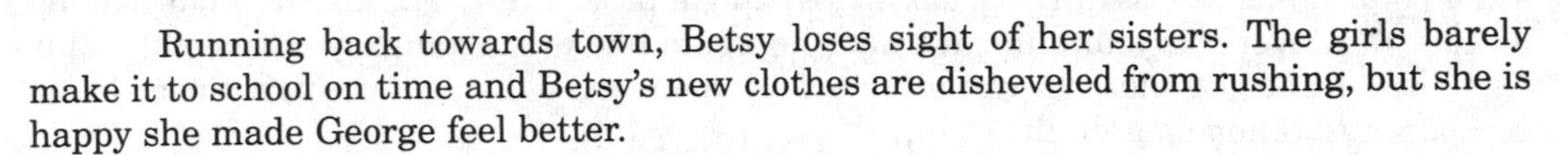

Running back towards town, Betsy loses sight of her sisters. The girls barely make it to school on time and Betsy's new clothes are disheveled from rushing, but she is happy she made George feel better.

What we will cover in this chapter:

[**Teacher's Note**: It might be fun to have a few peppermint sticks on hand to give to your student when this chapter is completed! Perhaps he will say, "Thank thee very much!"]

History and Geography: Quakers and the Church of Friends

Issues of Human Relationships: A Lifetime of "First Times"

Issues of Human Relationships: Caring for the Feelings of Others

Lesson Activities

History and Geography: Quakers and the Church of Friends

Nice Mr. Grant gives Betsy a peppermint stick for her first day of school. Unlike the Griscoms, Mr. Grant doesn't use words like thee and thou when he is speaking (page 37). This is because Mr. Grant isn't a Quaker. What's a Quaker? Has your student ever heard of this religious group?

The Religious Society of Friends, or the Quakers, was founded in England in the late 1600s by a man named George Fox. Fox became inspired to begin preaching and soon had a following of people who shared his views. Interestingly enough, the term Quaker was actually a derogatory term coined by Fox's opponents and was derived from Fox's belief that people should "tremble [quake] at the Word of the Lord."

Quakers believe in every lay person's ability to listen and respond to the Lord. Because of this loose organizational style, the Religious Society of Friends is able to make an impact all over the world in many different cultures.

The most significant defining features of the Quaker faith are 1) a simple lifestyle, 2) pacifism, 3) emphasis on education and learning, and 4) equality for all people.

Betsy's family lives in Philadelphia, Pennsylvania. In 1682, a Quaker named William Penn came to America from England and founded the colony of Pennsylvania as a refuge for Quakers escaping religious persecution in England. The Griscom family lived within these roots of faith.

Issues of Human Relationships: A Lifetime of "First Times"

Betsy's first day of school has finally arrived! Life is full of "first times." Certain activities are important milestones in your student's life. Walking, talking, riding a bicycle, the first day of school, driving a car, his first real job, and so many more moments in life are special and exciting! Growing up is sometimes a scary and uncertain prospect, but it is also full of interesting and new experiences.

Share with your student a few of your favorite or memorable "milestones." And when those moments occur in your student's life help him cherish them and celebrate!

If your student is interested, make a scrapbook of "First Times" with him of his life up to this point. Perhaps you can begin the book from a point in time before he can remember (his first words, first steps, etc.) by gathering information from his baby book, and then allow him to continue to add to it as he gets older. Somewhere in this book, it might be interesting for your student to keep a running list of things he wants to try at some point in his life: sky diving, sailing, writing a book, running a marathon, or baking a cake. Whatever it is your student thinks he would like to try someday can be put on his list. Then, as he gets older, he can mark achievements off of his list and add a page to his scrapbook to commemorate the event.

This project can extend into a lifelong project and provide your student with both goals for the future and memories of the past.

Issues of Human Relationships: Caring for the Feelings of Others

Poor George! We all know what it feels like to be left out of something. George desperately wants to go to school, too! Draw your student's attention to the meaning behind Betsy's action of giving her brother the peppermint stick. Children during that time of history (and certainly Quaker children) were rarely given candy. And imagine—peppermint sticks seem to be Betsy's favorite candy!

On page 41 we read about Betsy thinking about the delicious candy and the taste on her tongue. She is just about to bite into the precious treat when she thinks about her little brother. What a kind and gracious thing to do. Betsy defers her own pleasure and provides George with something special for his day, too! Encourage your student to think about the feelings of others and to be on the lookout for ways to brighten their days!

Writing and Discussion Question

Why do you think Betsy took the peppermint candy back home to George?

Internet Connections

To view current suggested links relating to this chapter's lessons, see www.fiveinarow.com/connections.

Chapter 4–The Wagon Ride

Parent Summary

The Griscoms have a new regular visitor—a young man named Edwin Bolton. Edwin walks Debby home from meeting and then comes over to their house. Betsy loves Edwin! Everyone welcomes him into the family. A few months go by and one day Betsy overhears some frightening news. Edwin and Debby are to be married! Doesn't that mean Debby will be moving away from the family? Betsy is furious and heartbroken. She and George decide to alienate Edwin the next time he comes to visit the family. That time soon arrives and Edwin wishes to take the entire family on a wagon ride to visit the new house he has chosen for Debby and himself. Betsy and George grudgingly agree to the ride, but neither of them enjoys it. Finally, the wagon comes to a stop at the new residence and Betsy is shocked! They are on Mulberry Street—just a few doors down from the Griscoms' home. Edwin tells Debby he chose the house because he thought she'd want to be close to her family. Betsy is so happy. Now Debby will be married, but she can still visit anytime she wants!

What we will cover in this chapter:

Language Arts: New Vocabulary Words

Language Arts: Literary Appreciation—Three Recommendations

Lesson Activities

Language Arts: New Vocabulary Words

On page 46 we read the Griscom family goes to meeting on First Day. Your student will probably be unfamiliar with these phrases. Take a moment to explain these examples of Quaker vernacular. *Meeting* is the Quaker term for their weekly time of worship (or church service). And Sunday, the day they hold meetings, is called *First Day*. Learning new phrases is interesting and helps us understand other groups and cultures better!

Language Arts: Literary Appreciation—Three Recommendations

Betsy is not happy about Debby's betrothal! She knows she *should* be happy for her sister, but mostly she feels sorry for herself! Betsy feels sorry that Debby will no longer be living with the family, sorry that Edwin won't be coming over anymore and most of all, sorry that everything is changing. The scene we read on pages 47-48 is a familiar one for children who have had older siblings leave to be married.

Perhaps your student is already familiar with the famous novel by Louisa May Alcott, *Little Women*. If so, this might be a reminder. If the book is new to your student, this is a delightful way to introduce the book. In *Little Women,* very similar feelings to Betsy's rise up in Jo March. Jo's sister Meg is to be married and Jo is not happy about it. Read the following excerpt from the book with your student:

"...poor Jo never got her laugh, for she was transfixed upon the threshold by a spectacle which held her there, staring with her mouth nearly as wide open as her eyes. Going in to exult over a fallen enemy, and to praise a strong-minded sister for the banishment of an objectionable lover, it certainly was a shock to behold the aforesaid enemy serenely sitting on the sofa, with the strong-minded sister enthroned upon his knee, and wearing an expression of the most abject submission. Jo gave a sort of gasp, as if a cold shower bath had suddenly fallen upon her—for such an unexpected turning of the tables actually took

her breath away...Rushing upstairs, she startled the invalids by exclaiming tragically, as she burst into the room, "Oh, do somebody go down quick; John Brooke is acting dreadfully and Meg likes it!"

And just as Betsy soon learned to love the idea of Edwin marrying Debby, Jo learns to love Mr. Brooke as well. *Little Women* is a fabulous book for read-alouds! It has enough for both boys and girls to enjoy and the writing is truly delightful! Consider reading this famous American classic novel together with your student in its entirety.

On page 46 we see the Griscom family walking to Meeting on First Day. If your student has enjoyed learning about the Quaker lifestyle, there is an excellent series of books available. Written and illustrated by the amazing Brinton Turkle, the *Obadiah* books are simply wonderful! Both the original *Obadiah the Bold* (Copyright 1965, Viking Press, No ISBN) and others, such as *Thy Friend, Obadiah* (Caldecott Honor Book, Copyright 1969, Viking Press, ISBN 670050628), are filled with sweet scenes of the Quaker lifestyle, beautiful illustrations and heart-warming stories of the Starbuck family (Father, Mother, Moses, Asa, Rebecca, Obadiah and Rachel). These books are a must! They will truly make thee glad!

Finally, a book recommendation purely for fun! The Griscoms live on Mulberry Street (page 56). If your student enjoys poetry and funny pictures, why not share with him the first (and some say the best!) book from Dr. Seuss, *And To Think That I Saw It On Mulberry Street*. Take turns reading it aloud and enjoying the whimsical story and tongue-twisting rhymes!

Writing and Discussion Question

Why did Edwin take the Griscoms on such a long wagon ride when the new house was right down the street?

Internet Connections

To view current suggested links relating to this chapter's lessons, see www.fiveinarow.com/connections.

Chapter 5–The Visit

Parent Summary

Betsy and George have heard wonderful things about a new printer in town—Mr. Benjamin Franklin. One day, the two children decide to go and see if they can sneak a peek at the man through his shop window. Betsy can't see anything in the shop, and neither can George. Suddenly, they hear a voice behind them. It's Mr. Franklin! Shocked and delighted, the children say hello and are promptly invited into the shop for a visit. Mr. Franklin is very nice and chats with Betsy about the Liberty Bell and the wonderful city they live in. After a glorious time of conversation, the children leave to go home.

"Thee has been very kind, Dr. Franklin. Thank thee very much for a pleasant afternoon," says Betsy as they leave. Betsy and George rush home to finish their chores. They can barely wait to share their exciting tale of meeting Benjamin Franklin with their family!

What we will cover in this chapter:

History and Geography: Benjamin Franklin

History and Geography: Philadelphia, Pennsylvania

History and Geography: Liberty Bell

Language Arts: Famous Sayings—Two New Phrases

Lesson Activities

History and Geography: Benjamin Franklin

Betsy and George are very lucky children! Imagine sitting and talking with Benjamin Franklin in his print shop (pictured on page 64). Discussing the life and times of Benjamin Franklin with your student could be an entire unit unto itself. If your student is interested in any of the following points, by all means take some time and study Franklin in greater depth.

Ben Franklin was born on January 17, 1706, in Boston, Massachusetts, the youngest of 15 children. The Franklins eventually ended up with 17 children in all! His father, Josiah Franklin, was a soap and candle maker in Boston. His mother, Abiah Franklin, tended to her 17 children, ran the house and cared for her husband.

Little Benjamin attended formal school for only two years. His poor grades led his father to the conclusion that Benjamin would better serve his family by working in the family soap and candle shop. But as he grew up, Benjamin Franklin never stopped learning. He was "self-taught" and read journals and newspapers of the day, gleaning information and insight into the world around him.

Franklin studied and spoke five languages including Latin, and became quite well educated in both math and science. Tending to tallow and trimming wicks was not enough for Benjamin. He left his father's candle shop and went to work as a printer's apprentice under his older brother James. By age 12 he was printing his own little newspaper and at 17, he ran away to Philadelphia to start his own career.

Working in various printing shops in Philadelphia and for a short time in London, Benjamin Franklin was happy! He was working at something he enjoyed and soon was publishing *The Pennsylvania Gazette* (a well-loved paper of the day). In 1730, Benjamin married Deborah Read. Deborah's maiden name was ironic because she was poorly educated and could neither read nor write well. The letters of their correspondence still exist. Deborah Franklin's poor spelling is apparent since she always signed her notes to Benjamin, "your afeckshonet wife."

Benjamin's most beloved and successful publication was *Poor Richard's Almanac*. Filled with news, weather, crop information and witty sayings, the almanac was published for more than 25 years. Franklin's pseudonym, or pen name, was Richard Saunders. Benjamin Franklin's famous sayings are still common to this day. Introduce your student to the following proverbs from *Poor Richard's Almanac*:

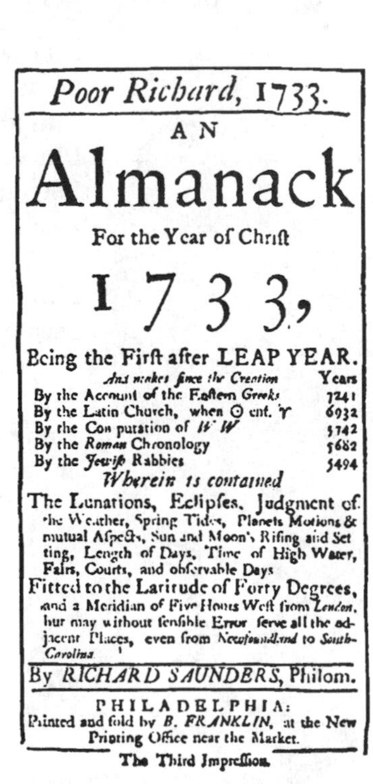
Poor Richard, 1733.

AN

Almanack

For the Year of Chrift

1733,

Being the Firft after LEAP YEAR.

And makes fince the Creation	Years
By the Account of the *Eaftern Greeks*	7241
By the Latin Church, when ☉ ent. ♈	6932
By the Computation of *W. W.*	5742
By the *Roman* Chronology	5682
By the *Jewifh* Rabbies	5494

Wherein is contained

The Lunations, Eclipfes, Judgment of the Weather, Spring Tides, Planets Motions & mutual Afpects, Sun and Moon's Rifing and Setting, Length of Days, Time of High Water, Fairs, Courts, and obfervable Days

Fitted to the Latitude of Forty Degrees, and a Meridian of Five Hours Weft from *London*, but may without fenfible Error ferve all the adjacent Places, even from *Newfoundland* to *South-Carolina*.

By *RICHARD SAUNDERS*, Philom.

PHILADELPHIA:
Printed and fold by *B. FRANKLIN*, at the New Printing Office near the Market.

The Third Impreffion.

"Early to bed, early to rise makes a man healthy, wealthy and wise."

"God helps them that help themselves."

"Little strokes fell great oaks."

"A penny saved is a penny earned."

"An ounce of prevention is worth a pound of cure."

But Benjamin Franklin was not just a writer, publisher, printer and philosopher. He was also a scientist! He is credited with discovering that lightning is electricity and the invention of the lightening rod.

He also invented bifocal eyeglass lenses, a heat-radiant stove and much more. Your student can research Franklin's inventions and make an illustrated report.

And yet, Benjamin Franklin's contributions to society did not stop there. He was also a great civil servant. Organizing the first City Hospital in all of America, founding the University of Pennsylvania (first known as The Academy), serving as Deputy Postmaster for the United States for more than ten years and radically improving the delivery of mail, founding the American Philosophical Society and finally, heading up a complete renewal of the police system in Philadelphia are just a few of the ways Benjamin Franklin sought to change the world in which he lived for the better.

Benjamin Franklin died in 1790 on April 17th at age 84. More than 20,000 people attended his funeral services.

If your student shows interest, find more books for him on Benjamin Franklin from your local bookstore or library. Try finding *Ben Franklin's Book of Easy & Incredible Experiments.*

History and Geography: Philadelphia, Pennsylvania

The Griscom family and Ben Franklin lived in Philadelphia, Pennsylvania. Discover, with your student, some of the wonderful and fascinating things Philadelphia has to offer.

William Penn

Founded in 1682 by Quaker William Penn, Philadelphia became the capital of Pennsylvania in 1683. The name comes from the Greek word *philadelphia*, which means brotherly love. For this reason, Philadelphia is known as "The City of Brotherly Love."

Often called the "birthplace of the United States," it was in Philadelphia (at Independence Hall) that the Constitution and the Declaration of Independence were created and signed. It was also in Philadelphia that such famous Americans as Benjamin Franklin and Thomas Jefferson lived and worked.

Before William Penn left England, he placed pamphlets and advertisements everywhere announcing his plan to found a city in the New World, free from religious persecution. Thousands of people followed Penn from Europe as a result, and the city of Philadelphia grew rapidly, becoming one of America's richest and largest cities. Philadelphia was actually the United States' Capitol from 1790 to 1800, before Washington, D.C. was founded.

Benjamin Franklin, the renowned civic leader of the new colonies and Philadelphia, moved to the City of Brotherly Love in 1723. His almanac and newspapers became famous and helped make Philadelphia the center of the budding publishing world.

There are still breath-taking sites and areas to enjoy in and around Philadelphia. Many of the original buildings from the late 17th and early 18th centuries are still present and the city provides a rich sense of America's heritage perhaps unmatched anywhere else. A good picture book of Philadelphia might make this study come alive.

There are many activities available for students wanting to know more about Philadelphia. They can do research to draw a simple map locating the most famous buildings of the 18th century. They can build a model of Independence Hall or do research and write a paper about the Declaration of Independence, the Constitution, Franklin or Jefferson.

If you live in or near the Philadelphia area, arrange for a trip to visit the historic sites! Philadelphia should hold a special place in the hearts of all Americans!

History and Geography: Liberty Bell

Benjamin Franklin and Betsy reminisce fondly together about the Liberty Bell (page 66). "It says 'Liberty!' every time it rings," says Mr. Franklin. Has your student every heard of the Liberty Bell?

Actually (note page 66), the famous bell was officially called the Liberty Bell after 1839. Before, it had been called the Old State House Bell, Old Independence or the Bell of the Revolution.

The story recounted in our chapter is indeed very close to the truth. The bell was brought over from England in 1776 and cracked during it's first set of rings. The second bell was then cast from the original and was inscribed with the same inscription.

The Liberty Bell's inscription reads "Proclaim Liberty throughout all the land unto all the inhabitants thereof." This quotation was taken from the Bible (Leviticus 25:10).

Today the Liberty Bell resides in the Liberty Bell Pavilion, right next to Independence Hall in Philadelphia, Pennsylvania.

Visit this historic site if you are able. The Liberty Bell is an American treasure!

Language Arts: Famous Sayings—Two New Phrases

Some of the most famous sayings or proverbs (words of wisdom) today are from the writings of Benjamin Franklin. Draw your student's attention to page 74. The Griscom's family motto is "waste not, want not." Ask your student what he thinks this Franklin saying means? (Of course, it suggests that we will not lack if we don't waste what we already have.)

This chapter also introduces the common phrase "dyed in the wool." Look at page 65. Mr. Franklin tells Betsy she is a "dyed in the wool" American. What does that mean? Has your student ever heard that phrase before? Describe to your student where that phrase comes from. When you dye fabric (after it is woven), the dye adheres for a time but will at some point fade. When, instead, you dye the raw wool first and then create the fabric, the color stays. Does this explain to your student what the phrase means? In other words, Betsy is an American through and through.

The phrase is often used in conjunction with political parties. Someone might say, "I'm a dyed in the wool Republican." This means that nothing can change his mind—he's been a Republican since he was born.

Learning new phrases increases your student's comprehension of the world around him. See if you and your student can find ways to use these two new phrases in your conversation today!

Writing and Discussion Question

If you were able to spend an afternoon with Benjamin Franklin, what questions would you ask him? Now do some research and discuss how you think Mr. Franklin might answer your questions.

Internet Connections

To view current suggested links relating to this chapter's lessons, see www.fiveinarow.com/connections.

Chapter 6–The New School

Parent Summary

The year is now 1782 and Betsy Griscom is 10 years old. She is too old for Miss Rebecca's class now. Now Betsy will go with her other sisters to the large Quaker school on South Fourth Street. The first day arrives and Betsy is very excited. But as she enters the schoolyard, she becomes increasingly nervous. These are all new children! Who will be her friend? Some of the children weren't Quaker children. Betsy feels very lonely and begins to cry.

Sarah, her older sister, comforts Betsy and soon things brighten up. Betsy learns to love her school. She has many friends, but she and Susannah Claypoole are especially close. The school day begins at 8 a.m. with two hours of academics, followed by two hours of art or trade work. Then from noon until 2 p.m. the children go home to eat lunch. Back at 2:00 each afternoon, the children work until 4 p.m. on academics once more. Finally, from 4 p.m. until 6 p.m. students work on their chosen trade or art once more. A ten-hour school day! But Betsy loves it. And she also discovers she loves sewing!

What we will cover in this chapter:

Science: Winter-Summer Solstice and Vernal-Autumnal Equinox

Language Arts: Vocabulary—Two New Words

Issues of Human Relationships: What Do You Most Delight In?

Lesson Activities

Science: Winter and Summer Solstice and Vernal and Autumnal Equinox

Draw your student's attention to page 79. Susannah is tired of school. "*It's dark when we leave home in the mornings. It's dark when we come home in the evenings*," she says to Betsy. Has your student noticed that light changes throughout the year and at times it's darker earlier in the day while at other times it doesn't get dark until later?

What happens?

Use this opportunity to locate a good book or encyclopedia on the seasons and the earth's rotation. Study the illustrations of the earth's tilting axis until your student understands the principles involved. Perhaps he would like to build a model of the sun and the earth and its axis and physically demonstrate how the seasons change as the earth makes its annual rotation around the sun. He can use Styrofoam balls, papier mache or even an apple and a grapefruit! Place a stick or skewer through the apple to serve as the earth's axis. If you use fruit, when you're finished with the project, take a break and eat the "earth and sun!"

Language Arts: Vocabulary—Two New Words

Betsy feels lonely and distant from the other children at her new school. But after all, it is only her first day! Sarah, Betsy's older sister, notices Betsy crying. Draw your student's attention to page 76 and the conversation between the sisters. Sarah asks Betsy, "*What ails thee?*" Does your student know what the word ail means? Ail is an Old English word and it means to be with a cause of pain or distress. In other words, Sarah is asking Betsy, "What's wrong with you?" Share with your student other words that comes from ail including *ailment* and *ailing*. These are good words to learn and use.

After Betsy tells Sarah she wants to go back to Miss Rebecca's school (page 76), Sarah uses another word that might be unfamiliar to your student—"Fie!" Fie is a word we gather from the French and means "Shame on you!" Found many times in Shakespeare's writings and other plays and writings from the 16th and 17th centuries, your student will come across this word more and more in his future studies.

Encourage your student to try using these new words in context a few times in his daily conversation until he masters them. It will help him enjoy building a broader vocabulary!

Issues of Human Relationships: What Do You Most Delight In?

Betsy's school on South Fourth Street sounds like fun! Betsy's favorite time of the day is when she is able to spend time working on "the art or trade she most delights in" (page 78). What a wonderful phrase!

What does your student most delight in? When something "delights" us, it means it gives us pleasure and joy. Part of growing up is learning what it is we most delight in. When we're young, we experiment and work with many different things. As we get older we begin to identify certain activities that we particularly love. Even though Betsy is young, she already knows what she loves—sewing!

Spend some time with your student discussing what it is he most delights in. Whether it is boats, computers, cooking, gardening, stamp collecting, making music, writing, woodcarving, etc., encourage your student to work on his "art or trade" every day, just like Betsy. It will instill in him a love of learning and may lead to a life-long interest. Everyone should discover what it is they most delight in!

Writing and Discussion Question

Betsy and Susannah debate the question, "do we do things well because we like to do them, or do we like to do them because we do them well?" (page 80) What do you think and why?

Internet Connections

To view current suggested links relating to this chapter's lessons, see www.fiveinarow.com/connections.

Chapter 7–Something Exciting

Parent Summary

Summer has arrived! Three long months for Betsy and Susannah to enjoy. To celebrate their vacation, the girls decide to go down to the wharf and see if any big ships are docked. Betsy loves the wharf. She loves the sea and the ships and the flags. Today, the girls are in luck. A huge sailing vessel from England has just docked!

The girls hurry over and admire the sweeping sails, the huge British flag and the sailors scurrying down the gangplank. Betsy wonders what it would be like to sail on such a ship! Someday, perhaps she'll find out.

Suddenly a young boy approaches the girls and strikes up a conversation with Betsy and Susannah. His name is Joe Ashburn and he tells the girls that the captain of the large ship is a friend of his uncle's. Joe seems nice and the girls enjoy their conversation. Joe asks Betsy and Susannah if they would like a tour of the ship. After some discussion the girls agree and they soon find themselves on the huge decks. Betsy is overcome with joy! The mighty sails, the captain's quarters, the gangplank, the bridge and the masts—it is all so exciting! All of a sudden, the wind whips up and rain begins pelting down. Betsy stands with her face to the wind and imagines she is out on the ocean. What a wonderful feeling!

Just then the captain approaches the children and asks them for some help. A little girl on the ship from England, named Mary Ellen, has come to meet her uncle. However, because of the rains he has been delayed in Baltimore and won't make it to Philadelphia for three days. The captain asks Joe, Betsy and Susannah if they would be willing to accompany Mary Ellen to her hotel. The children agree and set off.

What we will cover in this chapter:

History and Geography: Flags—State, National and International

History and Geography: Ships

Science: Turpentine

Language Arts: Learning and Using Appropriate Jargon in Your Writing

Fine Arts: Create Your Own Flag

Lesson Activities

History and Geography: Flags—State, National and International

Betsy is shocked that Susannah doesn't know the flags of other countries (page 86). Betsy tells her friend that each flag tells a story, like a page out of a history book. Betsy is right! Take this opportunity to share with your student the fascinating world of flags.

Flags have been around for a very long time. No one is sure when they began, but the oldest, recognized national flag known today is the flag of Denmark. With its red background and white cross, this flag has been used for more than 750 years. The study of flags, their history and usage is called *vexillology*, from the Latin word *vexillum*, meaning flag. Let your student try that word out on a parent or grandparent and see if they know what it means!

What country interests your student? One interesting way to learn about its history and people is to study its flag. For example, the Austrian national flag has a fascinating story that began during the Third Crusade in 1191. Reportedly, Duke Leopold V removed his blood-drenched cape after a battle and discovered that his belt had caused a strip across the middle of the cape to remain pristine white. Austria chose this design for their country's flag in 1919.

But countries aren't the only political entities to have flags. Each of the United States has a flag of its own too. Each Canadian province has a flag, and many organizations such as the Red Cross, NATO, the Olympics, etc., have their own flags as well.

You can devote much time to the study of the care and rules for proper display of your country's flag. In the United States, strict guidelines are in place for how the national flag is to be properly displayed, both during the day and at night. If left up at night, a spotlight should always illuminate the flag. If the U.S. flag is displayed on an automobile it must be flown from an antenna and is never allowed to be draped over the vehicle. You will also find lots of other guidelines for the proper display of the flag from a building, with other flags, in front of private homes, and much more. Use a good encyclopedia, or find a book at the library to learn more about how to properly handle our flag.

There is also much to learn about the various parts of a flag. Use your flag reference material to learn more about these things.

It would also be fun to take some time to study your state's flag. What is the design? When was it created? What do the various symbols stand for? Do you think your state flag accurately reflects your feelings about your state? For ideas about making your own flag, be sure to see the Fine Arts section of this lesson series. Have fun learning about flags with your student!

History and Geography: Ships

Betsy is quite enamored with ships! Ships make an excellent unit study unto themselves. From the huge sailing vessels of today to clipper ships, sailboats, passenger liners, and Great Lakes tanker ships, your student can find something that interests him. You might study the history of sailing, the role of ships in wartime, pleasure boating, water skiing, sailing, and much, much more. Begin with a general study of boats and as your student finds specific areas that interest him, narrow your studies and explore the wonderful world of ships and boating.

Whatever kind of ship you choose to study, you must find Stephen Biesty's book *Cross-Sections: Man-Of-War* (Copyright 1993, Dorling--Kindersley, ISBN 156458321X). Filled with extraordinary, detailed illustrations, this book explores the sea vessels from the 18th century (the exact kinds Betsy might have seen!). Each page reveals a deeper layer in the ship, and offers a wealth of facts and interesting notes about life aboard a British warship. The full-color pictures and activities appeal to any age. This book is simply fascinating!

Science: Turpentine

Betsy loves the smells at the wharf—tar, *turpentine*, paint and spices (page 83). Does your student know what *turpentine* is? Turpentine is a clear or golden liquid made from the Longleaf and Slash pine trees. Turpentine has a pungent (oily, piney) scent and is extremely flammable. Used primarily to thin paint, remove paint stains, and in disinfectants, turpentine is a common ingredient in many home products.

If you have some turpentine available, let your student smell its strong odor, and remind your student that Betsy liked the smell!

Language Arts:
Learning and Using Appropriate Jargon in Your Writing

Draw your student's attention to the amazing number of nautical terms used in this chapter (bow, wharf, gangplank, dock, captain's quarters, sea legs, harbor, mast, etc.). These words create a realistic setting and description for our story. An important term for your student to learn for his own writing is the word jargon. Although the word has several meanings, for our purposes define jargon to your student as "the specialized vocabulary, phrases or terms for a specific profession, region or place." In other words, this chapter uses nautical jargon.

Whatever your student wishes to write about in his stories, it is important that he consider the unique jargon his story might require. For example, a tale about a nurse in a hospital will demand a certain amount of medical jargon to seem realistic. Here are two examples of the same paragraph, the first without appropriate jargon and the second including it.

1.

As Nurse Tandy reached for her clipboard, she could hear someone yelling from down the hallway. Leaning over the patient, she checked to see if he was hot. Jotting down the information, she proceeded to check his cut hand. Nervous about her findings, she wrote a description of the hand and prepared to assist the doctor with the surgery. Handing the doctor the little metal clips he asked for, she took a deep breath and settled in for a long operation.

2.

As Nurse Tandy reached for her clipboard, she could hear someone shouting, 'Code Blue" from down the hallway. Leaning over the patient, she checked his temperature. Jotting down the information, she proceeded to check his hand laceration. Nervous about her findings, she wrote a description of the laceration and prepared to assist the doctor with the lengthy suture procedure. Handing the doctor the hemostats he requested, she took a deep breath and settled in for a long surgical procedure.

Often, research is required to understand and discover these new terms, but that is all a part of an author's job. Without this research, his writing will not "ring true" to his readers.

As a creative writing exercise, it might be interesting to have your student select a profession for one of his characters that is unfamiliar to him. Perhaps he will choose an astronaut, truck driver, baker, nurse, etc. Then, have your student do "jargon" research. Finally, have him write a short story, utilizing his newfound terminology.

For those who earn their living writing, there are actually specialized books, which include information about lifestyles, language and small details of everyday life from various periods of history or geographic regions. If a writer plans to write an entire nautical novel, for instance, he will need to do extensive research about sailing terminology and life aboard a ship. If a writer plans to write a period novel set during the Middle Ages, he had better learn about castles and jousting and much, much more!

Perhaps your student is familiar with the writer's phrase, "Write about things you know." Writing what you know about is an easy way to be sure you include jargon that is realistic, but so limiting! Sometimes it is exciting to write about new things, but always do your research!

Fine Arts: Create Your Own Flag

If you have done the lesson on flags listed above, your student already has some ideas about what flag designs include and where they come from. A great art activity for your student might be to create a flag for his family! By studying a book on heraldry (the art and study of coats of arms and symbolism in color), your student can design a flag which represents what his family stands for—the "story" behind his family.

The flag can be drawn on paper and framed, sewn into an actual flag from fabric, created in a bean or pasta mosaic (the beans and pasta painted or dyed into the required colors), or whatever else your student comes up with!

If you don't care to create a family flag, have your student copy his state flag, or one of his favorite foreign flags. This project might take some time and research to develop, but it will be well worth it!

Writing and Discussion Question

Betsy and Susannah are lucky to have found a nice friend like Joe Ashburn. However, we should be careful when a stranger offers to show us around. Taking into account Joe's strange actions and the fact he was a stranger to Betsy and Susannah, do you think it was the right decision to follow him onto the ship? What would you have done?

Internet Connections

To view current suggested links relating to this chapter's lessons, see www.fiveinarow.com/connections.

Chapter 8–The Sovereign

Parent Summary

Joe Ashburn, Betsy and Susannah go and meet Mary Ellen, the little girl the captain had told them about. Unfortunately, as Mary Ellen steps from the carriage, her dress is caught, torn and muddied! Heartbroken because it is her last clean dress, Mary Ellen realizes there is nothing to be done but to throw the dress away. Betsy steps in and offers to fix the dress, mending the torn places and washing it clean. Mary Ellen is skeptical of Betsy's ability but, of course, allows her to try. By the end of the afternoon, Betsy has done the "impossible." The dress is as good as new and Mary Ellen is overjoyed.

The following day, Betsy goes to say goodbye to her new friend as Mary Ellen sets off for Boston. Mary Ellen's rich uncle has now arrived and Betsy meets him. Betsy waits and waves goodbye as their carriage pulls away. Soon she sets off for home, but the innkeeper, Mr. Baker, calls after her. Mr. Baker has in his hand two shillings for Miss Susannah, two shillings for Joe, and a whole sovereign for Betsy—all from Mary Ellen's uncle as a thank you for their care of his niece. Betsy is surprised and very pleased! A whole sovereign! What will she do with all that money?

What we will cover in this chapter:

History and Geography: Crossing the Atlantic—How Long Does It Take?

History and Geography: Wigs—The Answer to "Perfect" Hair

History and Geography: Sovereigns and Shillings

Science: Physical Condition—An Important Element of Health

Language Arts: Writing Using a Diary Format

Issues of Human Relationships: Frugality—Another Example

Lesson Activities

History and Geography: Crossing the Atlantic—How Long Does It Take?

It took Mary Ellen two months to arrive in Philadelphia from England by ship (page 102). Imagine being on a ship that long? What would you do for entertainment? What kinds of food would you eat? Amazingly enough, this two-month voyage was a vast improvement over previous transatlantic voyages in history.

Share with your student a little about Christopher Columbus' trips to the New World. On his first voyage, Columbus sailed with a fleet of ships (the *Nina*, the *Pinta*, and the *Santa Maria*), a total crew of 90 men and only a few compasses for navigation. This first historic voyage took Columbus almost 7 1/2 months (August 3, 1492 to March 15, 1493)! Now that is a long time on a boat!

By the 1760s, in Betsy's time (approximately 250 years later), navigation had improved and ships were more seaworthy, thus cutting the trip by more than half. Mary Ellen made it in two months.

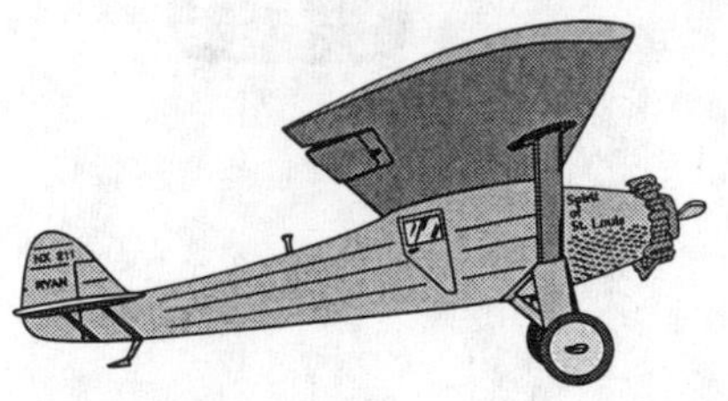

Less than 200 years later, by 1927, a man named Charles Lindbergh made the first transatlantic journey (more than 3,500 miles) by airplane in a mere 33 1/2 hours! Lindbergh's famous plane was named the *Spirit of St. Louis*. Wouldn't Betsy have been amazed? Technology had now shaved the trip Columbus had once made in over seven months down to less than two days. But history didn't stop there.

Today, major ocean liners like the *Queen Elizabeth II*, *Queen Mary* and others are able to consistently make the voyage in about four to five days. Even more incredible in terms of speed, however, is the new generation of supersonic (faster than the speed of sound) airplanes, the most famous called the *Concorde SST*. Beginning passenger service in 1976, the *Concorde* now makes transatlantic service for passengers and can complete the crossing in less than four *hours*! Wouldn't Mary Ellen have loved that?

Today, our thoughts on travel and travel time are vastly different than in Betsy's day. We pack the clothing we'll need for our vacation (not all the clothes we'll need for the trip to get there!). If your student has made a significant trip of some kind, talk with him about how long it seemed. Did he get bored? Did he enjoy the journey? What kind of travel is his favorite? Has he ever flown on an airplane before? Is that frightening or exciting?

Traveling can be a wonderful experience. Take some time to plan a real or imaginary trip with your student somewhere soon!

History and Geography: Wigs—The Answer to "Perfect" Hair

Betsy concluded that Mary Ellen's uncle was a very rich man by the look of his powdered wig (page 106). Every curl was in place and it looked fine! What is a powdered wig? Who wore them? Why?

The French (still fashion leaders even today) began the popular trend of wearing wigs in the 1600s. Worn by both men and women, the wigs were high and puffy, with spring-like curls hanging down and powdered snowy-white. Even today, the judges and counsel in England still wear these stylized wigs. The wigs of high nobility were kept much nicer than those of other people. Combed, set, and freshly powdered, the wigs were a sign of wealth. Because of this, Betsy knew something about Mary Ellen's uncle and his station in life.

In the early days of fashion wigs, they weren't cleaned frequently. The heat and sweat from people's bodies caused lice to nest in the fibers of the wig. The richest people hired full-time "lice-pickers" to remove the lice and clean the wigs daily. The less fortunate were forced to wear their lice-infested wigs.

Does your student think wearing a wig like that would be fun or difficult? If you are able, locate a book or encyclopedia on early French fashion and show your student examples of these interesting, signature hairpieces.

History and Geography: Sovereigns and Shillings

Mary Ellen's kind uncle gave Susannah and Joe two shillings each and gave Betsy a whole sovereign. No doubt these monetary denominations are new to your student. If you wish, take this opportunity to briefly introduce the British monetary system.

The British system centers around the denomination pound (also called pound sterling). Represented by the symbol £, this unit of money is available in a 1£ coin, 5£ paper notes, 10£ paper notes, and 20£ paper notes. One pound sterling is equal to 100 pence, in the same way that pennies are 1/100 of a dollar. Also, a shilling is similar to a nickel in the United States monetary system; each shilling equal to 1/20 of a pound.

Betsy received a sovereign. Although not in general circulation anymore (sovereigns are used mainly for international trade requiring gold), a sovereign is a gold coin, equivalent to 20 shillings or one pound sterling. Sovereigns were first minted under the authority of King Henry VII in 1489. At that time the sovereign was also known as a unite, in honor of the joining of Scotland and England in 1603 under the rule of James I.

Try to locate a coin shop in your area and plan a field trip to examine the coins and bills of other countries, including Great Britain. You can also exchange money at large banks. If you have a large bank nearby, perhaps your student would enjoy exchanging a few dollars for an assortment of British pounds and shillings. (You can also exchange money for most other foreign currencies including German Deutschmarks, Japanese Yen, Swiss Francs, etc.). Of course, you can always change your money back into dollars and cents later when you want to spend it!

Science: Physical Condition—An Important Element of Health

In our story we read that Mr. Baker, the innkeeper, is overweight and has a difficult time running after Betsy with the money (page 108). What a wonderful opportunity to discuss the importance of exercise and physical conditioning for our health! Just as important as maintaining a healthy diet (refer to the lesson in *The Boxcar Children*, chapter 1), getting exercise provides strong muscles, reduces body fat, provides better circulation and promises a higher quality of life.

There are so many fun ways to incorporate exercise into our busy lives. Gardening, bicycle riding, team and individual sports, swimming and more structured exercise programs (aerobics, walking, jogging, etc.) all provide great benefit to our minds and bodies.

Encourage your student to maintain a healthy exercise regimen using activities of his choice for one full week. Perhaps he would enjoy doing something different each day. Does he feel better at the end of the week? Family walks can also be a great way to blend exercise with family time spent together. Challenge yourself and your student to aim even higher in the area of physical fitness!

You may want to use this opportunity to do additional study about the human body and its response to exercise and diet. There are many good books available on the topic and any good encyclopedia will provide at least simple, introductory information. Learn about ideal body weights, calories burned per hour during various exercise activities, how muscle mass is built, how the human body's heart and lungs respond to exercise, etc. There is enough material in this one area alone to keep your student busy for several days. (If you study some of these topics, remember to add them to your Teacher's file—Human Body. This way you will have a record of what you have covered and in what depth.)

Language Arts: Writing Using a Diary Format

Over the course of history, one of the ways we have learned much about people's lives and thoughts has been from diaries. From Christopher Columbus to Abraham Lincoln, from Eleanor Roosevelt to Ernest Hemmingway, diaries have given us a glimpse into life in another time and helped us understand the feelings and struggles of other men and women.

As an interesting creative writing exercise, encourage your student to try to write a fictional diary for Mary Ellen. She spent two months on board that ship from England (page 102). Interesting things must have happened! This project can be as simple as four or five small entries, or as complex as your student wishes. The important part is that your student should think through what sorts of things Mary Ellen might have been thinking about and experiencing. He can then write the fictional diary passage from Mary Ellen's viewpoint, remembering that her parents have just died and she's sailing to meet an uncle in a new country! Here is an example of one such entry:

June 10, 1762

The trip is going smoothly thus far. I've been wondering what it will be like to eat fresh bread again—these crackers are getting a little boring. Every day the ocean looks bigger and darker. I know it's my imagination but it does look that way. Yesterday I met one of the sailors (I think his name was Edward), and he showed me around the sails on the starboard side of the ship. I think the sails are the prettiest part of the ship. I must go now. I hear the dinner bell. I certainly hope the meal is good. After conquering seasickness, I can't seem to get enough to eat!

This exercise can be delightful, and if research is done properly, quite historically accurate! Remind your student that the famous people whose diaries we read today did not know they would be famous when they began their journals. Perhaps your student should begin his own diary as well! One never knows who will become famous! Besides, keeping a diary or journal is a worthwhile exercise for anyone.

[**Teachers Note**: For an unusual look at a first-person memoir, try Newbery award winner *Hitty, Her First Hundred Years* by Rachel Field as a read-aloud. This is a remarkable story with many historic references.]

Issues of Human Relationships: Frugality—Another Example

Does your student remember Mrs. Terwilliger in *Homer Price*? Remember that she lived a frugal lifestyle? Betsy Ross has been raised to be *frugal*, too. She is careful with her belongings and tries to fix or repair them if she can. She is even able to help Mary Ellen with her problem.

Mary Ellen is sure her dress is ruined and fit only for the garbage (page 103). Betsy, on the other hand, understands her family's motto "Waste not, want not." She sets about fixing the dress, and does a wonderful job. Imagine the things we throw away that could be fixed and used again! Remind your student to always examine what he is throwing out before it is gone. The Griscoms are good stewards of their things. We should be, as well!

Writing and Discussion Question

Betsy received a whole sovereign from Mary Ellen's uncle. What do you think she will do with the money? Save it? Spend it? If so, on what?

Internet Connections

To view current suggested links relating to this chapter's lessons, see www.fiveinarow.com/connections.

Chapter 9–Ice Skates in July

Parent Summary

Betsy is thinking about what she wants to buy with her sovereign. Never before has she had so much money! Endless possibilities fill her mind, but she finally makes her decision—ice skates! She has been wanting her own pair of ice skates for a very long time and now she can buy a pair. She hurries to Mr. William's Blacksmith Shop, for she knows this is where ice skates are sold. But much to her surprise, no ice skates are hanging on the walls. Betsy asks Mr. Williams where the skates are, but he just laughs. Betsy seems to have forgotten the concept of *seasonal merchandise*. Skates are sold at his shop, but generally not in *July*.

Betsy is slightly embarrassed, but mostly disappointed. Mr. Williams, however, kindly offers to check his stock up in the loft. Soon he returns with the most beautiful pair of skates Betsy has ever seen! Sparkling and silver, Mr. Williams tells her they are the finest skates you can buy and that they are imported from England. After a few thoughtful moments, Mr. Williams tells Betsy the price is one sovereign. Delighted, Betsy plunks down her coin and takes her precious skates home. Ice skates in July!

For months Betsy waits for winter to arrive. She oils her skates to prevent rust and makes them glisten. Finally, she is able to go skating. Her first day out skating, Betsy bumps (literally!) into a nice young man named John Ross. John, a mutual friend of Betsy's pal Joe Ashburn, recognizes Betsy and offers to teach her how to skate. Betsy is grateful for the help and by the end of winter, John and Betsy are wonderful friends!

What we will cover in this chapter:

History and Geography: John Ross—A Hint for the Future

Science: Heat

Science: Oil–A Lubricant and Rust Preventative

Issues of Human Relationships: Kindness—Three Examples

Lesson Activities

History and Geography: John Ross—A Hint for the Future

While ice skating, Betsy meets a young man named John Ross. Without going into significant detail, ask your student who he thinks John Ross is. What role will he play in Betsy's life? For the older student, these answers should be obvious—John will be her future husband! For the younger student, it may be more of a stretch. Encourage your younger student to keep watching for more hints and to remember this name in later chapters!

Science: Heat

It is very hot in Philadelphia in July! Betsy grew hot just walking down the street. Draw your student's attention to the discussion on page 116 between Betsy and Mr. Williams about going up into the loft. Betsy kindly tells Mr. Williams, "Oh I wouldn't want thee to go up there, Mr. Williams, 'Twould be frightfully hot on a day like this." Why would it be hotter in the loft?

Science is founded on facts. One scientific fact is that heated air rises. When air is heated it expands, causing it to be lighter than the surrounding air. If you have a scientific thermometer, experiment with this concept by testing the temperature in your student's basement and then in the top floor (or attic) of his house. The top level should be a few degrees warmer (except for unheated attics in winter!). At summer camp, the top bunks are always warmer than the bottom bunks, for this same reason.

If your student has ever seen wave-like, moving lines above hot pavement on the highway, or above a candle flame, he has noticed how the heat rises. Light a candle and show this to your student. Has your student ever seen a hot air balloon? How does it fly? (The burner assembly heats the air inside the balloon—and since hot air rises, the balloon lifts off!)

Remind your student to remember this scientific fact: heat rises.

Science: Oil—A Lubricant and Rust Preventative

Betsy carefully oiled her new skates every month (page 120). Why did she have to oil them? Oil serves two purposes. It is first and foremost a *lubricant*. It helps gears and other pieces of machinery and metal move smoothly together. Second, it is a sealant. The oil provides a film or coating to seal and protect the kinds of metal which form rust.

[**Teachers Note**: If you chose to do the lesson, your student has already been exposed to the scientific principles and causes of rust in *The Boxcar Children*, chapter 5. If not, this may be an appropriate time to review that lesson.]

Betsy oils her skates for the second reason. She is trying to prevent the shiny new blades from rusting. Perhaps your student oils his bicycle chains and gears. If so, he is both protecting them from rust like Betsy's skates, and he is also lubricating them to operate more smoothly.

Oil is a very helpful substance for many things!

Issues of Human Relationships: Kindness—Three Examples

Being kind to other people is a sign of maturity, character and self-confidence. It is something we should all work to cultivate in our lives. This chapter provides three wonderful examples of kindness, by three different people.

Mr. Williams owns the blacksmith shop. When Betsy arrives, he is busy working, but stops to speak with Betsy. After he learns what she is looking for he offers to check through his back stock in the loft. What a kind thing to offer! Surely Mr. Williams has better things to do than help a little girl find ice skates in July! Mr. Williams displays a kind heart by his offer.

Likewise, Betsy returns the kindness by insisting that he not go up into the loft. It is so hot, she says; he needn't go to the trouble. Now imagine how badly Betsy wanted those skates! She had been dreaming of a pair for so long and here was her chance. But instead of being greedy and self-serving, Betsy tells Mr. Williams to think of himself and not to go into the hot loft. "I can get the skates some other time," she says. What kind and humble words!

Finally, at the end of our chapter, we see another example of kindness displayed by John Ross. After John asks Betsy if she does figure eights, Betsy replies "no." Instead of being prideful and showing off, John immediately offers to help teach her. Encourage your student to display acts of kindness like this in his daily life. It will cause others to love and respect him!

Writing and Discussion Question

Even though Betsy had many months to wait before she could use her new skates, she didn't seem to grow tired of them. Have you ever bought something, or received a certain gift, and grown tired of it quickly? What was it and why?

Internet Connections

To view current suggested links relating to this chapter's lessons, see www.fiveinarow.com/connections.

Chapter 10–Philadelphia Winter

Parent Summary

It is now the winter of 1766 and Betsy is fourteen. In Philadelphia, the winters are harsh and many people become ill. The Griscom house is no exception. This winter, Betsy and her mother are the only two who remain well, taking care of the house and everyone else. One night Mrs. Griscom wakes Betsy up and frantically tells her to go and fetch the doctor. Mr. Griscom is ill. Betsy is amazed. Her father is always the first one up in the morning and the last one to bed. She can't remember him ever being ill. Nevertheless, Betsy and George bundle up in the dark and set out in the cold night air to get the doctor. The wind howls and the snow blows at the children's faces. Amazed to discover it is only nine in the evening, the children press on, arriving at the doctor's house chilled to the bone. While the doctor harnesses the horses to his sleigh, his kind wife warms the children with mugs of hot milk. Finally, when all is ready the three people bound into the sleigh and set off for the Griscoms' house. Not a moment too soon, they arrive and the doctor sees that Mr. Griscom receives medication. The doctor tells Betsy she should get to bed, for fear she may get ill as well. As Betsy does what she is told, she is again amazed to discover only an hour has passed in all. It seemed so much longer! The next week passes slowly, but by the following week, the entire household is up and well again.

What we will cover in this chapter:

History and Geography: Illness—Putting Up a Fight

Issues of Human Relationships: Chores—A Pleasant Side

Issues of Human Relationships: Why Does Time Fly When You're Having Fun?

Career Paths: Pharmist

Lesson Activities

History and Geography: Illness—Putting Up a Fight

Many people get sick every winter in Betsy's town—even her own family! Why does it seem as though winters and illness were harder on people in the past than in today's world? There's a reason.

Modern medicines (antibiotics, immunizations, and effective over-the-counter medications) have helped control disease tremendously in the last 150 years. If you like, share with your student some of these interesting notes about medical discoveries:

Antibiotics (drugs produced by certain bacteria and fungi that work to fight against human disease) help greatly in maintaining health today. Antibiotics work by attacking the disease-causing bacteria and either breaking them down or preventing them from forming again.

The first antibiotic discovered was called penicillin. A British doctor and scientist named Alexander Fleming made the historic find in 1928. Fleming actually made his important discovery by accident! One day Fleming was working in his laboratory and he noticed a tiny piece of mold had fallen from its culture dish onto another. Where it fell, it proceeded to destroy all the bacteria around it. The bacteria it destroyed was harmful to humans, but the mold was not. Victory!

If he could somehow cultivate the germ-killing mold and extract it into a serum, it could prove life saving for humans. This idea indeed was correct, but the execution of it was harder than Fleming thought when he began. Nevertheless, by the time World War II began (approximately 11 years later), Fleming's antibiotic, penicillin was being used for ill and injured soldiers and saved many lives. His "accidental" discovery won Andrew Fleming the 1945 Nobel Prize in Medicine and opened a new era in modern medicine.

[**Teacher's Note**: The roots of Fleming's discovery are found in the work of Louis Pasteur, who discovered that bacteria spread disease and infections. Refer back to the lesson on Pasteur in *The Boxcar Children*, chapter 5, for more information on his other discoveries!]

Immunizations are another way we prevent many serious diseases today. Your student no doubt remembers having received an immunization at one time or another. An immunization works by injecting the person with a very light "dose" of a particular disease. The injection has enough of the substance to cause the body to react and trigger healing antibodies, but not enough of the substance to make the person catch the disease and become seriously ill. Slight side effects like a light fever or body aches may occur, but nothing as serious as the actual disease itself. Most immunizations provide life-long protection from the disease they are designed to fight, and sometimes a doctor can combine several immunizations into one single injection.

Immunizations were first created by Edward Jenner in 1796. Smallpox had been a serious, life-threatening illness for hundreds of years and England, in particular, had been through many plagues.

Before immunizations wiped out smallpox in the United States in 1977 (the last known case occurred that year), this deadly disease killed hundreds of millions of people worldwide and left millions more blind, scarred and crippled. The disease is passed by infected air vapor. Beginning with high fevers, the disease quickly proceeds to produce pus-filled sores all over the body and within three weeks the victim can die.

Mr. Jenner knew that once a person had contracted smallpox and lived through it, he was immune—that is, he couldn't contract the disease ever again. He decided if he could give people a very light case of the disease, they wouldn't get too sick and then they would be immune. In 1796 he did just that, by infecting a healthy little boy named James Phipps with diseased bits from the arm of a local dairy maid named Sarah Nelmes.

Jenner's questionable experiment, perhaps unethical and dangerous, threatened to ruin his entire medical career. But it paid off! Little James became slightly ill, but did not catch smallpox. It was official! Immunizations for a variety of illnesses (German Measles, measles, mumps, smallpox, polio, tetanus, diphtheria, and whooping cough) are common today and many diseases have been eliminated in the United States. Unfortunately, in other parts of the world diseases like typhoid, cholera and yellow fever are still a risk. For this reason, people are often required to receive extra immunizations when they are traveling to areas where the diseases are prevalent.

Beyond antibiotics and immunizations, another aspect of modern healthcare we have at our disposal (unlike the Griscoms and the other families in the 18th century and before) is a myriad of over-the-counter cold, flu, sore throat, cough, and headache remedies. Very effectively, these medications can often curb the symptoms of common illnesses so they do not weaken us and make us prone to more serious diseases.

As an interesting lesson, go with your student to a local pharmacy or drug store and count how many over-the-counter remedies are available for cold, flu, sore throat, cough and headaches. The numbers will astound you! Cough syrups alone can number in the dozens!

We are blessed to live in an era where modern medicine and science have provided us with so many protections and safeguards. Unlike living in Betsy's day, we can take measures unknown then to help us maintain our health. What a good blessing!

Issues of Human Relationships: Chores—A Pleasant Side

Betsy makes a funny statement to her sister Mary on page 135. She says, "...Eleven dirty dishes. They're beautiful...It means the family is together again." Betsy doesn't mind doing dirty dishes if it means the family is no longer sick and they're all together again.

It is easy to complain and dread doing chores, but we can always think of how much worse things might be. For example, when we have to sweep the kitchen floor we could complain. Or, we could think of having dirt floors. Imagine keeping them clean! And many people in the world have floors just like that. Betsy is right! There is a pleasant side to cleaning and helping the family, because it means we have things to care for. Encourage your student to think of what he could be doing, the next time he is asked to help out. Mowing the lawn can actually be a pleasant job if we think about all the children who don't have their own yards!

Learning to look on the positive side and beyond our present circumstances is a major step toward maturity and cultivating thankfulness. Challenge yourself and your student with this lesson today!

Issues of Human Relationships: Why Does Time Fly When You're Having Fun?

As she crawls back into bed, Betsy is shocked to discover only an hour has passed since her mother first woke her up to go and fetch the doctor (page 133). Time is a funny thing. There are always 60 seconds in every minute, 60 minutes in every hour, 24 hours in every day, 168 hours in every week and so forth. Time is an objective fact, but it does not always *seem* so.

Sometimes when we're frightened or nervous, time seems to drag along. It also feels longer when we are very excited about something—like our birthday. Yet at other times, when we are doing something fun (playing with our friends, watching a movie, or riding our bikes) time seems to rush by.

Has your student ever heard the phrase "time flies when you're having fun?" Does he think this is true? Why?

Certainly time is absolute and never really changes, but our minds sometimes make us feel otherwise. That is why we should appreciate and soak up every minute.

Many famous writers and philosophers have recorded their thoughts on time. Benjamin Franklin, the famous writer, scientist and Betsy's friend, wrote many sayings about time in his papers and in *Poor Richard's Almanac*. Perhaps the most applicable here is his witty, yet profound remark, "Dost thou love life? Then do not squander time; for that's the stuff life is made of."

Encourage your student to think about time and how it is spent, and remind him "time always flies when you're having fun!"

Career Path: Pharmacist

In this chapter we've learned a great deal about the important role medicines play in our modern world. If your student finds this interesting, perhaps he would enjoy learning more about people who spend their time in the exciting world of medicine–pharmacists.

Typically, aspiring pharmacists must complete either a five- or six-year college program and serve a one-year internship before taking their state test to become a

licensed pharmacist. Pharmacists prepare various medications for patient's use, based upon the written guidelines of a physician called a prescription. In many cases, pharmacists have a great deal of personal contact with the patient, answering their questions, explaining the proper use of the medication and making sure they understand the safety precautions necessary to safely use modern medicines.

If your student enjoys science, chemistry and mathematics, and enjoys helping others, he might want to learn more about this exciting career field. Check your library or encyclopedia for additional information about this field, and check with several area pharmacies to see if you can arrange a field trip to meet a pharmacist personally and learn more about what he does.

Writing and Discussion Question

Betsy and George are up past their regular bedtimes. When was a time you were up late? Was it for fun or because of a crisis (like Betsy)? What happened?

Internet Connections

To view current suggested links relating to this chapter's lessons, see www.fiveinarow.com/connections.

Chapter 11–The Contest

Parent Summary

Betsy is highly distraught. Her sisters notice and ask her to tell them what is bothering her, but she says nothing. Finally, after much coaxing, Betsy begins to cry and shares with her sisters. A great fair is coming to High Street Market in four months and the fair will include an exhibit of handiwork, which anyone can enter. Betsy finally reveals the true reason for her sadness. If *anyone* can enter, not just Quakers but rich, fine ladies, the exhibition will be filled with beautiful, elaborate gowns, bonnets and other finery made from expensive silks and satins. How can Betsy compete with her simple Quaker patterns and fabrics? Even if her sewing is the best, her work won't get noticed. She is heartbroken. Her sisters are strangely silent. They know Betsy is partly correct. But surely she can create something as eye-catching and beautiful as anyone, so her skill will be noticed. Suddenly Sarah has an idea—a sampler! Betsy could make the most beautiful sampler in the world. Betsy is excited at first, but remembers her parents' beliefs. They will say a large sampler is a waste, not being a useful garment. But Sarah has another idea! If Betsy includes a verse from the Bible in the sampler, her parents might approve. Her father has always told the girls, according to the Quaker religion it is important to keep the Word of God in front of you. If it were hanging on the wall in a sampler, it would surely be in front of them! Betsy is so excited and hopes her father will be, too!

What we will cover in this chapter:

Fine Arts: Sewing a Sampler

Fine Arts: Appreciating the Simple and Ornate

Issues of Human Relationships: Seizing the Day

Lesson Activities

Fine Arts: Sewing a Sampler

Betsy's sister, Sarah, has a wonderful idea! Betsy can sew a sampler for the contest (page 141). Does your student know what a *sampler* is? Often *embroidered*, a sampler is comprised of "samples" of the artist's work. Traditionally including a center panel of the alphabet and numbers, the border of the piece is made up of many different examples of stitches.

Betsy is right about samplers being for children. In the past, samplers were used as a kind of "test" to prove the child had mastered the different stitches and was ready to move on to garments and quilts. If there is interest, why not buy a simple sampler pattern or kit and help your student complete it? Boys and girls alike can make samplers that are beautiful enough to display—just like Betsy! If you don't want to actually take the time or expense to buy a sampler pattern and actually sew it, you can create your own simple sampler with a piece of scrap fabric and inexpensive fabric "puff paints."

Fine Arts: Appreciating the Simple and Ornate

Betsy is nervous and upset because she thinks her simple Quaker work won't get recognized alongside the rich, expensive gowns (page 141). Betsy's feelings of inadequacy are human, but how unnecessary! Throughout history the most exclusive art galleries and museums in the world have showcased both the simple and the ornate. Sometimes the most beautiful paintings involve a few pure lines and only shades of one color. Often the most striking sculptures are carved with just a *hint* of the details. Smooth lines and simple features can create a breath-taking sight. And who can deny the charm and beauty of an unblemished woodcarving done by hand?

Encourage your student to remember that "art" is not *always* a product formed from the culmination of years of training, expensive materials, and months of work. "Art" is the culmination of the artist's desire and love for the work. However long it takes, with whatever medium is chosen and for whatever goal is decided upon, love is what makes things memorable and lasting.

Never let your student forget that what he puts *himself* into, will *always* be meaningful and beautiful!

Issues of Human Relationships: Seizing the Day

Sarah is inspiring Betsy. Who's to say Betsy's sampler won't be the most beautiful sampler in the world? Betsy mulls this over. "Sometime, somewhere, someone" (page 143). Could the time be now? Could the place be Philadelphia? Could she be the person to make the most beautiful sampler in the world?

Made popular by recent movies and popular speakers, the Latin phrase "Carpe Diem" is a wonderful saying for your student to think about and remember. *Carpe Diem* [car pay DEE um] means "Seize the day." Ask your student what he thinks that means.

It can mean different things to different people. Sometimes it is used to describe conquering a fear—doing something for the first time. Other times it is used to describe taking an opportunity and making the most of it. Every day is filled with new possibilities.

Just as Betsy contemplated her ability to take the moment and create the most beautiful sampler in history, so we can decide to make the most of each day and activity. Your student could be the next famous scientist, astronaut, fireman, doctor, teacher or anything else he chooses. The only thing that stands between your student and success is making the most of each opportunity. The next time he feels unsure of himself or something he is about to do, remind him of Betsy and *Carpe Diem* and see what happens!

Writing and Discussion Question

Betsy is sure she will take some example of handiwork to the fair. If you were to choose something to take, what would it be? What do you love to put work into? (For most students, this will probably have nothing to do with sewing. Possible answers might include writing, cooking, painting, model building or any number of other things. Encourage your student to elaborate on what he might take to the fair and why he particularly likes that activity.)

Internet Connections

To view current suggested links relating to this chapter's lessons, see www.fiveinarow.com/connections.

Chapter 12–The Quotation

Parent Summary

Betsy is very excited at the possibility of sewing a sampler. She decides to approach her father with the question and then waits for his response. Mr. Griscom is thoughtful and reflective for awhile. Weighing all the sides, he comes to the conclusion, much to Betsy's delight, that indeed a sampler including a Bible verse might not be a bad idea. Betsy thanks her father and sets out to find the verse she will use. After a time she discovers the verse: Leviticus 25:10. Ask your student if he remembers this verse from earlier study. (The verse inscribed on the Liberty Bell!) Betsy eagerly anticipates beginning the sampler.

What we will cover in this chapter:

[**Teacher's Note**: Due to its brevity and content, this chapter is somewhat of a transitional break for you and your student. Enjoy the lessons listed below and review anything you may have missed up to this point.]

History and Geography: The Bible—A Very Popular Book

Issues of Human Relationships: Learning to Ask

Lesson Activities

History and Geography: The Bible—A Very Popular Book

The Quakers in general and Betsy's family in particular see the Bible as an important part of their faith (page 148). As Betsy is looking for her special verse, she notices how many little "books" there are in the Bible (page 149). Does your student know how many books there are? If there is interest, take this opportunity to share with your student the framework of this famous book and a little about its history.

The Bible is the single most famous book in the history of the world. Translated into more languages, it is the most widely read book ever written. More copies have been produced, distributed and sold of the Bible than any other book in history. What is in this famous book?

The Bible is divided into two major sections, usually called the "Old Testament" and the "New Testament." (The word testament is defined as a statement testifying to the worth or validity of something. Other words from the same root include testimony and testify—witnesses attest to what actually happened when they testify before a court, giving testimony.)

The Jewish faith recognizes only the Old Testament in their faith, and it is referred to as the Hebrew Bible or the Holy Scriptures. The Christian faith accepts both testaments.

Each faith's Bible includes the writings the members of that faith feel are inspired by God and integral to their worldview.

What books are included in the Old Testament? Divided into four sections the Old Testament includes 39 different books. Listed by section, they are: 1. The Pentateuch [PENta took—Greek, meaning "five books"] (Genesis, Exodus, Leviticus, Numbers and Deuteronomy); 2. The Histories (Joshua, Judges, Ruth, 1 Samuel, 2 Samuel, 1 Kings, 2 Kings, 1 Chronicles, 2 Chronicles, Ezra, Nehemiah, and Esther); 3. The Wisdom Books (Job, Psalms, Proverbs, Ecclesiastes, and Song of Solomon); and 4. The Prophets (Isaiah, Jeremiah, Lamentations, Ezekiel, Daniel, Hosea, Joel, Amos, Obadiah, Jonah, Micah, Nahum, Habakkuk, Zephaniah, Haggai, Zechariah and Malachi.)

The Old Testament was written by a variety of authors. It was first established around 100 A.D. and became standardized by 150 A.D.

This first half of the Bible deals mainly with the history of ancient Israel and lays the foundation for the Jewish and Judeo-Christian faiths.

The second half of the Bible, the New Testament, is also divided into four sections and 27 books. The divisions are as follows: 1. The Gospels [GOS puls—Greek, meaning "good news") (Matthew, Mark, Luke and John); 2. The Acts of the Apostles (Acts); 3. The Letters (Romans, 1 Corinthians, 2 Corinthians, Galatians, Ephesians, Philippians, Colossians, 1 Thessalonians, 2 Thessalonians, 1 Timothy, 2 Timothy, Titus, Philemon, Hebrews, James, 1 Peter, 2 Peter, 1 John, 2 John, 3 John and Jude); and 4. The Revelation (also commonly referred to as the Apocalypse—Greek, meaning "to reveal") (Revelations).

The first four books of the New Testament, the Gospels, were each named for their author. Though Matthew, Mark, Luke and John all wrote about the life of Jesus, each view is subtly different, and John's perception of the events is perhaps the most different. Matthew, Mark and Luke are referred to as the "synoptic gospels" because they are so similar. The Book of John, however, is more reflective and lengthy. Luke was also the author of the book of Acts.

The next section of books, the Letters (also referred to as "the Epistles"—Greek, meaning "to send"). Thirteen of these books were written by the disciple Paul, but the other authors are unknown. The final book, the Book of Revelation, is a complex, visionary text recording thought on the end times, the return of God and the spiritual triumph over evil.

Like many books from ancient times, the first known translations of the Bible were passed down through oral interpretations—or storytelling. The first complete English translation of the complete text is believed to have occurred in the 1380s A.D. by an English man named John Wycliffe. Many people over the next 250 years wrote different translations, but none were lasting until the King of England, James I, in 1604 commissioned a group of scholars to translate the texts into a more modern vernacular. The result, known even today as the "King James Version," is still considered one of the world's great treasures and is commonly used in many churches and parishes today.

The Bible is certainly complex. Filled with history lessons, reflections on the end of the world, love poetry, riddles, wars and battles, letters, meditations on the meaning of life, songs, prose and prayers, the Bible encompasses much more than meets the eye.

If there is interest, take some time and locate a Bible. Look with your student through the various sections and read some passages aloud. What does he think? If your student is familiar with a Bible, look at a few of the books he may know less about (Ecclesiastes, Malachi or Jude, for example). Unlike other books, the Bible does not have to be read from beginning to end. Because of its structure, any of the interior books can be read in any order. If you belong to a church, parish or synagogue and your student has questions about the Scriptures you feel unable to answer, a trip to visit your pastor, priest or rabbi can be an interesting and eye-opening adventure. A classic resource book you may wish to locate is entitled *What the Bible is All About* by Henrietta Mears.

Don't be intimidated by the Bible's history and breadth. Instead, have fun studying the most popular book ever written!

Issues of Human Relationships: Learning to Ask

Betsy isn't sure her father will like the idea of her sampler. However, Mr. Griscom, much to her surprise, is open to the idea. Has your student ever wanted something he wasn't sure he would get? How did he ask? Discuss with your student the different ways we can approach people with questions. Demanding, badgering, bribing, bullying and begging are all viable options, but do they bring peace and a satisfactory answer? Not usually.

All through our lives, with siblings, parents, friends, teachers, spouses and employers, we will have requests and wishes. The way we approach a person with our idea often determines the outcome. Ask your student how he thinks a person should ask. Keeping a cheerful outlook, humble heart and quiet spirit are all good ideas when we approach someone with a special request. Challenge your student to work on "asking" instead of "telling." Everyone can afford to try harder in this area!

Writing and Discussion Question

The Bible is the most famous and widely known book of all time. Why do you think this is true? What are your thoughts on this famous book?

Internet Connections

To view current suggested links relating to this chapter's lessons, see www.fiveinarow.com/connections.

Chapter 13–The Sampler

Parent Summary

The Griscoms are sitting around the fire. The girls are sewing and George gets up to fetch more firewood. When he returns from the brisk, cold wind with an armful of wood he tells Betsy it reminds him of the night they left to get the doctor. Betsy smiles and remembers how dark the night sky was and the beautiful Liberty Bell and the stars. Suddenly, Betsy knows just what she will put on her sampler. She will make a night sky scene with the Liberty Bell and twinkling stars all around it. Then she will sew the words from Leviticus right on the Bell, just like they really appear.

Betsy is delighted with her idea. She sets to work right away and spends many evenings drawing sketches of what she might want the sampler to look like. After many ideas, she settles on one picture and her mother helps her get the stars just right. Finally, after hours of work, her sampler is finished, and it looks beautiful! Betsy is very proud.

What we will cover in this chapter:

Science: Why Do Stars Appear to Twinkle?

Fine Arts: Making Your Own Five-Pointed Star

Fine Arts: The Creative Process and a Different Kind of Criticism

Lesson Activities

Science: Why Do Stars Appear to Twinkle

Betsy wants the stars on her sampler to "twinkle" just like the stars in the sky (page 153). Does your student know why the stars seem to twinkle?

To understand why a star twinkles, we must first understand what a star is. A star is actually a sphere of moving, shifting gases in the sky. The sun is a star, and is the only star close enough to Earth that we can see its "ball-like" shape. The other stars are so far away that they look like dots, instead of spheres.

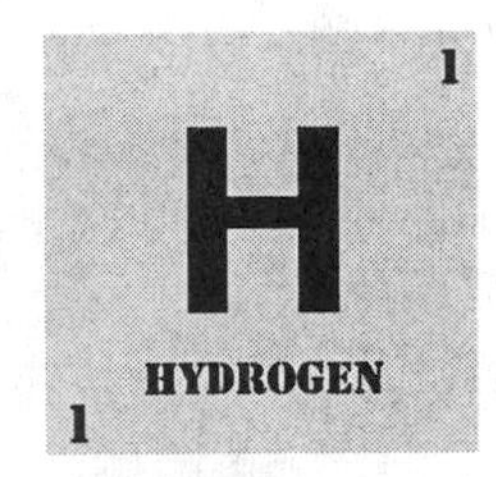

[**Teacher's Note**: Be sure to warn your student of the extreme dangers of looking directly at the sun!]

When we look at a star it twinkles because its light energy is passing through many shifting layers of atmosphere between it and the earth. Those moving atmospheric bands make the star's light almost appear to "glitter."

The two gases that make up a star are hydrogen and helium. They glow because of nuclear energy. After a long time some scientists believe a star will eventually burn up all of the gases and explode. When this happens, scientists say the star "died." New stars, however, are being born every day in the galaxies above our heads.

Have you ever tried to count the stars? Scientists estimate there are more than 200 million, million (200,000,000,000,000) stars! Isn't that amazing?

If you have access to a good sky-viewing area far from the city lights, go with your student on a clear evening and look at the stars. For an even better look, have your student keep his eyes closed for a few minutes before looking. Try to count them! And remember why they twinkle so beautifully!

Use this as an opportunity to do additional research on stars in general, and our sun in particular. Find a book at the library or use a good encyclopedia to learn more about the amazing world of stars! Two fine books on stars are *Find the Constellations* by H. A. Rey (Revised Edition, Houghton Mifflin Co., ISBN 0395245095) and *A Primer for Star-Gazers* by Henry M. Neely (Copyright 1970, Harper and Row).

Fine Arts: Making Your Own Five-Pointed Star

Betsy's mother knows how to make a beautiful five-pointed star. On page 155, our book gives us a nice illustration of how to make one ourselves. Why not take some time and help your student create his own five-pointed star. You can begin by using plain white paper, but if there is interest, beautiful stars can be cut from shiny silver or gold papers, hand- or water-colored papers, satiny or sequined material, etc. Your student can go wild with this project. Why not make little twinkling stars to hang from his bedroom ceiling? Or how about a paper star for his bedroom door (just like an actor's dressing room)?

Have fun and think of how grateful Betsy was to her mother for showing her how to make a lovely five-pointed star!

Fine Arts: The Creative Process and a Different Kind of Criticism

Betsy spends a long time thinking about what verse she wants to include on her sampler. Then it takes many evenings of hard work and planning for Betsy to draw what she thinks is a good pattern. Then she begins the actual project itself. This process of *dreaming, thinking, planning, trying* and finally *realizing* her sampler are all included in a process every artist goes through. It is often referred to as the "creative process."

Is your student the type who is easily frustrated if a project isn't going smoothly? Does he give up quickly if no ideas are coming to him? Encourage him by sharing with him the reality of hard work that must go into any art. Sewing, painting, drawing, carving, sculpting, composing, acting and cooking—all of these arts require thought and planning. And ideas don't always just hit us! Sometimes it takes a long time to understand what it is we're trying to do. Often just a feeling, an "inkling" might strike us, but it takes a slow, evolving process to make sense and become something definite. Contrary to most people's impression, very, very few creative projects just "happen" in a matter of minutes. Most projects take many, many hours of planning and execution and more than a few have been started over several times before their successful completion.

What happens when we complete a creative project but someone doesn't like it? What do we do when someone criticizes it? Or worse yet, what if we find fault with our own project? If your student suffers from self-criticism and frustration, creating art may be a tiring avocation for him. There is a difference between destructive criticism and artistic dissatisfaction.

Destructive criticism is an inhibitor. It blocks the creative thought process. Suddenly, everyone else is better than you, and your work is lessened. You feel powerless and afraid to try again. Adults can be very harmful to young budding artists. "No, do it this way." "That isn't right, try doing this." "What is that supposed to be?" "I don't understand this at all." All these comments can wound a child's creativity and hamper his self-esteem and talent.

On the contrary, great artists should always labor under artistic dissatisfaction. Artistic dissatisfaction is the knowledge that your work is complete and good—but it can always be better. If your student draws a picture of a horse, it would be odd for him to say, "That is a perfect horse. I could never draw a better one—that's it!" People who want to become great creators, might say, "That is a good horse. I like the way I drew the eyes. I think I'll send this one to Aunt Mary, but next time I try drawing a horse I'll work more on the tail."

The difference between destructive criticism and this new thought process (artistic dissatisfaction) is the end result. Now the child *wants* to try again. Artistic dissatisfaction constantly propels the artist forward, instead of squelching his desire to create.

What does all this mean to you? Learn to encourage and foster the creative process in your student. Allow him to hit and miss, make messes, try new things and find out what interests him. And most of all, remind him that it takes a lot of work to make something great! Thomas Edison (a man we've studied in depth) once made an important observation. He said, "Genius is one percent inspiration and ninety-nine percent perspiration." Work is what the creative process is all about! And artistic dissatisfaction, instead of destructive criticism, is what makes us want to go through it all again!

Writing and Discussion Question

Betsy worked long and hard to prepare a plan for her sampler. Have you ever worked long and hard on a project? Use this opportunity to write about that project, being careful to share how you felt about it when you were finished.

Internet Connections

To view current suggested links relating to this chapter's lessons, see www.fiveinarow.com/connections.

Chapter 14–Booths for the Fair

Parent Summary

The fair is coming to town! Every day after school, Betsy watches the workmen at the High Street Market build the booths and platforms. Finally May 1st arrives and Betsy carries her sampler to the handiwork booth to leave it for judging. The man at the booth abruptly tosses her sampler inside the booth and briskly asks Betsy for her name and address. Betsy is mortified! Surely the man thinks her sampler is no good, but instead of crying, she quickly gives him the information and hurries away. Because of the man's surly manner, Betsy is no longer excited about the fair. But by the next morning, all that will change!

What we will cover in this chapter:

Issues of Human Relationships: Believing in the People You Love

Issues of Human Relationships: Dealing with Self-Doubt

Lesson Activities

Issues of Human Relationships: Believing in the People You Love

Betsy is trying to be realistic about her sampler's chance of winning a prize (page 158). She isn't even sure it will be chosen to be hung in the booth. But her sister Hannah is extremely encouraging. "Won't hang it? Why wouldn't they? They'll put it right out in front. Wait and see." Sometimes, when we don't believe in ourselves, it is someone else's faith which helps us go on. Just like Hannah's faith in Betsy, we can encourage people in our lives. Encourage your student to cultivate this in his own life.

Believing in the people we love (family and friends) is something that can come naturally inside our own hearts, but learning to *communicate* that belief to them is the part we can work on. Challenge your student to look for opportunities each day to encourage and communicate his confidence in his family and friends.

Issues of Human Relationships: Dealing with Self-Doubt

Betsy is not confident her sampler is going to do well in competition. Betsy is suffering from self-doubt. But how do we conquer it? First, you can listen to the positive input you are getting. No matter how much negative feedback someone receives, there is almost always someone to encourage you! Whether the self-doubt is focused on ourselves and our abilities, something we've created, or something we are planning to do, there is always at least one person who believes in us! Listen to that person! Remember that you are a unique and special individual—like no one else on Earth! There is something wonderful and beautiful in each one of us.

Another way to combat self-doubt is to focus on the process instead of the end. Betsy forgot this concept! If you look at page 150, she is excited about her sampler, not concerned about the prize. But suddenly in this chapter she is nervous and doubting her sampler's ability to win. When we begin to worry about something we've created or worked on, we fail to properly focus on the fun we had making it, the joy we had thinking of it, the things we learned along the way and the inherent beauty it represents—all these things are more important than who likes it!

Sometimes a person who doubts his ability in a certain area is justified. Occasionally we try things we can't do or we aren't gifted at. Does this mean we should give up? Sometimes. If your student has tried singing in choirs for years but has never been selected from an audition, perhaps singing isn't his area of giftedness. There is no need to sink into a deep depression, but instead, we need to realize our limitations and our strengths and identify the areas in which we excel.

If your student labors under self-doubt, encourage him to listen to positive influences, focus on the process, and reevaluate his strengths and weaknesses. Adults, as well as children, can learn to deal better with self-doubt! It plagues the most confident of people!

Writing and Discussion Question

Betsy is upset by the man's reaction to her sampler at the booth (page 160). She thinks he doesn't like her work and that he probably doesn't like her. Why would Betsy assume that? What are other possible reasons for the man's reactions?

Internet Connections

To view current suggested links relating to this chapter's lessons, see www.fiveinarow.com/connections.

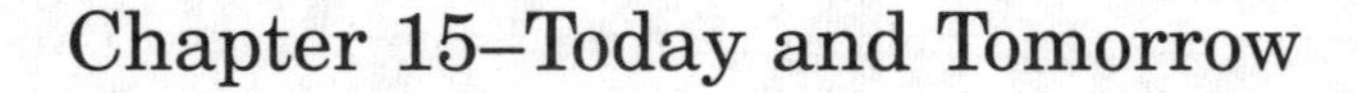

Chapter 15–Today and Tomorrow

Parent Summary

The day of the fair has finally arrived! Betsy wakes up early and shakes her sister Hannah awake, as well. The Griscoms finish all their chores and housework as quickly as they can and dress in their First Day's best. Setting off for the fairgrounds, Betsy begins to feel anxious. What if she does not win? What if her sampler isn't even hanging in the booth? She begins to walk slower and slower. George, her enthusiastic little brother, has run ahead of the others. Soon Betsy sees George rushing back towards them, yelling to hurry!

What is he so frantic about? Soon Betsy hears the good news. Her sampler is hanging right out in front of the handiwork booth. Delighted, she grabs George's hand and runs back with him to see. Sure enough, Betsy's beautiful Liberty Bell sampler is prominently displayed and many people are milling about admiring it. Betsy is pleased. The handiwork judging is set for later in the day, so the Griscom children head off to see the rest of the booths.

At five o'clock they return to the booth and arrive to see a throng of spectators. Betsy can't even see the platform! Soon the judges call a woman's name who made a beautiful evening gown and hand her a prize. Betsy knows it must be the first prize. Next, a woman's quilt is recognized. Suddenly, the announcer calls Betsy's name. Third prize! How wonderful! Betsy goes to the platform and is handed five pounds. Five pounds? But that is the first prize. Betsy is stunned. She was wrong about the other two women. They won second and third, and Betsy's sampler has won first place. The judges tell her they think her sampler is the best piece because it is made from American materials and has an American theme. Thrilled, she hurries back to her family and shows them the glittering gold pieces.

What we will cover in this chapter:

History and Geography: Nationalism

Lesson Activities

History and Geography: Nationalism

The judges like Betsy's sampler the best because it "...is an American design made from American materials." They tell Betsy, "America must learn to develop her own arts." This is an important statement. Remind your student that our story is set in the mid-1760s. The colonies were still fairly new, and Americans were struggling to find their own identity, apart from England. The British Empire still maintained tight control on the trade and economy, as well as influencing fashion and society.

But now the words *freedom, liberty* and *independence* were being used with increasing frequency. These words weren't simply intangibles either. Being chained to England was getting old. Americans were tired of paying taxes to their "mother country" without having any voice. Americans were tired of having British soldiers crowding the shores and cities in order to "keep an eye" on them. Americans were tired of giving allegiance to a King, rulers and governors almost 3,000 miles away! It was time to create strictly "American" things. It was time for America to develop her own, unique identity.

The actual separation did not occur until 1776 and resulted in the Revolutionary War. But wars begin with quiet revolutions in the hearts and minds of individuals, and that was what was happening when Betsy won her prize! A new recognition of American pride, culture and product was beginning.

Today, words like "Made in America," "Grown in the Homeland," and "Built with Pride" are all catch-phrases manufacturers use to assure Americans they are buying products made in the United States. Nearly 250 years after the Revolutionary War, America is now a major world influence in her own right, helping to set the trends in society, the economy and world politics.

Possibly a new term for your student, this emphasis on cultural pride and homeland development is called *nationalism*. Nationalism means to have a sense of pride and devotion to your country. Patriotism and independence also play a part in nationalism.

What does your student think about his country? What words would he use to describe it? What products does he feel best represent his country?

For more information on nationalism and cultural pride, the three following books are wonderful! The first, *I Love America*, edited by Shelagh Canning (Copyright 1990, Western Publishing Company, ISBN 0307868311) is filled with interesting essays and poems by famous Americans (Mark Twain, Robert Frost, Walt Whitman, Benjamin Franklin and many more). The book also features beautifully illustrated sheet music and lyrics to dozens of classic American songs. A treasure!

Another excellent resource is *Fireworks, Picnics and Flags* by James Cross Giblin (Copyright 1983, Houghton Muffin Co, ISBN 0899191746). This delightful book traces the history behind many of America's famous symbols including our flag, the bald eagle, the Liberty Bell and Uncle Sam. Great for the entire family, this book is filled with interesting facts and fun information!

Finally, a book your student will love is *If You Were There in 1776*, by Barbara Brenner (Copyright 1994, Simon and Schuster, ISBN 0027123227). A wonderful read-aloud for younger students, this book is written in a user-friendly format and includes information on all aspects of life in 1776, ranging from the foods they ate to the games they played. Covering topics all the way through the Revolutionary War, this book is one of the best—a must-find!

As you go about the day with your student, discuss nationalism and cultural pride. Because America is often referred to as the "melting pot" of the world we have created a wide variety of products and traditions that are our own.

Writing and Discussion Question

Betsy is proud of winning first prize! Have you ever won an award? What was it for? How did you feel?

Internet Connections

To view current suggested links relating to this chapter's lessons, see www.fiveinarow.com/connections.

Chapter 16–The Apprentices

Parent Summary

Betsy and John Ross have become good friends. John is an apprentice at Webster's Upholstery Establishment. Betsy thinks it would be exciting to apprentice there, as well. She knows they take girls and with her sewing expertise surely they would want her! If only Betsy could convince her father. Mr. Griscom doesn't think girls should work unless they have to, but after much discussion, he grants Betsy's request. If Webster's will hire her, she can be an apprentice.

Betsy enjoys her new employment. Being with John each day is nice and she learns much about upholstery. Beyond that, Betsy talks with the other apprentices and learns about the growing dissatisfaction in the Colonies with England. There is much talk about becoming independent from the mother country. John is a Patriot. The patriots believe America should go to war. Betsy tends to agree with him but is confused. Her own family, being Quakers, are pacifists and do not believe in war. Her parents are Tories and still believe in allegiance to the King. Betsy is gathering her own independence, however, and cannot deny her true feelings about the war. She agrees with John and supports his position.

Betsy is beginning to support John in other ways too. John wants to someday own his own upholstery shop and wants Betsy to marry him and work with him. Betsy could not be happier. She wants to share John's dream. She decides that if war becomes a reality and John joins the army, then she can run the store while he is gone! Betsy is certainly growing up.

What we will cover in this chapter:

History and Geography: Apprenticeship

History and Geography: Tories and Patriots

Lesson Activities

History and Geography: Apprenticeship

Betsy wants to be an apprentice with John at Webster's Upholstery (page 176). Does your student know what an *apprentice* is? An apprentice (a person serving an apprenticeship) works under a master craftsman for a legally binding amount of time. For example, in Betsy's day she might have signed a year apprenticeship. For that contract, she would have learned a skill and been paid a small stipend. An apprentice cannot break his contract until his time is up. Draw your student's attention to page 182. The book tells us John Ross had "served most of his apprenticeship." That means John's contract was nearly finished.

Today, apprenticeships are rarely bound by legal contracts, but instead involve a course of study under a master. For example, many universities that offer degrees in the culinary arts refer to their program as an "apprenticeship." A young cooking student might learn the art of pastry work from top chefs in their field.

An excellent example of apprenticeship in the late 18th century (similar to what Betsy might have encountered) is found in the book *Carry On, Mr. Bowditch* by Jean Lee Latham (Copyright 1955, Riverside Press). This book, set in Salem, Massachusetts in 1775, focuses on the apprenticeship of young Nat Bowditch. Filled with interesting nautical terminology, exciting action and sweet characters, this book will touch your heart and teach you a great deal about the Colonies and apprenticeships. The book is written at the 10-14 age reading level, but is a wonderful read-aloud for your younger student as well!

History and Geography: Tories and Patriots

John and Betsy enjoy discussing politics. John is a patriot and Betsy is, as well, but her parents are Tories (page 181). Does your student know what a Tory is? A Patriot?

[**Teacher's Note**: The following chapter's lessons will cover the Revolutionary War in much greater detail. This lesson is just meant to be an introduction to the two different political viewpoints in Colonial America.]

The Colonists were divided into two camps in the years leading up to the war. Many people felt a strong sense of liberation and independence. They wanted to separate themselves from England and unite under their own flag. The burden of taxes and paying homage to a King nearly 3,000 miles away was tiresome. The Colonists had enjoyed their own government for quite some time, but were now demanding complete independence. People like John and Betsy—rugged individualists—shared these ideas. They were known as *Patriots*.

But there is always another side. Some of the Colonists felt a strong sense of loyalty to their homeland. After all, they were *colonists*. They had come to America with the express goal of colonizing a new British Empire—spreading the power of England abroad. These people did not understand the patriots' desire to war against the very nation where their parents, grandparents and great-grandparents had lived all their lives. England was the colonists' mother country—their homeland. Why would they want to sever those ties? Why would they want to spread bloodshed among their own people? These were the thoughts of the other colonists. They were known as *Tories*.

Betsy's parents were Tories. They believed in allegiance to the King, and further, they did not believe in war because of their Quaker faith.

Too often historians do not give enough credit to the Tories. Today, we are all products of an independent, united nation so it is much easier to empathize with the Patriot side. But it was not an easy decision. There were no easy answers. And, like the Griscom family, many families were divided over these very issues (page 181).

If your student is interested in this discussion, there is a wonderful book written from the Tory perspective entitled *Katie's Trunk* by Ann Turner, illustrated by Ron Himler (Copyright 1992, Simon and Schuster, ISBN 0027895122). Set in the early days of the Revolution, Katie and her family are Loyalists. One day some patriots invade their home, and the family is forced to hide. Katie hides in her mother's wedding trunk. A beautiful turn of events happens, however, and the story ends by showing there is still goodness in the world. A poignant story told from the Tory viewpoint!

Writing and Discussion Question

We know America was granted independence from England through the Revolutionary War. What would America be like today if this had not happened? How do you think your life would be different?

Vocabulary Words

demur: to hesitate because of one's doubts or objection

rampant: spreading unchecked, widespread

turbulent: full of commotion or wild disorder

militia: an army composed of citizens versus soldiers

Internet Connections

To view current suggested links relating to this chapter's lessons, see www.fiveinarow.com/connections.

Chapter 17–A Famous Story

Parent Summary

In this chapter, two new characters are introduced, Ruth and Jim Wills. The story has suddenly jumped forward more than two centuries and this modern, American couple is visiting the historical site of Betsy Ross' home in Philadelphia.

Over 150,000 people visit the site every year just like the Wills. But why? What makes Betsy's home so intriguing? Mrs. Stewart and Miss Worrell, the tour guides, let us in on the rest of the story.

Betsy Griscom eventually married John Ross and they opened an upholstery shop in Philadelphia, just as they had planned. Betsy's brilliant sewing and John's business sense helped the little shop do well. The year was now 1776 and talk of war was becoming frequent. John, a Patriot, had an uncle who was under the command of General George Washington. His uncle, Colonel George Ross, had discussed with General Washington the possibility an American flag for the new army to fight under. General Washington was intent on obtaining a flag and even had his own designs for it already in hand, but didn't know who he could ask to make it. Colonel Ross quickly recommended his nephew's wife, Betsy, and the General and Colonel went to her house. General Washington showed her his designs for the first American flag and she agreed to sew it. According to the story, Betsy even suggested to the General using five-pointed stars instead of six-pointed. The design included six white stripes, seven red stripes, and a field of blue with thirteen stars in a circle. Washington loved the idea and Betsy set to work on the flag.

John Ross was not around to enjoy Betsy's accomplishment. Having joined the militia in the early stages of the war, he was killed when ammunition in a storehouse exploded. At 24, Betsy was a widow and running the shop alone.

Betsy Ross is a piece of American history. She has been remembered well.

[**Teacher's Note**: The chapter does not include information concerning the end of Betsy's life. Betsy Ross eloped with John Ross in 1773 (she was only 21 years old). Married a scant three years when John was killed, Betsy continued to run the couple's upholstery shop. Married two more times in her life, Betsy eventually had seven daughters in all. Betsy died in 1836 at the age of 84.]

What we will cover in this chapter:

History and Geography: Revolutionary War—A Brief Outline

History and Geography: George Washington—General and President

History and Geography: Legends of Famous Americans

Language Arts: Jump Shifts—A Literary Device

Lesson Activities

History and Geography: Revolutionary War—A Brief Outline

General Washington needed a standard flag for his army to fight under (page 188). The Revolutionary War, so long talked about, was beginning. Discuss this amazing piece of American history with your student.

America was ready to become her own nation at last! Wanting to sever all ties to England, the colonists took matters into their own hands and began the long fight for independence. Several specific situations precipitated the war and led to the military conflicts.

First, in 1763 Britain handed down a proclamation. On October 7, England sent thousands of soldiers to the Colonies to provide a constant army presence. The colonists were not consulted or notified of this major change. Along with this decision, England proclaimed the Appalachian Mountain range and much land west of it off limits for settlement. This area was to be reserved for the Indians and many colonists were outraged. They felt Britain had no right to interfere in colonial development.

Not three months later, on December 16, 1773, a famous event took place, which continued the animosity between America and England. Britain, having arranged a high tax on tea, sent a huge shipload of tea into the Boston Harbor. That night a large group of passionate Patriots, led by Samuel Adams, dressed as Indians, climbed aboard the ship and dumped over 300 crates of tea into the harbor. This event, known as the Boston Tea Party, was a slap in the face to Britain and they, in turn, continued to inflict more serious taxes and laws on the colonists.

As an interesting historic note on the Boston Tea Party, after that event, Americans drastically cut back on their tea consumption as a statement to England. Instead, Americans turned to coffee. To this day, Americans consume more coffee than any other nation in the world. All other European nations still hold tea as their hot beverage of choice.

The final event, which pushed the colonists to war, was the Restraining Act Britain introduced in 1775. King George III, enraged by the Boston Tea Party, commanded all trade between England and the Colonies halted and encouraged the British troops stationed in America to begin using force against what he felt were "mobs" of rebellious Patriots. The various decisions implemented by King George became known as the *Intolerable Acts*. The beginning of the end was at hand.

The British military forces included the British soldiers stationed in the Colonies (known as Redcoats), the Tories, mercenaries (hired soldiers from other countries), and several of the various Indian tribes. The Colonists, although facing a difficult battle, did hold several trump cards. They knew the terrain and countryside, had more than enough soldiers, weren't dependent upon the transport of supplies across the ocean, and were hoping to enlist other countries (chiefly France and Spain) who were enemies of England to come to their assistance on the naval front.

The Revolutionary War began on April 18, 1775. The Redcoats, led by British Lt. General Thomas Gage, began a siege on Concord, Massachusetts, trying to capture the Patriot's main supply station. Paul Revere, along with several other men, rode his famous ride from Lexington to Concord, warning the colonists of the danger. (If you can, read Ralph W. Emerson's "Concord Hymn," a great poem about this time in history.)

In the days that followed, many bloody battles were fought. (Famous battles include Concord, Bunker Hill and Lexington.) General Washington, leading the American forces, fought long and hard, surviving not only the battles but also the harsh elements. The winter at Valley Forge was a particularly difficult time for the American soldiers as they were faced with bitter cold and little food.

The war lasted nearly eight years, eventually ending with the Peace Treaty ratified on April 15, 1783. America was a free and independent nation at last! If there is interest, more in-depth research on the Revolutionary War is recommended. Also, making a timeline of important events and battles in the Revolutionary War can be a delightful and helpful endeavor.

An interesting book is the *Liberty Book*, by artist and author Leonard Everett Fisher (Copyright 1976, Doubleday and Co, ISBN 0385048920). Including quotes, songs, and famous poetry, this book unabashedly shouts out "Liberty!" from every page. For the older student, any of the poems and literary selections would be excellent for memorization.

It is important to note that although American political thought has gone through many evolutions since 1776, the principal rights and freedoms won more than 200 years ago are still recognized as the basis for America's national policy. Freedom of speech, freedom of religion, fair trials and equal justice all remain close to the hearts of Americans. We know the importance of listening to each other—holding other people's differences as sacred as our own beliefs, and welcoming a dialogue of views instead of enforcing strict codes and policies. America is an amazing nation and its future history can thrive as these freedoms are deemed important. A thought-provoking book on the topics of freedom and justice is *Are You Liberal? Conservative? or Confused?* by Richard J. Maybury (ISBN 0-042718-23-1).

History and Geography: George Washington—General and President

Betsy's relative, Colonel Ross, served under General George Washington (page 187). Most people know George Washington as America's first president and indeed he was, but his accomplishments and life before that assignment are as amazing as his time in office. Take this opportunity to share with your student some interesting facts and details of this famous American.

Born February 22, 1732 in Virginia, Washington was the son of wealthy plantation owner, Augustine Washington. George's father died when his son was only 11 years old and George lived off and on with various relatives. With no formal education, George Washington spent much of his late teens and early twenties working as surveyor. By the time he was 21 years old, Washington was a self-supporting professional and lived on his brother's plantation, Mount Vernon (a famous site he later inherited).

George Washington had a brilliant mind for the military. Interested in tactics and foreign affairs, he was anxious to begin serving in any way he could. Moving quickly through the ranks from Major to Lt. Colonel, Washington played an influential role in the French and Indian War.

By 26, however, George was ready to settle down and married the young and beautiful widow, Martha Custis. Never having any children of this own, George adopted Martha's two children from her previous marriage and loved them as his own. Throughout the first 10 years of their marriage, George and Martha worked hard at becoming successful plantation owners and succeeded. In 1761, after inheriting Mount Vernon, George brought his family to the farm and they worked to create a pleasant and prosperous farm. Society parties and hunting expeditions were routine at Mount Vernon, and his business success made George a well-respected citizen.

During those years he served in various civil capacities and learned much about legislation and political life and met many important figures including Thomas Jefferson and Samuel Adams (who was an orator and writer during the American Revolutionary period and who organized the Boston Tea Party).

With the Revolutionary War eminent, no one else in the Colonies was better qualified to serve as commander-in-chief than George Washington. Accepting the military post he never sought, Washington is quoted as saying humbly, "I beg it may be remembered by every gentleman in the room, that I this day declare with the utmost sincerity, I do not think myself equal to the command I am honored with."

With a commanding presence and loyal following, General George Washington led his troops through many historical battles including Trenton, Saratoga and Yorktown. Washington served his country as commander-in-chief from 1776 to 1783. By the end of the war, George Washington was ready to go home. But now America was a free country needing a new government and leader. Washington fit the bill. With reluctance, Washington accepted the office of first President of the United States on April 30, 1789. He is the only U.S. President in history to have been voted into office unanimously.

Forming many of the characteristics and expected services of the presidency today, Washington was forced to invent them as he went along. He was the first! What a daunting task that must have been.

After serving two terms (he could have been re-elected but refused), he was succeeded by his vice-president, John Adams.

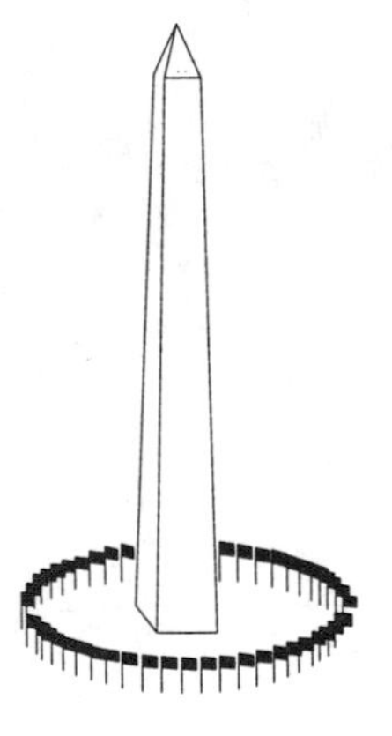

George Washington is remembered in the hearts of Americans today and honored with the Washington Monument, located in Washington D.C. His home, Mount Vernon, has been fully restored and is open to the public for tour. Both he and Martha are buried on the grounds.

If your student is interested, locate a good biography on this famous American—a fascinating person who faced many difficult decisions, but rose to the challenges before him. One excellent title is called *George Washington's World,* written by Genevieve Foster. Request it from your library system. Foster's book is a treasure-house of interesting information. Enjoyable!

History and Geography: Legends of Famous Americans

It is obvious in our story and from other sources on Betsy Ross, that many historians are not convinced she was the first flag maker. Even in our book, her involvement is not put into definite words (pages 186-188). There are many such legends in American history. Legends are stories so long told that they are now believed to be true. Share with your student some other examples of famous American legends.

For example, many people recount the story of the young boy George Washington and the cherry tree. Supposedly, little George's father found a cherry tree sapling, which had been chopped down. Augustine Washington asked whether George had chopped the tree down. According to legend, Washington answered, "I cannot tell a lie. It was I." No one really knows whether this conversation actually took place or not, but it has been accepted as fact over the years. Indeed, George Washington's life was a fine example of honesty and integrity, but whether or not this scrupulous behavior was evident at such a young age is unknown.

Another American legend is the story of Abraham Lincoln returning a penny he was given. The tale says a young Lincoln made a purchase and was given a penny too much in change. Not discovering the mistake until he had walked the mile home, Lincoln immediately turned around and walked back to the store to return the extra money. Is this story true? No one knows, but it makes for an excellent tale of moral character and fiber in one of America's most beloved presidents.

More examples of American legends are Daniel Boone, Davy Crockett ("killed him a 'bar' when he was only three") and Johnnny Appleseed (a real man, but his efforts have been somewhat exaggerated).

There is much evidence to lend credence to the story of Betsy Ross making the first American flag. If indeed she did not create the original, we have documented proof she sewed and sold many of the very first flags made in America.

For more information on Betsy Ross, her home and the story behind the legend, write to:

Independence Hall Association
Carpenters' Hall
320 Chestnut Street
Philadelphia, PA 19106

From this historical society, you can also order an 18"x12" exact replica of the Betsy Ross Flag for under $10. Attached to a 30" pole with gilded top, the flag is the famous red and white striped, five-point star bedangled banner of freedom. All proceeds go to the Independence Hall Association.

Whether or not Betsy Ross actually made the first flag for America is debatable, but her influence, kindness, devoted patriotism and never-ending optimism are what make her an American hero!

Language Arts: Jump Shifts—A Literary Device

In this final chapter of our book, we are spun into the future and shown what Betsy's later life and times were like through the eyes of her great-great-grand-niece, Miss Worrell (page 187). The author employs a classic literary device used to condense time and events—a flash forward.

Often used in writing, both flash forwards and flashbacks are referred to as jump shifts. Literally meaning "a jump or shift in time" this device allows the author to either fill in the reader with pertinent details from the past (a flashback), or condense future events into a manageable amount of text, as seen here in our biography.

Does your student like this device? What other books has he read where a jump shift was used?

There is no better way to understand this literary tool, than for your student to try it for himself. If there is interest, have your student write a short story where the plot is developed and then flashes forward or flashes back. He could even write the same story twice—once including a flashback to let the reader in on past details, and a second time including a flash forward.

Although this technique is more advanced, even the youngest students can understand its concept if led through some simple questions and answers. For example, here is an example of a teacher's conversation with the student.

Teacher: Your story is wonderful. The squirrel, Nutmeg, is already on her own. What was her family like?

Student: They all lived in the forest and Nutmeg wanted to move to the prairie.

Teacher: When did she decide to move?

Student: A long time ago.

Teacher: Did she discuss it with her family?

Student: Yes.

Teacher: How did she explain her plan?

Student: Well, she said she longed for the beautiful rolling grass.

Teacher: I think that is so interesting. You could include that in your story by adding it as a flash black. Then other people would know how Nutmeg made it to the prairies in the beginning.

By leading your student down a road of mental reasoning and allowing him to discover what he already knows about his character's past (or future) you can aid him in writing a jump shift.

Encourage your student to try this literary device in a story soon and to be looking for it in books he reads for himself.

Writing and Discussion Question

Do you think Betsy Ross made the first American flag? Why or why not?

Internet Connections

To view current suggested links relating to this chapter's lessons, see www.fiveinarow.com/connections.

Master Index

Scope of Topics for *Beyond Five in a Row* Volume 1

The Boxcar Children

History

Greek and Persian War
- Marathon, Greece
- King Darius

Hippocrates
Hippocratic Oath
Pioneer life in America
Industrial Revolution
- England, 1700s
- America, 1800s
- Mills
  (flour, steel, lumber, cloth)
- Dickens, Charles (protesting factory abuse

Potato Famine, Ireland
Irish immigrations
Transcontinental Railroad
- Union Pacific Railroad
- Central Pacific Railroad
- Golden Spike

The Great Depression, 1929
Dust Bowl, The Dirty Thirties
Philanthropy
- J. D. Rockefeller
- Andrew Carnegie
- James Smithson
- Cornelius Vanderbilt
- John P. Morgan
- Ford Foundation

Geography

America
- ME, MI fruit regions
- Route of Transcontinental Railroad
- Dust Bowl—KS, OK, TX NM, CO
- Hoover Dam, Colorado River
- Mapping types of mills, U.S.
- Mapping major railroads—U.S.
- Boston (Marathon)
- New York City (Marathon)

Canadian provinces—Maritimes
Europe
- Marathon, Greece

Science

Scientific Classification System
Human body and health
- Nutrition
- Vitamins
- Calories
- Health and cleanliness
- Sleep
- Fever

Medicine, field of
- Germs
- Scientists—men of medicine
  - Louis Pasteur
- First aid
- First aid kit
- Sterilization—autoclave
- Career path—Doctor

Water cycle
- Drought
- Evaporation
- Condensation
- Precipitation
- Water, valuable resource

Dams
- Hoover
- Aswan

Climates
- Temperate
- Tropical—Subtropical

Plants and agriculture
- Parts of flowers
- Parts of leaves
- Parts of fruit

Orchards—Pesticides, Pruning
- Organic farming
- Harvesting

Gardening
- Potato, tuber

Plants from temperate climates
- Plants—subtropical climates
- Plants—tropical climates

Egg, parts of
- Shell
- Membrane
- Albumen
- Yolk
- Grading eggs
- Sizing eggs
- Experiments with eggs

Animal
- Beaver

Measurements of
- Distance, Land
- Volume
- Water
- Time

Elements
- Oxygen
- Iron

Language Arts

Elements of mystery
Use of serialization
Description in writing
Learning to write in chapters
Learning to compare and contrast
Point of view
Periodicals: newspapers
- Reading foreign papers

Letter writing

Literature explored:

- *Incredible Journey* by Sheila Burnford
- *Haystack* by B. and A. Beisert
- *All Creatures Great and Small* by James Herriot
- *Moses the Kitten* by James Herriot
- Stone Soup (old folk tale)
- *Charles Dickens* by Diane Stanley
- "The Courtship of Miles Standish" by Henry W. Longfellow

Vocabulary Words

catalyst
hydrophilic
hydrophobic
evaporation
condensation
precipitation
Dust Bowl
transcontinental
timetable
serialization
amenities
cultivate
climate
acidity
cliffhanger
deciduous
evergreen
veterinarian
pasteurization
separation
homogenization
fortification
packaging
autoclave
flammable
tinder
kindling
oxidation

The Boxcar Children, continued

Vocabulary Words, continued
abrasive
encourage
watch
calorie
shell
membrane
albumen
yolk
candling

Fine Arts
Functional design
Cooking (three lessons)
Painting with blueberries
Making maps and models
Recycling for art
Collage
Dramatic interpretation
Drawing a scene
Picturing a poem
Charcoal drawing
Potato printing
Sewing a design
Design and illustration
Architecture
Portraits
Room decorating

Issues of Human Relationships
Listening
Assuming things about people
Reasons why people are difficult
Making fun of people
Being an encourager
Generosity
Being a good worker
Being flexible
Being helpful
Being inventive
Grandparents
Moving
Going the extra mile
Seeing past differences
Making friends

Career Paths
Veterinarian
Doctor

Thomas Edison— Young Inventor

History
Gutenberg
Printing press
Gutenberg Bible
Beginnings of Abolition Movement, late 1600s
De Witt Clinton
- Governor of New York
- Erie Canal
- Seneca Chief, first boat

Canals
- Erie Canal
- Suez Canal
- Panama Canal

Steam powered locomotives
Fred Harvey
George pullman
One Room Schoolhouses
Canadian History
- Vikings, Leif Ericson
- French fur traders
- French and Indian War

Telegraph
- Samuel Morse
- Morse Code

President James Polk
President Zachary Taylor
- Treaty of Guadalupe

Hildalgo
Presient Millard Fillmore
Abolition Movement
Underground Railroad, Pre-Civil War
- Sojourner Truth
- Harriet Beecher Stowe
  - Uncle Tom's Cabin
- Harriet Tubman

President Franklin Pierce
Commodore Perry
- Japanese Trade Agreement

President James Buchanan
Slavery
- Dredd Scott Decision
- John Brown

Geography
America
- Erie Canal
- The Great Lakes
- Niagra Falls
- Straits of Mackinac
- Huron River
- Lake St. Claire
- West Branch, IA
- Detroit, MI
- Port Huron, MI
- Melano Park, Greenfield Village, MI
- Newark, NJ
- New York City, NY
- Milan, OH

Canadian territories and capitals
- Yukon Territory, Whitehose
- Northwest Territory, Yellowknife
- Nunavut, Iqaluit

Canadian Provinces (Maritime)
- British Columbia, Victoria
- Alberta, Edmonton
- Saskatchewan, Regina
- Manitoba, Winnipeg
- Ontario, Toronto
- Quebec, Quebec City
- New Brunswick, Fredricton
- Prince Edward Island, Charlottetown
- Nova Scotia, Halifax
- Newfoundland, St. John's

Central America
- Panama Canal

Europe
Asia
- India

Africa
- Egypt
- South Africa

Diameter of Earth
Distance of earth from moon

Science
Biology
- Eggs
  - Fertile and unfertile
  - Incubation
- Human body
  - Ears, parts of
  - Deafness
    - Sign Language
  - Hypothermia
  - Frostbite

Botany
- Tree identification

Electricity, electrons
Static electricity
- Lightning

Current electricity
Speed of sound

Thomas Edison, continued

Science, continued
Speed of light
- Albert Michelson

Light bulb
- Light
- Heat
- Tungsten filament

Economics
- Savings
- Budgets
- Warning symbols

Regelation—ice skates, function
Dew point
Frost
Humidity
Pollution
- Air
- Water
- Ground
- Smog
- Pollution control projects
  - Landfills

The Scientific Method
- Observation
- Hypothesis
- Experimentation
- Evaluating results

Setting up your own laboratory
Different branches of science
- Math and Logic:
  - Arithmetic
  - Algebra
  - Geometry
  - Calculus
  - Probability
  - Statistics
- Physical Science
  - Chemistry
  - Geology
  - Meteorology
  - Astronomy
  - Physics
- Life Science—Biology
  - Zoology
  - Botany
- Social Science
  - Anthropology
  - Economics
  - Psychology
  - Sociology

Periodic Table of Elements, brief introduction
Elements
- Mercury
- Phosphorus

Language Arts
Descriptive word choices
Creative writing of life on a canal
Making a list of travel options
Autobiographical writing
Famous sayings
Penmanship review
Marketing: advertising
Similes and metaphors
Writing styles
Subscriptions
Newspaper editing

Literature explored:
- *Locs, Crocs and Skeeters* by Nancy W. Parker
- *Wind in the Willows* by K. Graham
- *Farmer Boy* by Laura Ingalls Wilder
- *Hans Brinker* or *The Silver Skates* by Mary Mapes Dodge
- *Hound of the Baskervilles* by Sir Arthur Conan Doyle
- *Gutenberg* by Leonard Everett Fisher
- *If You Lived at the Time of the Civil War* by Kay Moore

Vocabulary Words
pitch
parlor
light year
biography
autobiography
regelation
dew point
hypothermia
frostbite
cinnabar
entrepreneur

Fine Arts
"Erie Canal" (song) History Alive through Music
Cooking
Colored pencils, blending with
Drawing illustrations
Marketing, creating a look for your business
Drama and memorizing
Making your own newspaper printing block
Creating a panorama
Making a flip book
Filming your own movie

Issues of Human Relationships
Listening to people who are younger
Obedience
First times
Observation
Being neighborly
Focusing our attention
Differences and assumptions
How we respond to discipline
Observation
Being helpful
Your first job
Organizing your personal study
Problem solving
Speaking words of praise
Being brave

Career Paths
Journalism
Law enforcement
- Police
- FBI
- Secret Service

Homer Price

History
Trojan War 1200 B.C.
Homer (? 800 B.C.)
- *The Illiad* and *The Odyssey*
- Ulysses (Latin for Odysses) and Telemachas

Dutch settlement of New York, 1600s
Jean Henri Dunant, Swiss philanthropist
Austro-Sardinian War
- Solferino
- *Un Souvenir de Solferino*
- Red Cross, 1863

Clara Barton
- American Red Cross, 1881

United States Constitution

Homer Price, continued

History, continued

- Political parties
  - Republican
  - Democrat
  - Third party candidates
- Party mascots
  - Republican elephant
  - Democrat donkey
  - Thomas Nast, cartoonist
- President Andrew Jackson
- Woman's Suffrage Movement, early 1800s
  - National Woman's Suffrage Association
    - Elizabeth Cady Stanton
    - Susan B. Anthony
- American Woman's Suffrage Association
  - Lucy Stone
  - Henry Blackwell
- 19th Amendment

- Department of Housing and Urban
  - Development (HUD)
- Habitat for Humanity

Geography

- America
  - New York
    - Settlement by the Dutch
    - Catskills
    - Hudson River
    - Appalachian Mountains
  - Transportation
    - City streets
    - County roads
    - Freeways
    - Interstate highways
    - Junction

Science

- Bird Eggs
  - Colors and patterns
  - Incubating time
  - Laying time frame
- Inventing egg cracking device
- Simple machines
  - Pulley
  - Lever
  - Wedge
  - Inclined plane
  - Wheel and axle
  - Screw
- Horsepower
  - Foot-lbs. of work per second
  - James Watt, Scottish engineer
- Technology and labor saving devices
- Economics
  - Law of supply and demand
- Early radio
- Early television
  - RCA (Radio Corporation of America)
- French chemist
  - Louis Nicolas Vauquelin
- Element
  - Chromium

Language Arts

- Different fictional story formats
- Making headlines interesting
- Advertising slogans
- Formula fiction
- Literary device
- Enrichment through thematic studies
- Famous sayings
- Applying vocabulary words, ideas for

Literature explored:

- *The Illiad* by Homer
- *The Odyssey* by Homer
- *Souvenir de Solferino* by Jean Henri Dunant
- *Rip Van Winkle* by Washington Irving
- *The Sketch Book* by Washington Irving

Vocabulary Words

- Homer
- junction
- tourist camp
- bungalow
- sensationalism
- slogan
- validate
- chromium
- horsepower
- to coin
- foot-pound
- monogram
- melodrama
- disillusionment
- suffrage
- suburb
- urban
- rural
- receptive
- imperative
- arbitrate
- architect
- landscape architect

Fine Arts

- What's wrong with this picture?
- Cartooning
- Melodrama
- Sandwich boards
- Illustrating movement
- Cooking
- Making a collection
- Leaf art
- Designing and making your own checkerboard
- Learning about James Abbott McNeill
- Whistler, American artist
  - Whistler's Mother

Issues of Human Relationships

- Having parents who understand
- Dealing with disillusionment
- Developing discernment
- Frugality
- Special occasions
- Making a good appearance
- Making people feel comfortable

Betsy Ross

History

- Crusades
- Duke Leopold V of Austria
- Austrian flag
- King Henry VII
- Columbus
  - *Nina, Pinta, Santa Maria*
- King James I
- King James English
- King James Bible
- England

Betsy Ross, continued

History, continued
Quakers
George Fox
William Penn
Pennsylvania
King George III
British Empire
Nationalism
- Freedom
- Liberty
- Independence
- National pride

American Revolutionary War—Introductory Overview
- Tories and Patriots
- George Washington
- Intolerable Acts
- Boston Tea Party
- Paul Revere's Ride
- Declaration of Independence
- Samuel Adams
- Thomas Jefferson
- John Adams

Ben Franklin
Apprenticeship
Pennsylvania Gazette
Poor Richard's Almanac
Legendary Figures
- Daniel Boone
- Davy Crockett
- Johnny Appleseed (John Chapman)
- American pioneers—lifestyle

Foreign currencies
- England, sovereigns, shillings
- Germany, Deutch marks
- Japan, yen
- Switzerland, francs

Geography
America
- Bunker Hill, MA
- Concord, MA
- Lexington, MA
- Trenton, NJ
- Saratoga, NY
- Philadelphia, PA
- Valley Forge, PA
- Yorktown, VA

Europe
- Austria
- Denmark
- England
- France
- Spain

Crossing the Atlantic
- Boat
- Plane

Flags
- State
- National
- International

Science
Human body
- Five senses
- Physical condition and health
  - Muscles
  - Heart
  - Lungs
  - Body fat
  - Circulation
  - Diet
  - Exercise
  - Calories
- Fighting illness
  - Penicillin
    - Louis Pasteur
    - A. Fleming

Immunizations
- Smallpox (Edward Jenner)
- German measles, yellow fever, typhoid

Why stars twinkle
Winter solstice
Summer solstice
Vernal equinox
Autumnal equinox
Turpentine
Preventing rust
Heat and hot air rising
Perception of time
Element
- Hydrogen
- Helium

Language Arts
Personification
Different literary voices
- First person
- Second person
- Third person

Jump shift—a literary device
Famous sayings
Learning and using appropriate jargon
Writing a diary or journal

Literature explored:
- *Little Women* by Louisa May Alcott
- *Hitty, Her First Hundred Years* by Rachel Field
- *Declaration of Independence*
- *Cross-Sections: Man-of-War* by Stephen Biesty
- *I Love America* edited by Shelagh Canning
- *Katie's Trunk* by Ann Turner
- *George Washington's World* by Genevieve Foster
- "The Concord Hymn" by Ralph Waldo Emerson

Vocabulary Words
ailment
ailing
demur
rampant
turbulent
militia

Fine Arts
Drama—sensory awareness
Cooking
Appreciating the simple and the ornate
Sampler
Five-pointed star
Creative process
- Destructive criticism
- Artistic dissatisfaction

"The Concord Hymn" by Ralph Waldo Emerso

Issues of Human Relationships
Parental decisions
Responding to judgments
Finishing what you begin
Caring for feelings of others
Learning delights
Frugality
Kindness
Chores—A pleasant side
Making the most of your day
Learning to ask
Believing in people you love
Dealing with self-doubt

Career Path
Pharmacist

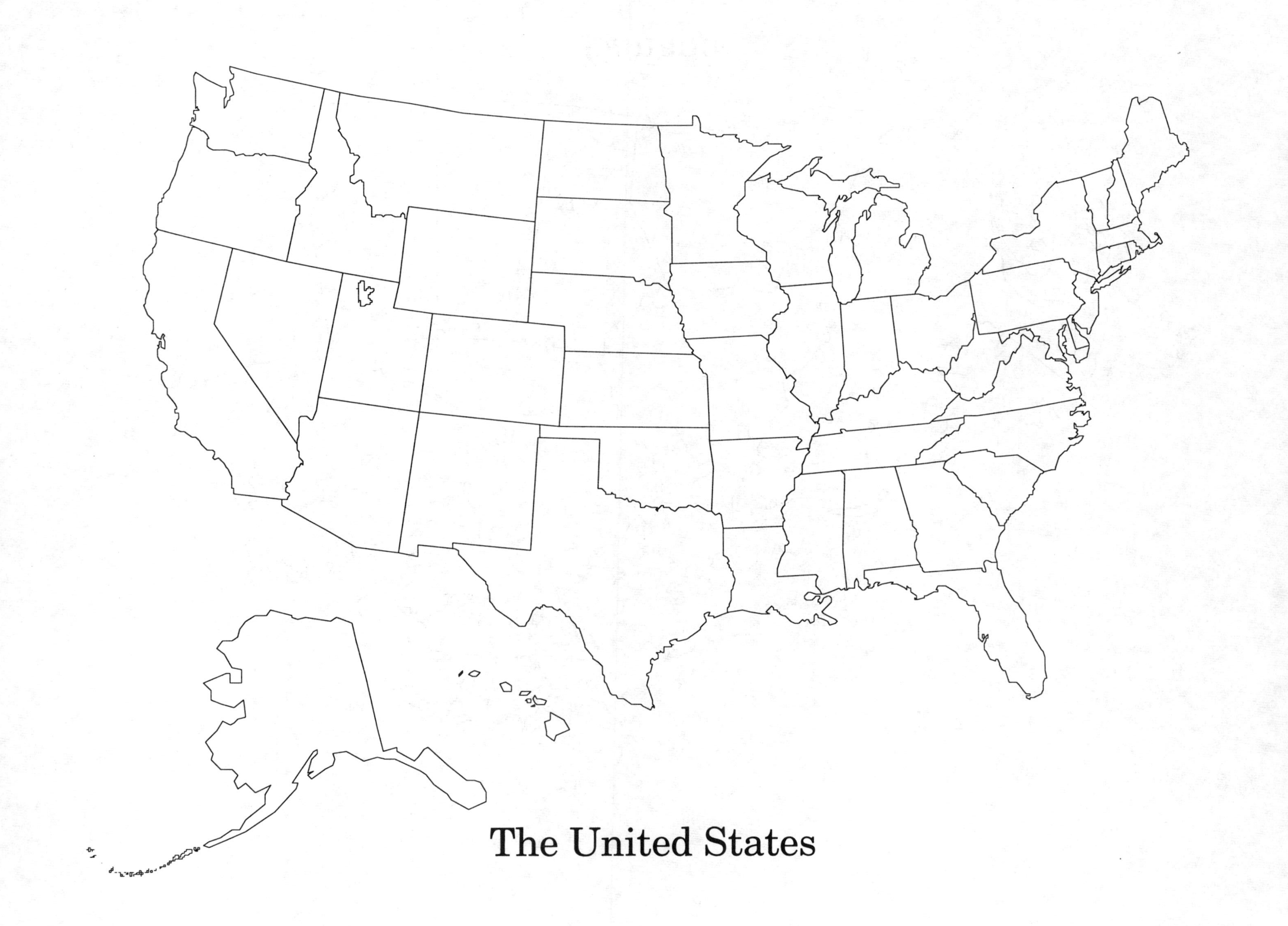
The United States

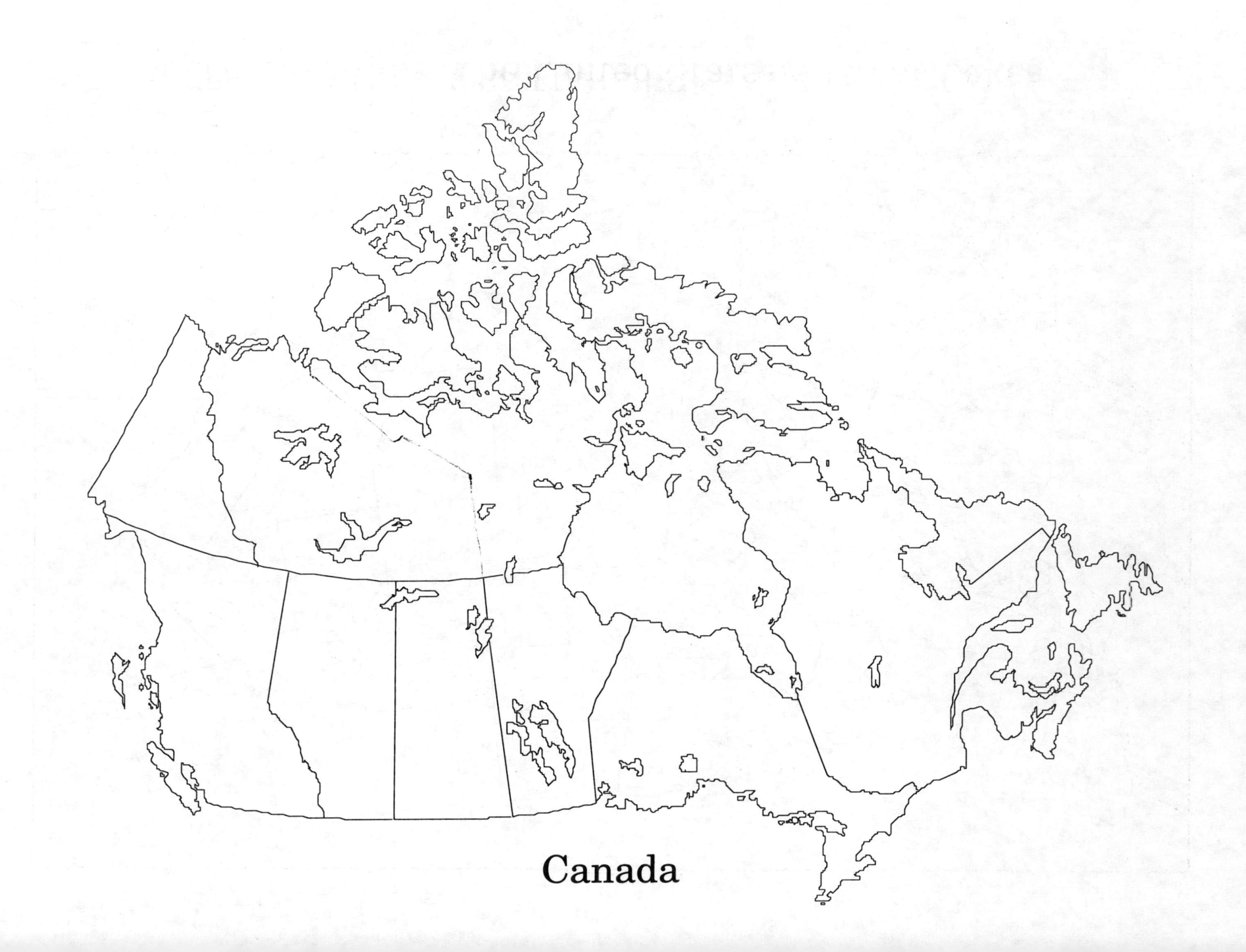
Canada

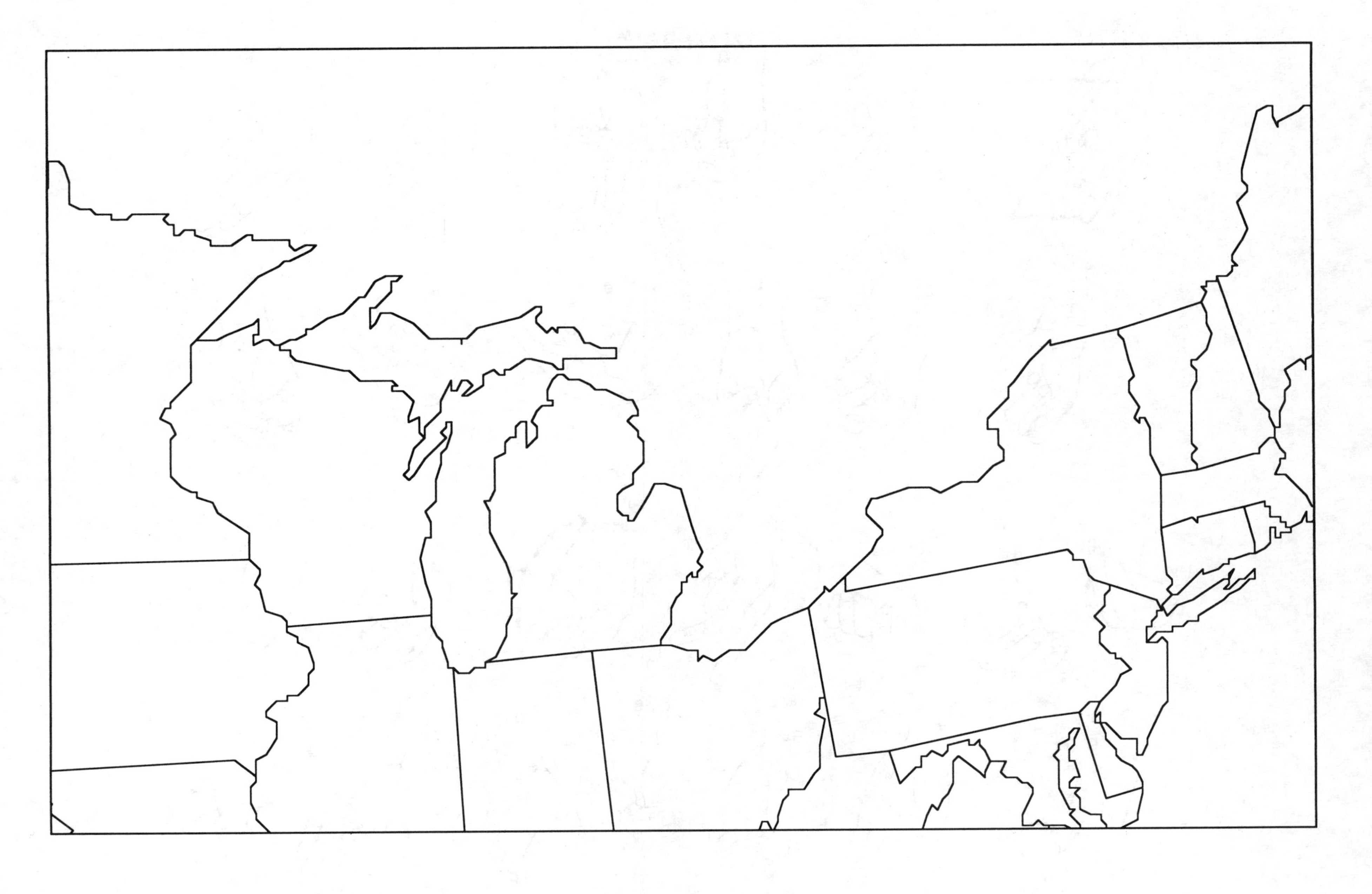

Thomas Edison Regional Map and Great Lakes

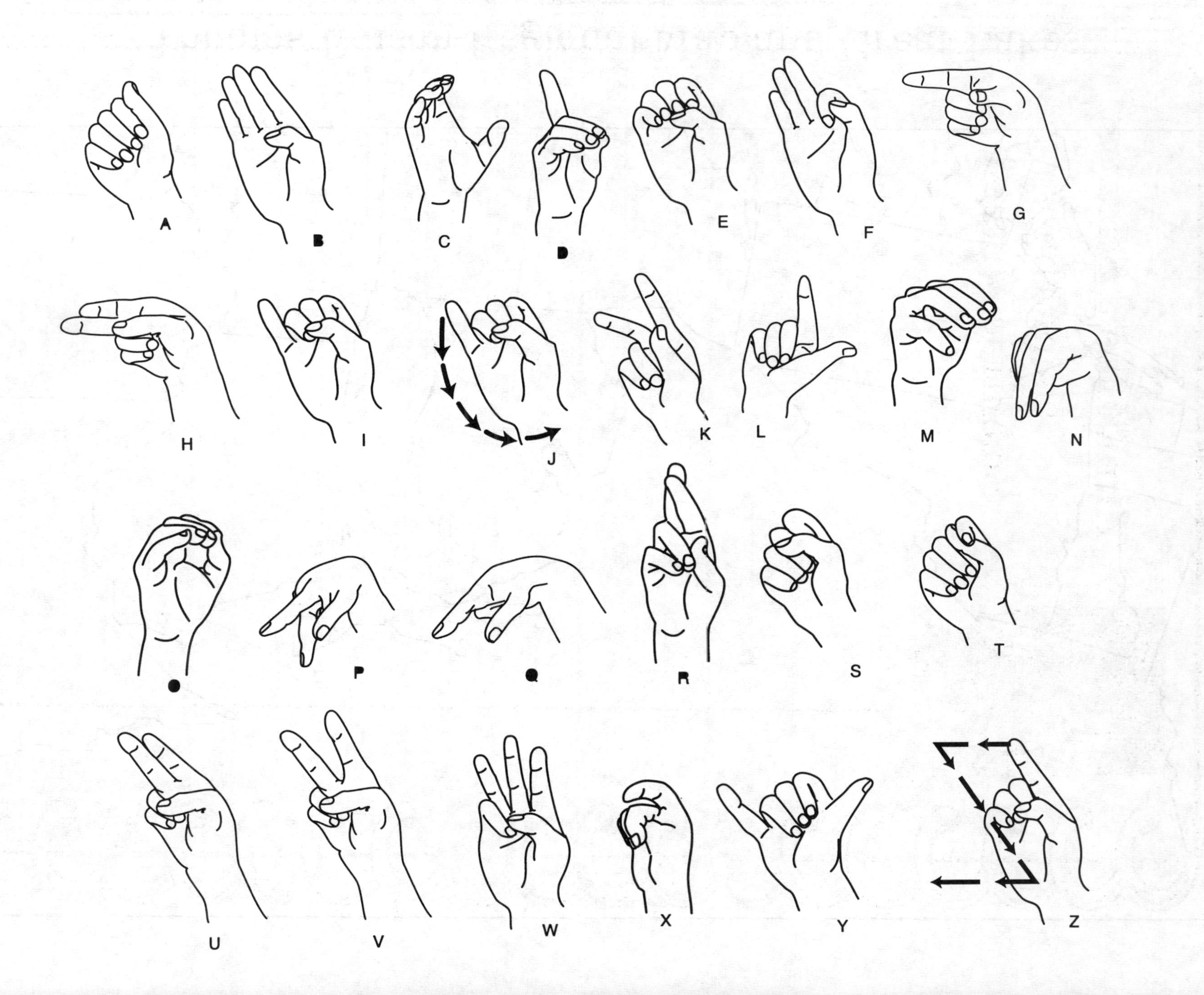
A
B
C
D
E
F
G
H
I
J
K
L
M
N
O
P
Q
R
S
T
U
V
W
X
Y
Z

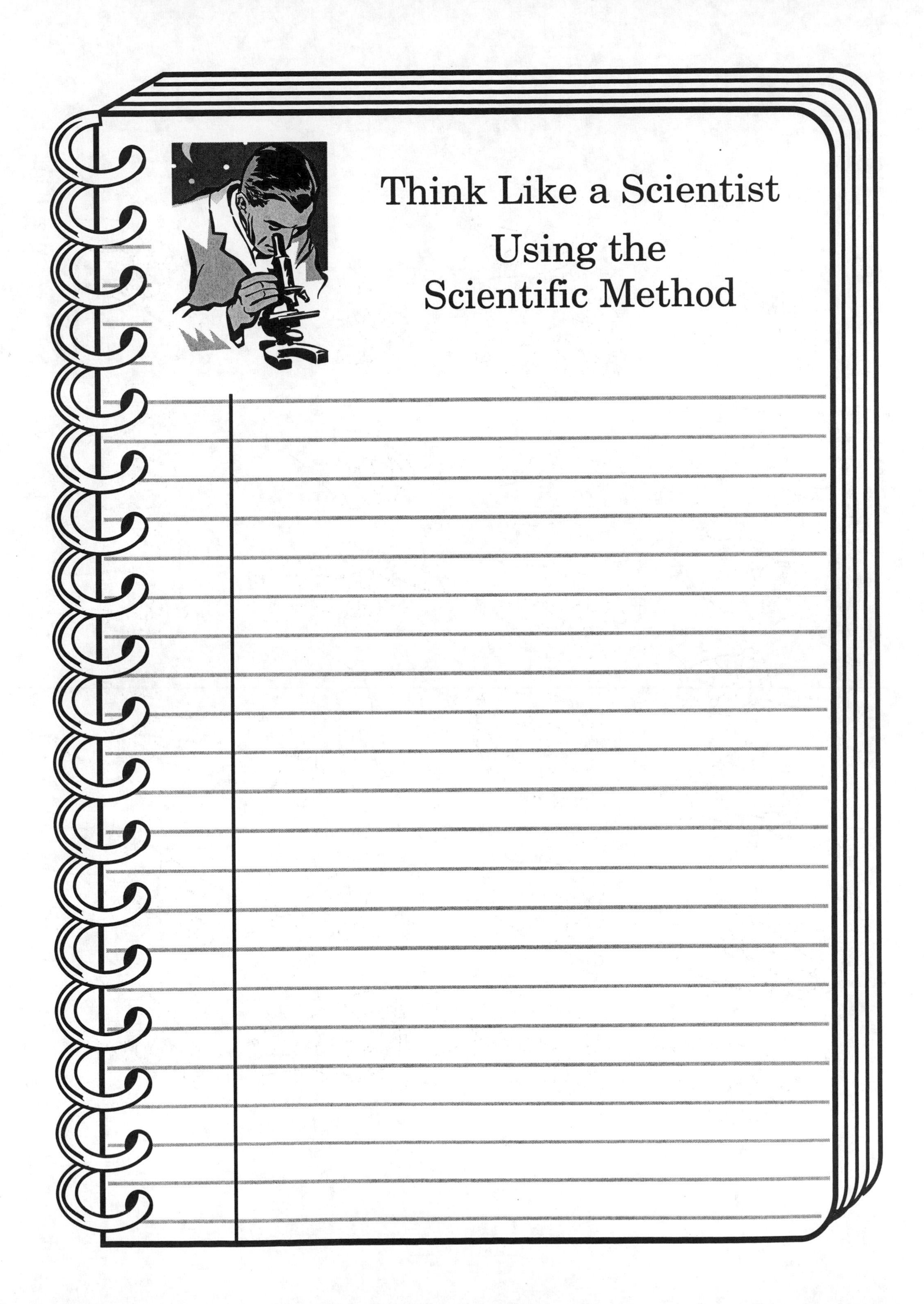

Think Like a Scientist
Using the
Scientific Method

This Award Certifies

that ____________________

has successfully completed

Beyond Five in a Row, Vol. 1

on this ___ day of _______, 20__

Teacher _______________

Author Becky Jane Lambert

Other Products from Five in a Row

Before Five in a Row by Jane Claire Lambert- This treasury of learning ideas was created for children ages 2-4. Enjoy exploring 24 wonderful children's books while building a warm and solid foundation for the learning years just around the corner. ISBN 1-888659-04-1 $24.95

Five in a Row *Volume 1* by Jane Claire Lambert- Volume 1 contains 19 unit studies built around 19 of the very best children's books ever printed. Each unit takes five days to complete. Created primarily for children ages 4-8 but don't be afraid to include other ages too! ISBN 1-888659-00-9 $19.95

Five in a Row *Volume 2* by Jane Claire Lambert- Volume 2 explores 21 more outstanding children's books. Each unit takes five days to complete. Created for ages 4-8. ISBN 1-888659-01-7 $24.95

Five in a Row *Volume 3* by Jane Claire Lambert- Volume 3 explores 15 additional outstanding children's books. Each unit takes five days to complete. Created for ages 4-8. ISBN 1-888659-02-5 $19.95

Five in a Row Christian Character and Bible Study Supplement by Jane Claire Lambert- This wonderful resource teaches hundreds of non-denominational Bible lessons and concepts using the first *three* volumes of *Five in a Row*. Teach your children about obeying parents, kindness, generosity, good stewardship, forgiveness and more. Ages 4-8. ISBN 1-888659-03-3 $17.95

Laminated Full Color Story Disks by Jane Claire Lambert- Each volume of *Five in a Row* contains black and white *story disks*. Use these little half-dollar sized drawings to teach children geography by attaching them to your own large, world map as you explore each new *Five in a Row* story. Just cut out the disks, color and laminate them. *However*, we offer this *optional* set of already colored, laminated disks for those who prefer to save the time needed to prepare their own. These disks are printed in full color and heat laminated—ready to use. One set of these disks covers all *three* volumes of *Five in a Row*. Beautiful and ready to enjoy! $15.00

The Five in a Row Cookbook by Becky Jane Lambert. This companion volume to *Five in a Row* (Volumes 1-3) and *Beyond Five in a Row* (Volumes 1-3) provides complete recipes and menus to complement each story you study. You'll enjoy the opportunity to wrap up each unit with a family meal, a time of celebration, and the opportunity for your students to share their achievements. You'll also appreciate the scrapbook area for photos, notes and homeschool memories.
ISBN 1-888659-11-4 $22.95

Beyond Five in a Row *Volume 1* by Becky Jane Lambert- Here is the answer for all those moms who have asked, "What do I do after *Five in a Row?*" You'll find the same creative, thought-provoking activities and lesson ideas you've come to expect from *Five in a Row* using outstanding chapter books for older children. Volume 1 will keep your students busy for many months with history, geography, science, language arts, fine arts and issues of human relationships. Each unit also includes numerous discussion questions, career path investigations and much more. Volume 1 requires *The Boxcar Children, Homer Price,* and the *Childhood of Famous American Series* biographies of *Thomas A. Edison- Young Inventor* and *Betsy Ross- Designer of Our Flag.* Created for ages 8-12. ISBN 1-888659-13-0 $24.95

Beyond Five in a Row *Volume 2* by Becky Jane Lambert. Requires *Sarah Plain and Tall, The Story of George Washington Carver, Skylark,* and *Helen Keller.*
ISBN 1-888659-14-9 $24.95

Beyond Five in a Row *Volume 3* by Becky Jane Lambert. Requires *Neil Armstrong-Young Flyer, The Cricket in Times Square, Marie Curie- and the Discovery of Radium,* and *The Saturdays.*
ISBN 1-888659-15-7 $24.95

Beyond Five in a Row Bible Christian Character and Bible Supplement by Becky Jane Lambert- This companion volume to *Beyond Five in a Row* provides a rich selection of the wonderful Bible references and strong character lessons you've come to expect from *Five in a Row*. This valuable supplement teaches traditional Christian values such as honoring parents, forgiveness, generosity, etc. Covers all three volumes of *Beyond Five in a Row* in one handy volume. Effective and easy to use!
ISBN 1-888659-16-5 $17.95

Above & Beyond Five in a Row *The First Adventure* by Becky Jane Lambert. This latest offering from Five in a Row Publishing is based on Rachel Field's Newbery award winning book *"Hitty: Her First Hundred Years."* This stand-alone unit study is aimed at students ages 12-14 years of age and includes a wide variety of learning opportunities in the best *Five in a Row* tradition. Each "adventure" will take several months to complete.
ISBN 1-888659-17-3 $19.95

Five in a Row Holiday: *Through the Seasons* by Jane Claire Lambert and Becky Jane Lambert *Five in a Row Holiday* is by far our most personal, intimate book, sharing our own family's values, traditions and memories in a way that we hope will inspire you to take whatever seems good to you from our experience and combine it with your family's unique traditions as you create your own family holiday heritage. Filled with individual holiday unit studies, activities, recipes, projects and memories, this book is more than just curriculum. You'll discover a delightful treasury of holiday enjoyment.
ISBN 1-888659-12-2 $24.95

Name____________________

Address*____________________

City/State/Zip____________________Phone__________

Item	Qty.	Price Ea.	Total
Five in a Row Holiday-through the seasons		$24.95	
Before Five in a Row Ages 2-4		$24.95	
Five in a Row Cookbook		$22.95	
Five in a Row-Volume 1 Ages 4-8	*pkg*	$19.95	
Five in a Row-Volume 2 Ages 4-8	*pkg*	$24.95	
Five in a Row-Volume 3 Ages 4-8	*pkg*	$19.95	
Five in a Row Bible Supplement	*pkg*	$17.95	
Laminated Full Color Story Disks	*pkg*	$15.00	
Five in a Row Cookbook	*pkg*	$22.95	
Complete FIAR Pkg. (Save 10%)		**$108.00**	
Beyond Five in a Row Vol. 1 Ages 8-12	*pkg*	$24.95	
Beyond Five in a Row Vol. 2 Ages 8-12	*pkg*	$24.95	
Beyond Five in a Row Vol. 3 Ages 8-12	*pkg*	$24.95	
Beyond Five in a Row Bible Supp. V.1-3	*pkg*	$ 17.95	
Five in a Row Cookbook	*pkg*	$22.95	
Complete BEYOND Pkg. (Save 10%)		**$104.00**	
NEW *Above & Beyond Five in a Row*		$19.95	
The First Adventure "Hitty" **(ages 12-14)**			
6-Cassette FIAR Conference Tape Set		$32.40	
4-Cassette Steve Lambert Tape Set		$21.60	
Five in a Row Book Tote		$12.95	
Reading Made Easy Phonics		$45.00	
by Valerie Bendt			
		Merchandise Total	
		Shipping Charges*	$5.95
		MO Residents add 7.10% Tax	
		Order Total	

Make Check Payable To:

Five in a Row
P.O. Box 707
Grandview, MO
64030-0707

Thank you for ordering *Five in a Row*

*** IMPORTANT** - Please be sure to include your street address for UPS shipping. They cannot deliver to a Post Office Box!